the day I went missing

the day i went missing

jennifer miller

st. martin's press ✿ new york

Permission for the following passages is gratefully acknowledged: pages 240 and 241 for Gavin De Becker's *The Gift of Fear* © copyright 1997 by Little, Brown and Company; page 242 for Alanis Morissette's "You Learn," written by Alanis Morissette and Glen Ballard, © copyright 1995 by Universal Music Publishing Group.

ISBN 0-312-26571-9

For my parents, Derek and Doreen, who did their best.

And for Jonathan and Jane, my family.

Acknowledgments

My special thanks to:

Bill Fitzhugh, who believed in my story and my ability to tell it. Your notes, advice, and friendship were invaluable.

Lewis and Baby, the sweetest distractions.

Rod Lindblom, who is much more than just my lawyer.

David Willis, you know why.

Michele Wolff, who I hope forgives me for immortalizing her in these pages. Thanks for being there without hesitation, and for being pretty funny for a girl.

Matt Hansen, for his faith in my work, and support in helping me finish it.

Deborah Swisher, David and Leslie Regal, and Kendall Fitzhugh— for being my friends in the aftermath and beyond.

Larry Silverman, who was there for the craziness. Sorry about the handcuffs.

Joan Rossman (Peapod!), who's known me forever, and shares the secret.

My agent, Jennifer Rudolph Walsh, who helped make this happen.

My editor, Jennifer Weis, who gave me great notes and the freedom to address them.

Joanna Jacobs for graciously fielding my numerous phone calls.

Sylvie Rabineau for her patience and hard work.

Henry Kaufman, who did a great job without making me lose what was mine.

My copy editor, Judith deRubini, for appreciating my style.

Paul Brooks, for the song.

And last but not least, my sister Jane, who knows my story better than anyone, and helped me remember.

Tuesday, January 28, 1997

It was around five in the afternoon. I'd been in Beverly Hills meeting with my literary agent and was driving north up Coldwater Canyon toward the valley and home. I called my phone machine to check my messages. There was just one.

It was from the private detective. He wanted me to call him.

I quickly dialed his number. "Mr. Hanks, it's Jennifer Miller."

"I found David," he answered abruptly. "He's dead."

I pulled over to the side of the road. I was numb, shaking, yet it was not totally a shock. After all, wasn't it my fault?

The detective continued, "They're investigating it as a homicide."

Wednesday, July 19, 1995

I had sold a screenplay. Just a few days earlier, less than twenty-four hours after it went out on sale, my first feature had sold to Warner Bros.

Prisoner of Love was a romantic comedy about a lonely woman, unlucky in love, who, under the influence of too much homeopathic medicine, accidentally kidnaps a guy. She decides to keep him, believing if he gets to know the real her, as no one else has been able to do, he'll fall in love with her. And of course, in a Hollywood happy ending, he does.

I had actually written *Prisoner of Love* over a year earlier. My feature agent at the William Morris Agency, Alan Gasmer, read it and had some notes for me. I, being the positive person I am, heard these notes as "Your movie sucks, there's not a word worth reading," and I put the script in a drawer for over a year.

I always thought about it, though, and finally got back to it. Alan's notes were good. I addressed most of them, and gave him back the script. It went out on a Monday, and by Tuesday it had sold. My first spec.

I'd actually come to L.A. to be an actress. Nine years earlier I'd arrived here from Kansas, via London, Michigan, New York and Chicago. My British parents had crossed the Atlantic on three different occasions before finally settling in the United States; and the three kids in my family, my brother Jonathan, my sister Jane, and myself, had been born in three different countries. Since my father wasn't in the military, I used to joke that he had been on the run from the law, but in fact he was a psychiatrist. Not that one precludes the other.

My brother was born in Saskatchewan, Canada, while my parents were living on the grounds of a mental hospital, where my father worked. I was born in Topeka, Kansas, while my father trained at a mental hospital. And my sister was born in London, England, where my father ran a mental hospital. I was short, Jewish, had big brown eyes, pale skin, dark curly hair (picture Bernadette Peters and Cher having a daughter), from the heart of the Midwest. A sunflower girl from the Sunflower State.

Within days of arriving in Los Angeles, I got my first job, the cliché for a would-be actress—a waitress. I ended up at a place called Ed Debevic's, an erstaz fifties diner where the sassy waitress danced to Buddy Holly music; in between mouthing off to customers, delivering them food when they felt like it, and bossing them around. I was one of the most popular characters; people would come in and wait to be seated at my table. It seemed they liked being abused, and the meatloaf wasn't enough.

Unfortunately my sassy attitude toward the customers started to spill over into my attitude toward management, and I was not-so-politely told they wouldn't be needing me anymore (I was escorted out lest I steal my uniform). Good-bye coffeepots and one-dollar tips, I was off to teach comedy traffic school.

Talk about the blind leading the blind; I was averaging a speeding ticket a year. Still, I got to stand in front of twenty to thirty people a day, imparting my wisdom, and have them pay total attention to me. Which after a while led me to stand-up comedy, performing in clubs, late at night, trying to make people laugh. Very similar to traffic school, except in traffic school the audience wasn't drunk, presumably.

I was a good stand-up. I performed at all the major L.A. clubs, did a few TV shows, and other comics respected me, and they are the harshest critics. But there was no money in it. I didn't want to go on the road to do colleges, and it didn't look like getting my own sitcom was in my future. There had to be a better way to make a living.

I partnered with a woman, Amy Sherman, who I met at the Groundlings Comedy Theatre, famous for such alumni as Paul Rubens (Pee Wee Herman), Lisa Kudrow, and the late Phil Hartman. Frustrated with our failing acting careers, Amy and I wrote a spec *Roseanne* script and, remarkably, though we had no credits, we ended up represented by William Morris. I had gotten an introduction to them from a guy I met in traffic school, an executive in TV comedy development at one of the studios. Taking advantage of the fact that I now knew his home address from the sign-in sheet, and—as I told him—wasn't afraid to use it, I persuaded him to read our *Roseanne* script, which he did. He liked it, and let us use his name at several of the biggest agencies. We signed with William Morris, and, not knowing any better, cockily told them we wanted to get on *Roseanne* as writers.

We were told it could never happen—we were too inexperienced, and we didn't have a personal relationship with Roseanne or Tom. Personal relationship meaning someone Tom had wronged during his drinking days and was now making amends to; or someone who found no problem with all of Roseanne and Tom's wacky antics, i.e.: firing a crew member because he laughed at what Roseanne considered an inappropriate moment; or writing obscene messages and leaving photos of their bare asses on the car of a pregnant woman who accidentally parked in their space.

In spite of our agent's prediction, Amy and I got on *Roseanne*, then the number one show in America. I stayed two years. Fifty insane episodes, often working seven days a week, frequently past four in the morning. Among a staff of twelve, Amy and I were the only women. We were quickly nicknamed "The Go-Go's," and given an office which contained a huge, noisy pinball machine. We'd be on deadline, typing frantically, a script due in days, and the other writers would tiptoe in apologetically, assuring us, "Just one quick game, I promise." This would be followed by twenty minutes of whoops and hollers of joy or dismay, depending on their skill.

In our second year on the show, and only our second in the business, Amy and I were nominated for an Emmy for writing the Becky-goes-on-the-pill episode, thrilling the men on the show who'd been in the business for years, to no end.

"A Bitter Pill to Swallow," was an episode where Roseanne, at Becky's request, takes her to get on birth control, later finding out that her daughter has already had sex. Among the staff it was nicknamed the "Becky Gets Popped" episode. There were either three or even four *Seinfeld* episodes nominated, and one *Roseanne*. It turned out to be the only writing nomination the show would receive in the entire run of the series.

I had no date to take to the Emmys, so I took my mother. I wore a hot-pink tuxedo (what was I thinking?) that I'd had specially made for the occasion. Amy's boyfriend sprung for a limo, and we were off to Pasadena.

It's nerve-wracking sitting there, and at the same time tedious. There seemed to be hundreds of categories before they got to ours, and long, rambling acceptance speeches by people we'd never heard of. Finally, "Best Writing in a Comedy Series" was announced, and my name and Amy's went out over the air to millions of viewers.

We didn't win. We were beaten by one of the *Seinfeld* episodes. Amy and I watched the writers go up on stage to accept their award, with definite twinges of envy. I don't care what anyone says, it's *not* enough to be nominated.

Amy and I ended up splitting as a team, though we remained friends. I wrote a pilot for CBS that went nowhere; wrote for a year on *Dave's World*; worked on a few other shows; then partnered up again, this time with a guy named Mark Brazill. After being together for about two months, we sold three sitcom pilots, to ABC, NBC, and FOX. Writing three at one time was a mistake, crazy and chaotic. I'd be typing one script, putting in names of characters from others.

At the same time, I was finally addressing Alan's notes on *Prisoner of Love*.

It looked like I was finally making it in Hollywood. I was a successful comedian. I was selling movies. I was writing TV shows. And it all meant nothing.

———

My friend Paul Avery took me out to dinner to celebrate the sale of my script. In the course of talking about the sale, Paul commented that I didn't seem very excited for someone who'd just sold her first screenplay. "This is a big thing, Jennifer," he said, "you should be ecstatic."

I shrugged it off. "You know me, I don't get excited about anything."

As I thought about it, it occurred to me that I really didn't care very much about the film. I'd pretended to be excited, accepting congratulations from friends, thanking my agent effusively, acting like this was a major big deal, but the truth was, except for the help the money would be, it really meant nothing. And my main thought about the money was that it wasn't enough. Money had always been a huge issue for me. My whole life I'd had a sense that I'd end up taking care of myself, that I'd be alone. The being alone part was something I'd come to accept, it was just a known fact, but the idea of being alone and *poor* was terrifying. I had this image of myself as an old woman, pushing a shopping cart and screaming obscenities at people who offended me (as opposed to now, without the cart). So that was my predominant thought, that I wished the movie had sold for more.

I think in the back of my mind was a vague sense that my reaction probably wasn't normal, but I had no idea or even any desire that I was aware of to do anything about it.

Paul thought it was sad that I was so emotionally untouchable. I said, "Yeah, I guess." Since sadness was a feeling I didn't comprehend, I couldn't really agree with him.

He asked how my parents had reacted to the sale. My father had said something like, "That's very nice," which was his reaction to virtually anything I accomplished. When I had given him the script to read, he never got around to it.

But it was my mother's reaction that had struck me. She'd been asking over and over if the movie was ever going to get made, when would it get made, who would be in it? And I'd told her repeatedly that I didn't know, that some movies never get made, in fact *most* movies never get made.

"You have to understand," I told Paul, "this was in conversation after conversation, the same exact questions." As usual my mother was not listening to me. Finally I told her she had to stop bugging me, it could be years before I knew anything. "Mom, sometimes these things are in development for years. It could take ten years."

"Good," my mother replied, "that'll give me something to live for." There was a pause. "I mean to look forward to." She'd corrected herself, but it was too late. And to me that was the summation of our relationship in a nutshell. I was there for her benefit. She basically had nothing in her life but to live through me. And now she had the idea that this movie could get made so that she could tell her friends that her daughter had a movie made. There was no awareness of how great it could be for me, or how frustrating it might be for me to have to wait that long, or to not have it made at all, but only how it would make her happy and give her something to live for.

"That's really fucked up," Paul said. I laughed. "That's my mother," I said.

We started talking about families, and somehow the conversation got around to therapy. Paul asked if I'd ever been. Uncharacteristically I admitted, which I had to no one else, including my parents, that since my twenties I'd tried therapy five different times with no success. My attempts had ranged from one hideously uncomfortable visit with a silent, distant man who reminded me of my father, himself a psychiatrist, to almost a year of once-a-week visits to a woman with whom

I mostly discussed shopping. Admittedly one of my favorite activities, but still . . .

I told Paul how boring therapy was to me, and how worthless it had been. It had made me no happier, no less frustrated, my life no more satisfying, I had learned nothing. I couldn't believe I was actually admitting going. Seeking therapy means I must want something. I have desires, needs. I'm not strong. I'm weak. Weakness was a big problem for me, hating it in others almost as much as I hated it in myself. I figured that now Paul probably despised me.

Instead he said, "You should try my therapist. David. I've been seeing him five years; he's the greatest guy in the world. He changed my life."

"Okay," I said. My instant acquiescence shocked me. I hadn't even been thinking of trying again. I'd pretty much given up the idea that anyone could help me. But something made me say yeah. Later I was to call it a miracle.

In Paul's car after dinner he called his therapist, Dr. David Cohen, leaving him a message. "Hey, David, it's Paul. I'm with a friend, and she could really use some help." In the background I yelled out, "I'm crazy!" Paul told Dr. Cohen that I'd call tomorrow and leave my number.

After he hung up I felt embarrassed. Did I really want to do this? "Don't worry," Paul reassured me. "You're going to love him."

The next day I felt like a fool. I think I called him just to be polite. I left the briefest of messages on his pager. "Hi, Dr. Cohen, I'm Paul's friend Jennifer Heath, my number is . . ." I didn't even use my real name, but my professional name.

When he called me back, we barely spoke, making an appointment for Saturday. He said I could call him David. I asked if there was a charge for the consultation, he said no. He suggested I take his last appointment of the day, in case we needed to go a little longer. About to ring off he said, "Well, I'll see you Saturday, Heather."

"My name's Jennifer. Maybe you should take a look at your life and see who you know named Heather, and why you'd call me that."

David very pleasantly agreed that maybe he should, and we'd talk about it Saturday. And that was it.

Saturday, July 22

I was in the waiting room of a small, rather dowdy office in West Los Angeles. I was nervous, having second thoughts, feeling ashamed, humiliated, stupid.

Still, I had decided to keep the appointment, with total conviction that I was only going to go this once, to be polite, then I'd be done with it. Meanwhile I was sitting here just hating myself.

One of the four inner doors opened and a man came into the waiting room. He was young, maybe thirty-five, shaved head, stubble on his face, a small, gold hoop in his left ear, scarily brightly colored surfer pants, a mismatched T-shirt, and sneakers.

Okay, this was interesting. My dad's a shrink. He wears a dark suit to work.

David smiled and invited me into his office. It was cheaply decorated, with an ugly floral-patterned couch, matching chair, a big swivel chair, and cheesy paintings that looked like rejects from those art sales at the Airport Marriott.

I sat in the corner of the couch, uncomfortable. David sat crosslegged in front of me in the swivel chair, toying with a MontBlanc pen.

"Did you figure out why you called me Heather?"

He said he supposed he got it from my last name Heath. He apologized, saying he'd never, ever made that kind of mistake before. I wondered if I was supposed to be flattered.

"Why isn't your name on the outer door?" I wanted to know. Other therapists were listed there, why not him? He explained that he'd just moved here from offices in Beverly Hills, and he hadn't gotten around to it yet. He asked if having his name on the door was important to me. I said I didn't care. David chose to stay away from the obvious question—if I didn't care, why did I bother asking, or even notice? We sat in silence for what seemed like an interminable amount of time, probably thirty seconds. Finally David asked me why I was there.

I shrugged. "I don't know, why does anyone go to therapy? I guess I'm just not as happy as I could be." He waited for me to go on.

I told him I'd just sold a screenplay, and I didn't really care about it, that all I cared about was the money. I told him the story about my mother, and how much that pissed me off. I said she was chronically depressed, and had been for as long as I could remember, refused to admit it or get help for it, but just reveled in the attention it gave her. And how that pissed me off, too. I told him briefly about my emotionally distant father. David wanted an example. My father is sooo distant . . . How distant is he?

It was an impossible question to answer. We were so far apart, so removed from each other's lives, that I couldn't even think of a time there was something between us to be distant about. I realized I could sum up my father's and my relationship with two photographs. One is of the only time I remember sitting with him. I was around ten. My father is in a big easy chair, and I am perched uncomfortably on the arm next to him. We're both staring straight ahead, not touching. The other is where he's handing me money.

When I would be going home at Christmas or Fourth of July, I would frequently tell my friends, "I'm going to my mom's house," and have to correct myself, "I mean my parents' house."

I told David that I never remembered once being hugged by my father, rarely by my mother, and that kisses in my family were always cheek to cheek. As a child, I have no memory of putting my head on my parents' shoulders, cuddling with them on the couch, creeping into bed with them.

I used to see children walking down the street holding their parents' hands, amazed at how natural it looked, how easy. And later, I would watch my three youngest nieces run to their father with glee and jump into his arms, and I would be filled with curiosity. I was like an anthropologist, observing unfamiliar behavior. Did they think before they ran or was it instinctive? Was there any doubt that he might not want them there? Was being held comforting or just fun? Did they feel shame at showing that much pleasure?

I was not looking with envy; it was so far from my experience that I couldn't even imagine it in relation to me.

I pointed out the irony that my father was not only a psychiatrist but an adolescent psychiatrist in particular, and that (at least in my experience) kids of shrinks always seem to be fucked up. Years earlier I'd had a joke in my stand-up act:

"My father is a psychiatrist. Whenever I tell people that they always say, 'Ah, so that explains it.' It *is* different having a psychiatrist as a father. Here's an example—it's four A.M. and you've just awoken from the worst nightmare of your life. You're lost in the world's biggest supermarket and there's monsters and your dog is dead and you don't have any parents, and you come screaming into your parents' room in the middle of the night. 'Daddy, daddy, I've had a nightmare!' 'Hmm,' he says, 'you felt betrayed, didn't you?' 'Yes, daddy, I did feel betrayed, but I could really use a hug.' 'Hmm,' he says again, 'tell me about your mother.' "

A joke of course, but, like many jokes, not just a joke.

I was hesitant to talk much more about my father, who was fairly prominent in his field. I wanted to protect him, concerned that David might have heard of him and think badly of him. It was why I had not used my real name.

David wondered why I was protecting my father, but the fact was I didn't blame him. He had had the worst life of anyone I ever knew. His own father died when my father was four. His sister died of leukemia. His brother died in a plane crash on the way to his honeymoon. His mother died of breast cancer. His other sister died of a brain tumor after losing her son, my father's nephew, to suicide by self-immolation. No wonder he was distant.

I remembered an even bigger irony than my father being a psychiatrist. This day, July 22, was my parents' anniversary. The day they got married. Started a family. I told David I considered that event the worst thing that ever happened to me.

At some point I informed him very calmly, off-handedly, that I had no needs and no desires. I wanted nothing, and felt nothing. I felt no happiness and no pain. He asked me about sex, which, frankly, therapist or no, I thought was none of his business. I'd had another joke in my stand-up act:

"I bought a remote control for my vibrator. That way I don't have to get so emotionally involved."

I told David I'd had sex of course, plenty of times, but never had a boyfriend, which was something I'd never admitted. I found myself telling him things I'd never told anyone, including every other therapist I'd had, and I was surprised at myself. He just seemed easy to talk to. I liked him, even on that first day. He seemed kind, intelligent, he had a sense of humor. He didn't exactly laugh uproariously at my jokes, but sometimes I thought I caught a glimmer of a smile.

But I refused to tell him my age. I told him that was something he'd have to guess. I was very vague about it, maybe because he was sort of cute and young and it just emphasized how old I felt I was. I'd always had an issue telling people my age, and in fact not even my best friends knew how old I was. It was a quirk that I didn't fully understand myself. When I learned to pay closer attention to what was going on inside, I came to believe it stemmed from the fact that I felt I'd had such a desolate existence, both emotionally and experientially. If people knew how old I was, somehow it would make it more true that I'm this old and my life has been so barren. That the everyday experiences other people took for granted were so alien to me.

I felt that if I was twenty then things could be different, my life could get better, I could one day maybe even be happy. But after thirty I knew it was too late for me.

I had never expressed these thoughts to anyone before. I'm not even sure I knew they were thoughts.

"We need to stop soon, Jennifer," David said. "But I think I can help you."

"Well, I doubt that. No one can help me. It's too late." No feelings attached to the words, just the facts, ma'am.

With a little snottiness I asked how he thought he could succeed where five others had failed. He asked if I'd be willing to give it a try, and I told him fine, whatever, that I supposed I had nothing to lose.

He wanted me to come three times a week, which flipped me out. I'm figuring I'm a little unhappy; he must think I'm really crazy. And he wasn't even done. He wanted me to commit to twenty sessions. "Would you do me that favor?" he asked. It felt like a huge commitment, and I was really hesitant.

I was also concerned about money, and he told me his normal fee was one hundred and fifty dollars. "Oh my God, I can't afford that," I said, trying to add it up in my head. I suck at math in the best of times, and all I could see was lots of zeros.

"Look, I feel like I can help you and I'd like to help you," he said. "And if money is what's coming between that, then let's see if we can work something out."

Now that I was faced with the reality of it, suddenly the thought of twenty sessions seemed overwhelming, even at a reduced price, and

I started to hedge. Maybe I *was* happy. You know, come to think of it . . .

"Let me put it this way," David said, "I'm going to ask you to commit to twenty sessions and I'm going to ask you to pay for them, but if at any point during the twenty you change your mind, I'll give you all the money back. So you don't feel trapped."

I was shocked into silence. How could that be? He didn't even know me. In my experience, people didn't go out of the way for me, I took care of myself. And here was this stranger, making this amazing gesture. Save my soul, with a money-back guarantee.

I told him if I can get my money back, then I'm not really committing, am I? And he said he felt I was making a commitment, because he believed I'd stick with it.

I don't know how he arrived at the figure, but he came up with ninety-two dollars a session, a total of eighteen hundred forty dollars for the twenty sessions. "But you promise I can get my money back?" I asked.

"You can get it all back," he said. "I don't care. It's not about money. That's the least issue here, I want to help you." He paused. "You're a special person, Jennifer."

I asked him what he meant. He said, "I wasn't going to tell you this, but I want to tell you something. Is that okay?" I said sure. He went on, "In that first conversation on the phone, I felt there was something about you. Your spirit. It seemed very strong, very special."

"You felt that on the phone?" I asked. "We talked for less than a minute." No one could feel that way about someone so instantly, and particularly about me. He must be just saying that. Somewhere deep down, though, was there a faint flicker of hope? Could he be right? Could he see something where no one else could? And then another flicker moved in, a reminder. "You must have been drinking," I told him.

"I can't explain it, Jennifer," David said. "I just felt it. I even told my wife about it, that I couldn't stop thinking about this new patient, and I was really interested and curious to meet her because I had a strong feeling about her, a connection. I just had the weirdest feeling I'd spoken to someone really special."

That was unfathomable to me. I never thought anyone had ever thought about me when I wasn't right there in the room in their face. "You really feel that about me?" I asked. I was incredulous, but also trying not to smile.

David nodded. "Your spirit feels really strong to me, Jennifer," he said, "but it's in hiding. I'd like to help you rescue it."

We agreed to start in a week and a half, after he got back from a business trip, and that I would pay for all twenty visits at the first session. David felt if I paid up front, I'd be more likely to keep the commitment. In addition, he was making a commitment to me by lowering his fee so drastically, and in return he wanted to see I was making the same commitment.

"But Jennifer, if you change your mind, you can get all your money back. Do you believe me?" I said of course.

His idea made sense to me. Knowing myself, I knew it was very possible to just not go again, or go once or twice and then quit. In all my other (failed) attempts at therapy, I'd paid the standard way, billed at the end of every month, and look how those had turned out. Therapy had always seemed casual to me, take-it-or-leave-it. Maybe this way I was more likely to see it through. I was inspired by David's belief. He was the expert. He saw hope where I had seen none. And of course if he was wrong, I had the fail-safe of being able to get out of it. If I thought at all that it was unconventional, I probably welcomed it. My father was so formal and distant, and had such rigid rules on standards of behavior, and about what you can and cannot say and do, both in his home life and with his patients, and here was David with his T-shirt and goofy pants and looking sort of like Andre Agassi and it seemed cool. I agreed.

David said he was glad I was doing this, and was looking forward to starting. Then he said, "We really do need to stop now," and I looked at the clock. I had been there three hours.

As I was leaving he said to call him if I needed anything, that his pager was always on, even while he was away. And I turned back and said, "Don't worry, I won't call you. I'll never cry and I'll never call you." And I left.

It was true that I never cried. Not over never having a boyfriend or even dating, never going to a prom or a school dance, never having a boy tell me he loved me or thought I was pretty. I shed no tears because my parents and I had never had a conversation much more meaningful than how's the weather. Nor because my siblings and I rarely spoke, or because I had few close friends. I didn't cry that I'd pretty much only had sex when drunk, usually with men I knew little about and cared to know even less, that life held no pleasure for me, or for the certain knowledge that I would live and die alone.

Crying about my life was pointless. Weak, pathetic, an indication that something mattered.

Maybe I had cried as a child, but I have little memory of my life before around age eleven or twelve. I used to joke that I must've been kept locked in a closet my whole childhood, and had blacked out the horror of the experience. I came to learn that was true, although it was not a closet of normal construction.

"I read in the newspaper where this girl was found locked in a closet, covered in her own feces. I don't know what the big deal was. I was locked in a closet covered in someone else's feces."

Now I cried only over animals—seeing them die, seeing them suffer. Their pain I understood. Mine was unknown and unconnected to me. True, in the past I had wanted a close family, a boyfriend, love, support, to feel special, pretty. I dreamed of it. But the longing was so balanced with knowing it would never happen—that I was too ugly, too boring, something was so wrong with me—that eventually I pushed the desire away, and soon stopped remembering what it had even felt like.

Now when I would meet men I would instantly turn on them, with wit, hardness, boredom, superiority. I showed no interest. No vulnerability. I had no belief they could ever find me attractive, and no idea what I would do if they did. It would only prove there was something terribly wrong with them.

I subscribed heavily to the Groucho Marx creed, "I wouldn't want to belong to any club that would have me as a member."

The only men that ever did seem drawn to me were married. It happened with amazing regularity. Later I came to understand it was probably because I was the most myself with them, the softest, the least threatened. But then I believed it was because they saw me in such huge contrast to their wives, the type of girl no man would ever marry.

And I would flirt with them, as much as I knew about flirting, which was not much. I was hardly known as a coquette. I was safe in knowing it would go no further, enjoying the belief—even if for only a second—that perhaps if they had someone else, they weren't total losers, and maybe I *was* a little desirable.

But it didn't even matter if I was desirable, because they were married, and if they *did* become available or showed interest in going beyond flirtation, I would fall back to my normal position, becoming sarcastic, brash, crude, moody, loud. I was always proud that I swore like a truck driver and ridiculed men who didn't have as big balls as me.

———

I started seeing David on Mondays, Tuesdays, and Saturdays, standard fifty-minute visits. Prior to starting I'd had serious second thoughts about whether I really wanted to do this, but I thought about my friend Paul, and how much he said David had helped him. Maybe I should at least try. David was young, enthusiastic, passionate. And he'd told me I was special.

I wondered if maybe this wasn't my last hope. All that week before my first appointment I vacillated between that glimmer of hope, and having it squashed by my own cynicism and negativity and history.

David had called me the day before our first session to say he was looking forward to seeing me tomorrow. It pissed me off, like he was feeling I needed a phone call to remind me, like I was an idiot. Besides, why would anyone look forward to seeing me?

In spite of my anger, I kept that first appointment, and the ones after that. And for the first time in all my attempts at therapy, I was arriving on time (instead of up to thirty or even forty minutes late), and even started looking forward to going.

Even so, information about my life was coming out only in dribs and drabs in my sessions with David; vaguely, matter-of-factly. Mostly the sessions consisted of the same litany, "My life sucks. It's not going to change. I could be shopping with this money. Why am I bothering?"

Of course there was more to it than my life merely sucking, there were particulars, but I couldn't articulate what they were.

Besides my life sucking, another standard topic was my career; how I hated being a writer and wanted to give it up. David felt I should do things that made me happy. I pointed out that if I gave up writing, and with no other apparent skills, I'd probably end up living under a freeway overpass. I supposed that at least with my training my cardboard sign would be grammatically correct.

"It'll be your fault and I'll end up living in your basement," I told David.

"You can have the nanny's room," he said, smiling.

Okay, good, he had kids. A wife. So maybe he wasn't a loser. Maybe him finding me special was not so creepy.

"Aren't you sick of my complaining?" I asked David at the beginning of every session. "I'm boring myself, I must be boring you. Even that question is boring. Even me saying that question is boring, is boring." I could have gone on, but David stopped me.

"You couldn't bore me, Jennifer," David said. "I like you. I like being with you."

Yeah, right.

I have an idea, Jennifer," David said to me one day. I waited. He pointed out that the end of our sessions were always better than the beginning, that toward the end I'd really get going in terms of talking about meaningful and emotional issues. We were always going long, fifty-five minutes instead of fifty, even if he had other patients after me.

"I'd like to formalize that," David said. "I want us to go fifty-seven minutes." That would still give enough time for me to leave and the next patient to arrive. He didn't want to cut our sessions short, he explained; they were too important. And besides, as he said again, he really enjoyed talking with me.

There were only a few occasions in my life where I'd made any real attempt to talk to my father, maybe about my work, or what was going on in my life, and they would always end the same way. Almost without exception, sometimes after even less than five minutes, I'd look over at him and he'd be falling asleep.

Later, when I moved away and I would talk to him on the phone, in the middle of conversations he'd abruptly say, "Here's your mother," and hand her the phone. I would literally be in mid-sentence.

Extending the therapy hour meant David would have no time to himself between sessions, but he wanted to do that for me. I said okay. "Now I can bore you for even longer," I said.

———

One of the first things David said he wanted to teach me was to learn to pay attention. "What do you mean? I pay attention to you," I said.

"Not to me," he explained, "you need to pay attention to yourself." I had no clue what he was talking about. He asked how I felt about things I was telling him—that I'd never been happy, could never imagine being so. "It's just the way it is," I would tell him. "I don't know what you mean, 'How do I feel?' "

"How do you feel about it *inside*?" he asked.

"Well, I think it sucks," I said, always coming back to thinking, instead of feeling.

"My therapist is teaching me to be more vulnerable. Last week he hit me in the head with a two-by-four, and I was able to say, 'Yeah, that hurts a little.' "

To me, pain applied only to the physical. David said he wanted me to really try to feel things, in my body as well as in my head. "It's hard at the beginning, but I know you can learn this."

I was confused, but I said I would try.

Little by little, I was starting to explore my life, talking more about my family, my lack of connections, my loneliness. One day I told David that I had always felt like a ghost, drifting through life on another plane.

"I'm outside with other people, walking among them, but they don't see me. I'm not like them. I don't experience the things they experience. I don't know what they know. I don't belong with them. I just exist, invisible."

This was something I'd never been able to verbalize before. I hadn't even known (at least consciously) this feeling existed at all. I was learning all this amazing stuff, and I looked at it very clinically, with fascination, as if I was learning it about someone else. Even though I was describing things that to some might sound sad, there was no emotion tied to them.

Although the therapy seemed to be going well, and David said I was doing great, I was having a problem remembering the sessions after they were over, and sometimes even within the sessions I'd forget what we spoke about at the beginning. I'd leave, and as soon as I was out the door I'd have forgotten everything we talked about. Sometimes I literally couldn't remember a single line of conversation.

I brought this up to David, and also my concern that I remembered little of my life in general. Whole events, things I know I did, major life moments, I had no recollection of. Even as I was getting older, my memories are few. I don't recall my high school or college graduation, or a trip I took to Hawaii with my parents when I was twenty. I was there, my sister tells me I was, but I know nothing of it.

Jane and I had talked about this before, that fact that neither of us remembered much from our childhoods. Her first memory is of being eight years old, at a friend's house. I can't pinpoint mine.

As a child in England I had a pony. Getting a pony is a huge deal for any little girl, probably the biggest deal, yet I remembered nothing of being told that I could have the pony, of going to buy her, of seeing her and riding her for the first time; and nothing of the day I was forced to sell her so our family could move to America. I was thirteen years old, but I don't recall saying good-bye to her, or the last time I saw her. Big things in my life were known to me only in stories, as if they'd happened to someone else.

David had minored in neurology or neuropsychology, something to do with the brain, and he explained that when a person is deprived or neglected there's actually a ramification on memory because their synapses don't connect as well. But, he added reassuringly, "With attention, and someone paying attention to you those things will get better and your memory will improve. I promise."

Shortly after starting therapy, I'd gone out and purchased a journal. One of my first entries was of something that had come to me one night as I'd been drifting off to sleep. A story fully complete, as if it were already written. I got out of bed and wrote (copied?) it down.

The best way I can describe it is that it was like automatic writing; except for holding the pen, something I had nothing to do with.

"WIFE"

There is a gardener in a garden. He is old. He doesn't remember how old. He wears a straw hat against the sun. He takes out a handkerchief and mops his brow. He hears laughter down the path. He follows. In a clearing is a young girl. Young? Twenty. Not a child, to him a child. He tells her, "I am the gardener, I live here too. This is my house." She is so young and beautiful he can't stop speaking. She is laughing in a summer dress, thin, pure white, white with white flowers. He sees through the dress. She knows. Laughs. He asks, where did you come from? From her bag she pulls a cowboy hat and holster. "It's for my son," she says, and hands it to him. He's surprised she has a son, but he doesn't say. "Go on," she says. He puts on the hat and holster. An old man, like a cowboy. She laughs. He watches. She starts to dance, faster and faster—takes off her clothes. She's naked. Laughing. Dancing. Stops, breathless, beckons him. He knows she means him, he reaches for her, but she's gone.

He is awake, the shovel in his hand, leaning against the dirt. He looks down the path but it's silent. A car pulls up in the gravel. His wife. Old. Real. She has a bag for dinner. She crosses in front of him. He stops her. "I must tell you my story." He tells her the story of the young girl. "Maybe it was you," he says. She smiles. "Maybe it means something," he says, "Maybe I'm dying." "We're all dying," his wife says. He says, "I don't want to not be." She shrugs, as if to say, you can't make that happen. "Hold my hand," he asks her. He clasps it, but there's nothing there.

He wakes under a bush, remembering her, his straw hat fallen to the side. His daughter looks down at him, "Poppa, what are you doing under the bush?" He looks at her, he doesn't answer. It's hot. She smiles. Bends down and kisses him on the top of his head. Turns to leave. He grabs her. He says, "I am the strangest dream."

It was wondrous to me. I had no idea where it had come from, it was not even my style of writing. What did it mean? Was it about my father? My mother? Who was the girl in the white dress? David explained that the story was about me, that all the things I wanted, everything I had grasped for, seemed an illusion. That my life felt unreal to me; and that I, like everyone, was afraid of dying, of not existing in the world. It seemed to fit with my idea of being a ghost. But, I wondered, then why was the protagonist male? Why did I call the piece "Wife"?

I didn't really understand David's explanation, and I was too early in my therapy to push for more clarity. I did know that I loved that it was written so purely from my unconscious. If I could only write scripts so quickly and easily. They would not be the least bit amusing, and no one would be able to understand them, but how prolific I would be.

———

Writing had always been agonizing for me. Slow, torturous, every word the wrong choice. I was critical of everything and convinced that I was incompetent. I think that's one reason I preferred writing with partners, so I couldn't be totally blamed for the results if they were bad. Now I had a partner, Mark, with whom I had written three pilots the year before. An animated show for FOX, titled *Hollyweird*, about a family that moves from the Midwest so the father can become a low-level game show host; *Three the Hard Way*, for NBC, about three cute young women who buy a hunting lodge in Alaska and start a dating service between Alaskan men and women from the lower forty-eight states (NBC approved the premise, then after we wrote it told us it was too much like a prostitution ring); and *Strange Bedfellows*, for ABC, about a young, female MTV veejay who moves to D.C. to join the White House press corps. All good ideas (for television anyway), all went nowhere.

Now Mark and I were busy thinking up other ideas, hoping this year we'd at least get a pilot produced, if not actually to series. It was my dream to get a show on the air, as it is every sitcom writer's. A successful show, staying on the air long enough to syndicate, means money for the rest of your life. I could retire young, buy a horse, leave L.A., maybe even, someday, find myself a boyfriend. At least, I *think* a boyfriend was what I wanted. Not that anybody would want me. Not that I cared. Although maybe I did.

First, of course, I had a few issues to work on.

———

Hello, Jennifer, it's David." Okay, what in the hell was this? He was *calling* me? I was stunned to hear his voice on the phone. After every session he would remind me as I was leaving to call if I needed to, and I would just look at him like he was crazy. So what was he doing?

He said he felt like today's session had been particularly hard and he wanted to see if I was okay. I couldn't even remember that day's session, and certainly had no recollection that it was harder than any other. They all seemed the same to me, fairly inconsequential. I said as much.

"You seem angry, Jennifer," he said.

"I'm not angry," I said. "I just don't think the session was hard. I don't understand why you're calling me."

David said this would be a great opportunity for me to explore my feelings about his call and why I was mad. And I said, fine, I don't think I'm mad but I'll think about it. And we hung up.

I sat on the couch and really did try to feel if I was angry, and I realized I was. And I just sat there and sat there until little pieces of thoughts (feelings?) started to come to me. I grabbed a piece of paper and wrote them down.

> What's wrong with you?
> Leave me alone.
> Don't you have a life?
> You're obsessed with me.
> Stop being so concerned. Stop bothering me.
> I don't need you, you think I do so
> that means you're stupid.
> You don't know what you're doing.

It was just beyond me that anyone could care enough to call and see if I was okay. He must be crazy. I was excited. I had figured something out! I'd explored *feelings*! I knew I'd have to tell David. But how was I going to tell him I thought he was stupid and obsessed?

Right from the beginning David had made me promise to try to be honest. He emphasized over and over how important honesty was. So the next day I took in my piece of paper and read it to him. It was really hard, and I was really nervous, but I told him I thought he was stupid and obsessed and had no life and was a loser. And then I quickly qualified it, "I don't think you're really stupid, I just get these *thoughts* that you're stupid."

David smiled and said he wasn't offended, and he knew I didn't really think he was stupid. He was proud of me for being honest.

"I'm not obsessed with you, Jennifer," he said, "but it's interesting you think that." He pointed out the similarity between him calling me, meaning he's obsessed; and of guys liking me, meaning they're losers. "You don't feel you deserve someone paying attention to you, Jennifer," he said.

"Maybe," I said, uncertain. I didn't know yet what I knew.

He smiled. "We're making progress."

That night I thought more about that notion, that I didn't feel I deserved attention. I'd known vaguely that men were losers if they liked me, but had never been able to pin it down further than that. I tried to zone in on what that was really about, and I realized I had this sense that I simply wasn't fun enough, nice enough, interesting enough, pretty enough to have men care for me unless it was really easy. If I was too difficult, it would be too much trouble for the amount of return.

"I always hear men talking about women being good in bed, but I'm never quite sure what that means. I try to be good, but after we're done I always feel like maybe instead I should've just brought 'em a pot roast."

David wanted to add a session. He said I was doing really well at the end of each appointment. I'd start to really open up and my defenses would be lowered, and then three days would go by and I'd be all closed up again and distant and not knowing what to talk about. He wanted to add Fridays.

Four days felt overwhelming to me. Just how insane did he think I was? Plus Mark and I were working on sitcom ideas, and trying to come up with movie premises, and it just seemed like too much time. We had one sitcom idea, tentatively titled *Beverly Hills Biker*, about a rough biker bodyguard, who ends up marrying his rich client's daughter; another for Lily Tomlin, where she would play not only the tough-minded creator of a soap opera, but also several different roles, some within the soap opera itself (ultimately Lily decided she didn't want to do a series, she then went on to do *Murphy Brown*). And a third idea, about a public defender.

Mark and I were just starting to pitch these ideas to the networks, as well as meeting with film executives, trying to get rewrite work on film scripts. Pitching involves a lot of meetings that are frequently getting changed at the last minute, and you had to be flexible and available.

But maybe David was right, it *was* true that Saturday always seemed tough after not coming since Tuesday. Maybe another day would be good.

"Is that going to cost me more money?" I wanted to know. As always, my primary concern. David reassured me we would add this extra day at no charge. We were already more than halfway through the initial six weeks/twenty sessions, and it would really only add two more days. We weren't even talking about what would happen once the twenty sessions were up, but I think we both knew I was going to keep going.

We added Fridays. I was now going to therapy four days a week.

––––––

I was home one night, and I was having this weird feeling of not being comfortable, an unease in my body, and I couldn't shake it. It occurred to me that maybe this was what David was talking about, the mind-body thing. Was this some sort of anxiety? I didn't know, I just knew I didn't like it. I tried to get my mind on other things, but the feeling of unease remained. I was getting more and more uncomfortable and I just wanted the feeling to go away.

I felt like a teenage boy calling a girl for the first time (as much as I knew about that, which was not much). I picked up the phone and dialed six times before I actually let it ring. It was his pager, and I said in this croaky, strangled voice, "It's Jennifer. It's nine o'clock. Good-bye." That was it, name and time, click.

He called me back within five minutes. I felt sickened and humiliated that I'd called. My skin crawled. I wanted to take it back, pretend it never happened. He kept reassuring me and telling me it's okay to ask for help. "I'm not asking for help." I said. "I just felt uncomfortable and wanted to know how to get rid of it."

We talked for almost an hour, about anxiety and what could've caused it, and by the end of the conversation the uncomfortable feeling had gone. I still felt horribly embarrassed, and told him I'd never call again. I apologized for keeping him on the phone that long. "I'm a grown-up, Jennifer," he said. "If I didn't want to talk to you I wouldn't. I like talking to you." He said good night, and we hung up.

The next day of course I wondered how much he was going to charge for that phone conversation, and when I asked he said it wouldn't cost anything. If it was so hard for me to ask for help, why make it more difficult? I liked that I'd save money, but even for David that seemed overly generous.

"I don't understand why you're doing this," I said. David asked me what I meant. "Why you spend so much time with me, why you reduced the price, why you would talk to me free on the phone, everything." I was getting that feeling again like something was wrong with him. I knew it was related to my lack of self-esteem, and I felt it would be good to talk about it.

"I like helping you, Jennifer," he said. "I told you I think you're very special. Do you believe me?" He asked that question a lot, whenever he would tell me something or promise me something. He was always trying to reassure me. I said I guess I believed him. He went on to explain that he could do those things for me because money wasn't important to him. His wife was wealthy; he didn't even need to work.

"She wants me to retire," he said. "And in fact, before I met you, I was phasing out my practice."

He told me he was planning to give up private practice in order to write books and spend time with his family. "Contrary to your belief that I'm a loser, I have a really wonderful and interesting life," he said, smiling. He said that when he met me it was only for a consultation, and that he had in fact been planning to refer me to someone else.

"But if you're ready to quit being a therapist, what if I need to keep seeing you for a while or something?" Was he going to just leave me?

"Jennifer, come on," he said, "I've made a commitment to you. However long it takes. If it's five years, fine. If it's ten, fine."

"But then I'll be your only patient. You'd drive all the way here just to see me?" He lived in Dana Point, a wealthy community one and a half to two hours away, but had a condo in Santa Monica where he stayed part of the week in order to see patients.

"Jennifer," he said, "what's more valuable, a little time spent in a car, or saving your spirit?" He smiled at me, waiting.

"I guess you can always deduct the miles," I told him.

It was almost the end of August. We had four more sessions to go, and I knew we'd soon be talking about the idea of continuing. It was the beginning of the hour, and as usual I was having a hard time getting going. "You start," I'd frequently joke with David when I'd be stuck. This time he volunteered on his own.

"I want to talk to you about something, Jennifer," David said. He smiled. "It's about our therapy. I've had a really great idea."

"You're doing really great, Jennifer," David said. "You're making incredible progress. In a month you're where most people would be in a year."

"Really?" Very matter-of-fact.

"You work really hard. You're a real warrior," David went on.

"Yeah, I worry a lot," I said.

"No, a *warrior*," he said, and he spelled it. "You're fighting really hard for your spirit, Jennifer, and I'm really proud of you. We have a long way to go, though," he said.

"I'm pretty fucked up, huh?" I said, proving that writers are not always good with words.

"You were just never taken care of, Jennifer," he said, seriously. "And you should've been. You deserved it. You're very special. You know I think that, right?" I said I did. He told me that almost every time we met.

"I have an idea," David said, "but first I want you to know that I don't do this for everyone. Do you believe me?" I said, of course. "I'd like you to commit to a year," he said. "And I know you have a problem with money, so I've thought hard about what I can do to help you." He paused. Smiled. "This is really good, Jennifer, it's really good."

He'd come up with a figure that would reflect a drop in his fee from ninety-two dollars a session, already a reduction, down to eighty dollars.

David had told me that when he got his degree from Pepperdine University, he'd been the youngest Ph.D. ever in the state of California, so I knew he must be really brilliant. Even though he was phasing out his practice, he was still extremely busy. Not a session went by where his pager didn't go off at least seven or eight times. He consulted to corporations, and worked at different hospitals with terminally ill cancer patients. He was not lacking for work, and could certainly make more money off someone else if he chose to. "Are you sure?" I asked.

"I want to tell you something about myself, Jennifer," he said. "I never do things I haven't thought about very carefully. I don't want to make a commitment I could ultimately resent." He went on, "And when I make a commitment, just so you know, it's for life. Forever." But, he added, this decision actually didn't take that much thought at all. In fact, it was easy.

"There's one thing," David went on. "In order for me to do this, I want you to pay upfront. I need to see you're willing to make the same commitment as me."

I was silent for a long moment. Four days a week, fifty weeks a year. He wanted sixteen thousand dollars. That seemed like an enormous amount of money. On the other hand, as David pointed out, this was now almost half his normal fee. If he was willing to do this for me, didn't I owe myself the same?

I'd had a fairly good year professionally the year before, and had enough money in the bank, but even so ... My Writer's Guild insurance only paid twenty-five hundred dollars a year for psychotherapy (ironic, considering people in show business needed therapy more than anyone—or perhaps that's why; we would bankrupt them), so I'd be shelling out thirteen and a half thousand dollars in cash. Admittedly this was my spirit I was talking about, but did I really want to be doing this for a year?

I had written a poem in my journal a few weeks earlier:

WALK
I took a walk
So tired I wanted to sleep
Down a road, hard, cracked,
rising up in chunks
Built by a juvenile chain gang
I met someone
Not a man, a shadow
I have so much
to show you, he said
I heard the smile (tears) in his voice
I sat down by the side of the road
to make my decision.

David said he would make the same offer he'd made before. If I changed my mind at any time, he'd give me all the money back. "I don't care about the money, Jennifer," he said. "I only want you to pay because you'll feel weird if it's free, and it won't be as helpful, but

I still want you to feel safe that you can get all your money back if you change your mind."

I thought about it for a minute. "Okay, I'll do it," I told him. "And I won't change my mind. I know this is helping me."

And it was. For the first time I was paying attention to what was inside me, exploring my feelings, learning what feelings even were. I was learning about my mind and body being connected. I was trying to understand sadness, to comprehend my lack of desire, my negativity, and my anger, which was my predominant emotion. I was learning all these things, and they were going to change me forever. Sixteen thousand dollars seemed a small price to pay for a life.

One of the things David was teaching me about was anxiety and the benefit to be gained by examining it.

Without knowing what they were, I used to have these mini anxiety attacks whenever I was out to dinner with my parents. If I was visiting with them at their house I'd be okay, but if we were in a restaurant, or even at the suggestion of going out to eat, I'd get this inexplicable feeling of unease inside my body, a faint, vague churning in my stomach. I came to realize it was because if I was with them in the house I could watch TV or read or go to bed, but in a restaurant I was stuck with them, trapped with these two people to whom I had nothing to say. Nothing.

I remembered occasions when my father and I would go out to a movie (my mother would rarely want to go, she would only see movies that were totally happy, with nothing distressing in them at all), and we'd drive to the theater, completely silent in the car. If anything was said at all it was my father telling me to slow down, or to keep both hands on the wheel. Except he'd never actually say, "Slow down." He'd say gruffly, "Jennifer, there's lots of police on this road."

And I'd respond, "Good, maybe we'll meet some."

My father's criticisms of my driving were the longest conversations we ever had. I'd always be going too fast, or in the wrong lane, or not paying attention, or driving too close to another car. Eventually, after my sarcasm didn't work, I'd ask him to please stop criticizing, and he'd ignore me. Only when I would scream "Okay, you fucking drive!" would he stop.

At the movie we'd sit in total silence, and then we'd leave and drive home. Sometimes I'd say, "Did you like it?" And he'd say, "Yes, it was good," or "Not really." That was it. I didn't know if he even registered what the movie was about. Those were my evenings out with my dad. Just pointless.

Until I started exploring things with David, I'd had no idea how little there was between me and my parents. And didn't know that that wasn't normal.

One day David told me he wanted to share something with me

about his family. He asked me if that was okay. I thought it was a little unusual, but I said fine.

"You know I have twins," he said. I said I did. He said they were a year old, a boy and a girl.

I'd always wanted to be a twin, but I didn't know why. David theorized that everyone knows twins have a special bond, and maybe I wanted contact with someone who really understood me.

David went on to describe how each morning he'd take his twins swimming in his pool for an hour each. He wanted to spend time with each of them individually before he went to work, even though that meant getting up two hours earlier.

"My daughter loves the water and loves to splash and gets really excited," David said, "but my son is very tentative and timid, and needs to be held close and to just touch the water with his toe."

He told me they were also very different in the ways they'd fall asleep. His daughter liked to be held perfectly still in order to fall asleep, while his son needed constant rocking. "They're twins, but they're very different," he said, "and I take that into account when I'm with them." He went on, "If I'm in my office at home working and one of the children comes in, crawls in, I can tell who it is, even without looking. I can feel their presence."

I thought it was really amazing that he cared for his children that way, took that much time with them, knew them so well. "But that's the way it's supposed to be, Jennifer," David said. "That's what parents are supposed to do."

I was completely taken aback. That had never crossed my mind.

My father had never set aside an hour a day to spend with me. As far back as I could remember, when I was around him he was usually reading or asleep. I believed I could walk in a room accompanied by a live band and he still probably wouldn't know I was there.

My mother took me to ballet and violin lessons and made me do my homework and all the things you're supposed to do, but she knew nothing about who I was, or what those things meant or didn't mean to me. She took me because those things were expected of her; that's what mothers do. The minimum daily requirement. She never had the energy or desire to go beyond that.

I barely remember this but as a child I was very good at ballet, even exceptional. I loved it, and I am told I adored my teacher, although I have no memory of that. At the age of nine or ten, I was dancing with ballerinas twice my age with twice as much experience and I received the highest honors at every test level. Now, at just over five feet tall, I am obviously too short to have become a professional dancer, but at the time, with my final height uncertain, I clearly had at least some potential. I don't know the details, but my teacher died suddenly. My mother couldn't be bothered to find me another ballet school, she never encouraged me to keep it up, and I never danced again.

My sister was a very gifted violinist as a child in London, maybe even a prodigy. Yet when we moved to America, my mother never made an attempt to find her another teacher.

I never recall my parents asking me to show them or tell them what I did in ballet or at my riding lessons or anytime, although I do remember that when I was around eight we had a little routine where I'd walk into the living room and announce that I wanted to sing them a song I learned in school; and I'd stand in front of them and sing gibberish and they'd laugh.

While I had been unhappy and angry and solitary my whole life; while I believed I was ugly and worthless; while all other kids were dating and having boyfriends, in high school, in college, and as an adult; while I hated my career and saw no hope for my future; not once, ever, did my parents (my psychiatrist father) seem to notice or ask me what was wrong.

I confronted my father on that point once, far into my therapy. "You never even knew I was unhappy my whole childhood," I shouted.

"We most certainly did!" he shouted back.

What David had described had simply not been my experience. "Well, thanks for pointing out my fucked-up family," I said. David didn't laugh. He waited for me to go on.

"Okay, fine, you want me to admit it, I'm jealous that you're that good to your children," I said. Of course I would have wanted a father like that. To have my father take me in the pool for an hour. I would have accepted *looking* at a pool for an hour with my father. Looking at a *photo* of a pool.

"I didn't tell you to make you jealous," David said, noting that talking about their children was something most therapists don't do.

He had told me because he wanted me to know that's the way it should've been for me, as opposed to the way it was, and that maybe I could understand why I had become the person I was.

I had a puppy once, I was fourteen. A Golden Retriever. We'd had him only a few days, but already I loved him. One night, in the middle of the night, the puppy started screaming. Spinning in circles and screaming and foaming at the mouth. This tiny, sweet puppy, suffering terribly, going mad. My parents locked him in the bathroom and he just kept screaming, the worst sound I've ever heard. I couldn't bear it. The vet came and said the puppy had distemper, and he took him away and put him to sleep. I watched the puppy leave and my parents said good night to me, and I went back to bed. Neither my mother nor my father comforted me.

———

I was out to dinner with a friend of mine, Deborah Swisher, a fellow stand-up comic and actress. She was the only person besides Paul Avery who knew I was in therapy. I was excited about what was happening, what I was learning about myself, and what a wonderful guy David was.

I told her the story about his twins, about the way he treated them, his ability to feel their presence. Swish thought David sounded very cool, and she was happy that he seemed to be helping me.

The next day I started to freak out. David had shared something personal about his family, and I'd just blithely told someone else. He'd made a point of telling me I was the only patient who even knew he had children, and that he kept his life very private. "There's a reason for it, but you'd be shocked if you knew how private my life is," he'd told me. And here I had just blabbed about his family to someone he didn't even know.

I panicked. I'd betrayed him. He was going to hate me. Our therapy was over. I was convinced of it.

I went to the session and I was paralyzed with fear. I could barely talk. I couldn't even tell him I'd betrayed him by talking about his family without his permission, so I had to write it on a piece of paper. At the bottom I wrote that I understood that the therapy was over. I handed him the paper and watched him read it.

"It's not over, Jennifer," David said. "It's fine. I'm not mad. It's okay."

I let out a huge breath. "Really?"

"There's only one reason I would ever end our therapy, Jennifer," he said, "and that's if you purposefully did something to hurt me or my family. Nothing else would ever cause me to leave you. Do you believe me?"

I told him I'd never do anything to hurt his family, and he said he knew that. "You're much too good a person, Jennifer."

———

David had a collection of MontBlanc pens, one of which he'd bring in to the office every day. He played with the pen constantly throughout each session, turning it round and round in his hands, flipping it end to end, rolling it in his fingers. One of the pens had a snake on it, entwined around the end. Sometimes, David confessed, he was actually a little scared of the snake.

"What do you think about the fact that your therapist is afraid of his pen?" David said. He laughed lightly, embarrassed.

I'm not a big fan of snakes myself, but admitted, "Honestly, David, that's weird. It's just a pen."

He laughed again, and said he wasn't really afraid of it, just that sometimes it looked a little spooky. "Most of the time I really like it," he said.

———

I was starting to feel more secure in therapy, and was even able to call David occasionally and ask for help if I felt anxiety, or was upset about something. It was still very hard for me to call, and my message would be the same strangled "It's Jennifer, it's nine o'clock, 'bye."

The number I had was his pager, rather than a home phone. The message on the pager was: *"Hello. You've reached the office of Dr. David Cohen. If this call is urgent, you can activate my pager by putting in your phone number followed by the pound sign. Thank you."*

I used to tell him that he must have a hell of a lot of crazy patients with a lot of problems because his pager went off constantly during sessions, sometimes eight or nine times. He'd check the number, then press some buttons to quiet the beeping. I asked him if he couldn't turn the pager off so we wouldn't be interrupted, but he was reluctant. He wanted Roxanna to be able to reach him at any time, especially because of the children.

"Why don't you have a separate beeper with a number only she knows?" I suggested.

"That's a really good idea, Jennifer," David said, and he promised to think about it.

Despite all those calls, I seldom saw other patients of David's in the waiting room. There was an older woman I saw once or twice, and a younger woman who I saw maybe four or five times. She seemed to hate me, giving me hostile looks whenever we encountered each other. I privately called her the "evil witch," and I told David I didn't like her. Even though new to the kind of therapy that actually led to any kind of introspection, I was astute enough to wonder if I was just being jealous, and imagining her nastiness, but David admitted that she wasn't the most pleasant person. She had been his patient for quite a while, from before his marriage. "I probably shouldn't be telling you this," he said, "but when I told her I was getting married, she told me she hoped my wife would die on our honeymoon."

Lovely. And I thought *I'd* been rude when I cut in front of her going into the bathroom. I wondered if that wouldn't have affected the way he felt about her. David admitted that although he didn't like her very much, he still worked very hard on her behalf. She had children, David explained. "I'm helping her get well because of her children."

"Well, I think she's a bitch," I told him.

David laughed and agreed, "She *is* a bitch."

When I would call David, even though I'd never enter my phone number, or ask him to return the call quickly, he'd always call back right away. I'd apologize for disturbing him, and he'd say that he liked talking to me, he *wanted* to talk to me. He was always patient, gentle, reassuring. We never hung up without me feeling better and secretly being glad I called.

He told me the only time I might not be able to reach him would be on Thursday nights, because that was the night the whole family went out on their boat and frequently his pager didn't work.

"But you can still call me on Thursdays," he explained. It was just that he'd leave the pager at home, so it might take him longer to return the call.

One Saturday night I was having a lot of anxiety that I couldn't shake and I really wanted to talk to him. I'd never called him on a weekend.

He called me back almost immediately. There was static on the phone, and he explained he was talking on a cell phone from a friend's driveway. He'd been at a party and there was nowhere private to make the call, so he'd gone out to his car. I felt terrible ruining his evening; and I apologized profusely. He told me I didn't ruin his evening at all.

"But it's Saturday night," I said, "I shouldn't be calling you on a Saturday."

"Jennifer," David replied, "your soul doesn't know it's Saturday."

I once told David that it was my belief most people in the world were evil, not good; citing horrific animal abuse, child abuse, abuse of the elderly, war, greed ... I expected him to disagree with me, but surprisingly he didn't.

He said he was afraid I was probably right, that his belief was that of, say, two hundred people, probably only three were good—meaning kind, loving, passionate, and "impeccably honest" (he stressed honesty above all else). It became a catch phrase for us—"Three and one-ninety-seven." You were either one or the other.

With his constant support, enthusiasm, and generosity, David was proving to me that he was one of the three.

———

It was the end of September, and things were going well. I'd been in therapy a little over two months, and already my friends were noticing a change in me. I was too unaware to notice it in myself, but they said I seemed happier, more relaxed.

Out one night at the movies with my friend Matt Hansen, a group of people behind us talked loudly through the entire opening credits of the film. This has always been one my pet peeves, and is usually enough to send me flying over the seats threatening bodily harm if they don't "please shut the fuck up!" A ridiculous threat considering I'm not even an inch over five feet. As they yammered away, Matt waited for the inevitable blowup, and wondered as always if he was going to have to step in to defend me. When I did nothing, Matt, who had no idea I was in therapy, looked at me in disbelief. "Okay, what have you done with Jennifer?" he asked.

Mark and I had been pitching pilot ideas to the networks, and there was a strong possibility of doing one for NBC. They had made a deal with a stand-up comic named Tom Rhodes, who one of the comedy-development executives had seen at the Montreal Comedy Festival. They wanted to know if we had an idea for him.

Going into a pilot with talent attached is always preferable to just writing one and casting it later. Sometimes a great pilot is written, but the right lead actor or actress can't be found, or isn't available, and the pilot simply disappears. More importantly, the networks feel much more inclined to pursue pilots with talent they have a financial commitment to.

Tom had long hair, and his stand-up showed a sort of irreverent attitude toward life. I came up with the idea of putting him into our public defender show. It would be an ensemble show that would allow the free-spirited Tom the opportunity to preach his beliefs, defending the poor and the weak and the scummy, in the conservative courtroom venue. The old "fish-out-of-water" deal, which is the staple of so many sitcoms.

NBC loved the idea and suggested we pitch it to Tom. He would be hearing lots of different ideas from lots of different writers and deciding which one he wanted to go with. He was in the enviable position that stand-ups long for, where the network really liked him and was looking to put him on TV.

Mark and I got together to flesh out the idea and work out our pitch. This could be a big opportunity for us.

I had had some hesitation about continuing to work with Mark because he had a temper that when it erupted could even scare me. But he had promised to work on it, and David agreed that with the payoff being my own show it was worth trying to stick it out. Mark and I had done some really good work together in the past. He was a friend of Tom's from his stand-up days, and this looked like it could actually happen. David promised to support me through Mark's occasional outbursts.

———

Every session with David seemed now to be jam-packed, sometimes even going over an hour if he didn't have another patient. He was frustrated by not being able to spend even more time together.

"I've been thinking, Jennifer," he said to me one day, "I don't want to waste any more time rescuing your spirit. It's too important. I've come up with another idea."

We made Tuesdays a double session. Since we frequently ran over anyway, David thought it'd be a great idea to formalize it. "The more we meet, the faster we can get your spirit back," he said.

"How will I know my spirit?" I wondered. "How will I recognize it?" David reassured me I'd know. It was hard for me to know what he meant. Spirit? Soul? I was just this person who existed. Was there really more?

For the year, I paid David an extra four thousand dollars for this additional hour.

I came in to a session one day very excited, or at least as excited as I ever got. Things had taken a good turn financially.

It was around mid-October, and Mark and I had just gotten a rewrite on a Disney movie (*That Darn Cat*), which would bring each of us twenty-five thousand dollars. Of course, as I told David, with taxes and commissions to my agent and lawyer, I'd end up with closer to twelve, thirteen thousand. Still, I was pleased. I'd been trying to break into the lucrative arena of movie rewrites, and maybe this was the start.

———

Mark could display an angry and at times bitter side, yet he had a lovely wife and a child, and what looked like a happy marriage. My anger, although a predominant emotion, was not as vehement as Mark's could be, yet I had managed to find no one.

Likewise I never understood how my sister's and my life turned out so differently. Hadn't we had the same parents, and presumably the same experiences? Yet Jane always had lots of friends; and always had a boyfriend, starting in high school, through college, and in law school. At her first professional job, she met her husband. She was now happily married, with three beautiful girls.

I had relatively few close friends, never dated, never had a boyfriend, had absolutely no interest in having children, loved only the animals I'd had as a child—dogs, cats, pony, horses, mice; and the two cats I had now. My barren life must be my own fault. I obviously hadn't taken what my parents offered me.

As my therapy with David progressed, I started carefully confiding in Jane, hesitatingly sharing with her some of the things I was talking about. Never having had discussions of any private nature before, we weren't really sure how to talk to each other, the intimacy was so unfamiliar to us. I wondered if maybe this was how sisters were supposed to be.

We tiptoed around the subject of our growing up, both of us joking and making light of things, laughing about how difficult Mom could be; how distant Dad was. I was surprised to learn that Jane and I had experienced childhood in a very similar way. Rather than feeling sad for her, I felt relief. Could it be I wasn't the ungrateful daughter I thought I was? Or, then again, maybe we were both just spoiled brats.

As we talked further, I realized that although we had indeed felt the same abandonment and disinterest, we fled from it in opposite ways. Jane didn't just have lots of boyfriends, but ran from one to another, searching desperately for a boy (father) to love her, take care of her. She couldn't bear to be alone.

I couldn't bear for anyone to be near me. I pretended I needed nothing, and indeed came to need nothing.

But why did Jane and I react so differently? David theorized that along with differences in our basic temperament, birth order could have played a role. While not the oldest child, I was the oldest girl. Maybe all my parents' anxiety flowed into this first tiny, needy female. During my sessions, I started to examine how their own unhappy lives might have affected me.

My parents' life seemed one half-lived. I saw no passion in it, no exuberance, no sense of the thrill of life. No sense of adventure. No daring. No joy. My father particularly seemed unhappy, dull, half-real. He had no friends, only colleagues; no hobbies except the solitary ones of reading and gardening; it seemed he wanted nothing more than to not be bothered. To live oblivious. The only time I ever saw him animated was when he was talking to other psychiatrists about some new way he'd come up with to handle troubled adolescents.

As a child when I would act out, my father would tell me to settle down, to relax, stop. As an adult, David told me, "Acting out has magic in it. It has storytelling in it."

David thought I learned to contain myself so I would not threaten my parents' one-note lives. If they were taken care of, if I caused them no stress or anxiety, maybe then they would be able to take care of me.

About two months into therapy I had a dream. I got up and wrote it down, and the next I day showed it to David.

I'm in a building, trying to get away from someone, a man, chasing me. I make it down some stairs, but they dead-end into a wall. I run, finally I make it to another room, a tiny room no one knows about. There's a window, I push it open, it's in many weird sections, they're very heavy, they keep falling on me so I can't get out. I wriggle my way out and I escape. I run, ducking down paths, behind cars. When I am spotted, I act like a zombie so no one will know. Everyone walks around like zombies. There is a squirrel, it's not supposed to be with me, it's too wild. Too fun. The grounds of this place are immaculate, with beautiful, perfectly manicured grass, flower beds, etc. The place is huge, vast, so huge it's hard to even know which direction is out. I see this beautiful mosaic-tiled tower, on the edge of the complex. I head in that direction, always acting zombie-like, vacant and wide-eyed, if spotted. Finally I get to a big wide street, others are there making their escape. We have to cross this street, which will expose us to being seen. We're cautious, we're scared, we must not get caught. We wait, then run. We arrive at a tunnel-like building, disused, very dark inside, almost pitch black with a dirt floor. I get used to the dark. The escape is down drainage pipes. I ask if they're sewer pipes, am told, not really sewer, but they're very dirty. On the other side we know a barbecue is going on, that's where we're headed. We change clothes to go through the tunnel. I put my other clothes in a trunk along with everyone else's. The trunk will go with us so we can put on our own, clean clothes on the other side. I close up my purse tightly. I will sling it across my body on my trip down the tunnel. I'm ready to go. But I woke up before I escaped.

I remember as a little girl in London going to see the Beatles with my mother. All the kids around me were screaming, and I wanted to scream and to be a part of that, but I was too embarrassed in front of my mother. At one point I asked her, "Can I scream?" And she said yes, but I couldn't do it. I had to ask my mother's permission to scream at the Beatles when all the kids around me were going completely berserk, and I still couldn't bring myself to do it, because it was too much pleasure to show, too much enjoyment, too much being out of control. So I just sat silently and watched the Beatles.

I found out much later that I was not the only one to carefully control and contain my life. My sister told me once that as a little girl she used to pack a little suitcase, get on her bicycle, and ride around and around the driveway, pretending to run away.

My parents' lives from childhood had been very unhappy, what little I knew of them. I was aware that my grandmother, my mother's mother, did not care very much for my mother, and clearly preferred my two uncles.

As a child and teenager in her small northern England town, my mother desperately wanted to be an actress. It was her dream, she longed for it, and she had shone in school productions. Her father told her that if she passed the test for the Royal Academy of Dramatic Arts in London, they would find a way to pay for her to attend. The day of the test came, and her mother refused to let her take it.

Without knowing many other details, I knew that my grandmother as a rule treated my mother horribly, ignoring her most of the time, only paying attention to her when she was ill.

My mother broke her wrist once in a car accident, and her back was also causing her a lot of pain. Rather than call her doctor and ask for pain medication, she preferred to tell my sister and me how terribly she was suffering. When we suggested she call her doctor for help, she said plaintively, "Stop yelling at me." When the pills finally arrived, she delayed taking them. The effort was too much.

She wanted to suffer. Suffering brought her so much more attention than if she was feeling good.

In her life, everything was a trauma, was going to turn out badly, was too difficult. But she was clever with her complaints, always adding, "I'm fine, it doesn't matter, I'll be all right," in a way certain to show you the opposite. To ensure the most effort would have to be put out by the person trying to care for her.

As a child and teenager, with my father rarely around, and my brother not being (at least at the time) the most nurturing type, it was up to me, the oldest daughter, to make her happy.

Of course, as David pointed out, my attempts to do so were futile, only temporary at best. That's why as I grew up I tried to control everyone else in my life, because the one job I had been assigned, I had failed at.

Until David explained it to me, I had had no idea it wasn't the child's job to take care of her mother. That it should've been the other way around.

It never occurred to me to wonder why my sister and I grew up with nannies. My mother had no career, no job, no hobbies—virtually nothing to do but take care of us. Why did she need a nanny to help her? She told my sister once that she was glad her three children had each been born five years apart. "That way," she said, "when I had a new baby, the older ones could take care of themselves."

As I had told David, my father's life was filled with loss—losing his father, mother, sister, brother, sister-in-law, another sister, nephew . . .

He was cursed. It was not surprising he had learned to shut down. How else could he not go insane with grief? I felt sorry for him. In fact, the only sadness I ever felt in session was for my parents, particularly my father, never for myself. I told David over and over, "They didn't mean any harm. They did the best job they could."

David disagreed. He believed they were irresponsible and lazy. If you're not prepared to take care of your children, and put passion into it, he said, don't have them.

And I would argue and argue that I'd heard way worse stories than mine; kids beaten, sexually abused, screamed at, ridiculed. I had nothing like that to tell. How could I complain? At the same time I told David that sometimes I wished my parents *had* done something like that, starved me, left me with dirty diapers, something. Something concrete that I could get my mind around, so I could understand why they meant so little to me. But there was nothing concrete to their behavior. There was almost no behavior at all.

It was so hard for me to get across to people the idea of my family, the complete barrenness. Because there was nothing they could see. As children we wore beautiful clothes, went to the best schools, lived in lovely homes. But our family was a shell, a beautifully decorated piñata, hollow inside. And in our case, if you broke it open, it would fall empty to the ground.

David agreed that it would have been easier for me in a way if I'd been physically abused, but for a different reason. He told me, "You know, Jennifer, I would never hit my children, and I think people who hit their children are horrible. But in a weird way, it would almost have been better for you to have been hit, because at least your parents would've shown some passion toward you. Shown *some* interest in you."

"My therapist asked me if my parents ever sexually molested me when I was a child. I said, no, of course not. (PAUSE) Was I so unattractive to them?"

David talked a lot about passion. Not in a sexual sense, but in a life sense. Energy, enthusiasm, daring, a leaping into the fray. He believed that people who are afraid of passion cannot bear to see it in others.

I had written in my journal:

WANTING

I'm turned inside out, a mass of flesh, bloody, exposed, quivering. I'm twelve, eighteen inches long, on the ground. Angry delinquent boys with sticks surround me, poking at me. They will kill me for wanting something 'cause they have nothing. Fuck her we have nothing, why should she have anything? They're so angry that I want something when they have nothing, how dare I? Who does she think she is? So I pretend I want nothing so they won't kill me out of anger. I tell them I want nothing and lie there still, pretending to be dead, beaten, then I crawl into a hole and hide and choke and finally fall asleep. And the flesh turns in on itself, becoming more and more rotted and putrid, and it becomes smaller and smaller, squirming in on itself in shame.

This vision had come to me one day, unbidden, a vision both in pictures and in words, as if I could almost see them written down in front of me. I was startled. Amazed. Intrigued. Those thoughts were inside me? Those images?

More importantly, could my parents be the boys with sticks?

I protested to David, "My parents never told me I couldn't want things."

And of course they didn't have to. As David explained, your parents don't have to tell you how to live, you learn by watching the way *they* live. Or don't.

One of my only childhood memories in London is of being in our neighbors' car. I must have been about five or six. The father was driving up the street and he would take his hands off the steering wheel and clap his hands, and all the kids just thought it was so great. And I remember thinking, my dad would never do anything like that. So outrageous and daring and silly. And I was just amazed that this man would take his hands off the steering wheel and clap and make us all laugh.

My father had no sense of playfulness; he was never fun to be with. I remember once as an adult being in a car with my parents and another couple, Etan and Caroline Schwartz, who were two of my parents' few friends (Etan was a fellow psychiatrist). I had always liked them, particularly Etan, who was very funny. Etan was driving us home from a restaurant. He made a game of telling us his car wouldn't turn left, so in order to get home every left turn became three rights. It was funny and silly and we were all laughing, except my father, who was furious. He saw it as ludicrous, a waste of time. He kept saying, "Could we just go home, please, and stop this?" Etan kept teasing him and telling him, "I can't help it, Derek, it's the car," and my father just became more and more angry. And of course it was ruined. It stopped being fun, and it became miserable and uncomfortable and so typical of my father, and as I did so often, I wished he wasn't my father.

My parents got into a huge fight with the Schwartzes sometime later, because of something Etan did that offended them at a party. I never understood exactly what happened, only that Etan had drunk a little too much and criticized them somehow, and it blew up. The couples didn't speak for months, and the friendship never fully recovered.

David had suggested a name to describe the place my parents inhabited—Pluto, the coldest planet. And that voice in my head that told me over and over it was too late for me, I was too old, too ugly, I could never be happy, I would always be alone, that my life was a waste and would forever be one—we called the Pluto Dude.

I had written another poem in my journal:

THE PLUTO DUDE
The Pluto dude
He's got candy
Come inside (whisper)
Your eyes are safe with me
Don't look. There, there
see now,
foolishness
The Pluto dude's a big Doris Day fan
And he's got candy.

The Pluto dude told me not to look at my life, that looking was pointless. He believed in "Qué Será Será," that nothing could be changed. And his argument was both enticing and persuasive.

When I would get negative thoughts in my head; about my future, about David being a loser because he cared about me, that I was fat and ugly and worthless and tiresome, I learned to step back and say, that's not me, that's the Pluto dude.

Toward the end of October, David suggested increasing our time together even more. "Look how much you're learning, Jennifer," he enthused. "I can't believe the progress you're making." We made Monday a double session, and added a whole other day, Wednesday, which would also be double. Three more hours a week.

David's normal days in L.A. were Monday, Tuesday, Friday, and Saturday. He and his wife and twins would leave Dana Point early Monday morning, stay in their Santa Monica condo, and return Tuesday night. Then they would come back to L.A. Friday morning, and stay until after his last Saturday appointment. Which was me.

Before we added the Wednesday, David said he needed to talk to his wife about it, because it meant changing his family's schedule. They wouldn't be going back to Dana Point on Tuesday nights, but instead after our Wednesday appointment.

"She's happy for me to do it," David told me the next day. So we added the time, and I paid David twelve thousand dollars, making my total almost thirty-four thousand. Luckily I had the money. In fact it seemed cosmic; it was almost exactly what I'd made on my Disney rewrite. Maybe even the gods were finally on my side.

In a session one day I asked David if he believed in angels. He wanted to know why I asked. "If there are angels," I said, "I want to know where mine has been all my life. Who's been looking out for me?" My throat tightened as I asked the question. It was the first time I ever felt sadness for myself.

David said he didn't know if he believed in angels or not. "You seem sad, Jennifer," he said.

"No," I said, "I was just thinking about it, that's all."

November 28. It was my birthday. Not a great day for me. I was sitting on the couch, not really knowing what to talk about, when David said he had something for me. A birthday card. I was surprised and flattered.

My name was sprawled in big purple letters across the front of a white envelope. I opened it and pulled out the card. It was a colorful abstract of a cat. David knew I had two cats, Lewis and Baby, whom I loved dearly.

"Open it, Jennifer," he said, explaining that he had written it the day before.

NOVEMBER 27, 1995

Dear Jennifer—
    Happy Birthday!
    Battling 2 release your spirit (and the passion that belongs 2 your spirit) from the sordid grasp of the Pluto Dude will B the hardest battle of your life. In spite of the inherent difficulty, you—we will win, quite decisively, although I submit a military strategy that will minimize bloodshed to our army.
    First, and most importantly, **you** (whatever we call that you— soul, spirit, or essence) **R more important than anything**, including comfort, interpersonal conflict, or the needs of others. The Pluto Dude will continue 2 remind you otherwise, in a myriad of tricky and insidious ways, but you-we must keep our collective eye on the 2 truths that possess a capital T . . . **You own the deed 2 your spirit and you-we must minister to its most authentic desires.** Provid-

ing your spirit with the twins of time & space is our joint & ultimate responsibility, with you as the owner & me as the advocate. Given that time & space, your spirit will bloom, like a perfect lavender rose, in all of it's gigantic & original radiance, anything else would violate the most immutable law of nature. But don't B fooled—as the Pluto Dude, in the banal monologue that defines his existence, mumbles otherwise.

Jennifer—on this, the eve of your birthday—I invite you 2 join me in a massive commitment: 2 squeeze 50 years of life into your next decade. I know it can be done, if you-we continue 2 give your spirit the space it needs to stretch, the nutrition your spirit needs 2 develop, and the curiosity your spirit needs in order 2 comprehend it's (sic) own divine specialness.

My spirit salutes the courage of your spirit & is in awe of its titanic resilence.

Namaste—
David

I was completely taken aback. I'd never seen anything like it. Virtually every birthday card I'd ever received from my parents was signed by my mother and said only, "Happy birthday, Love Mum and Dad." Occasionally my father would add his signature, or there would be a printed verse from the Hallmark writer saying what a nice daughter I was, but even that was rare.

I asked David what *namaste* meant. He told me it was a Japanese word meaning "The spirit in me salutes the spirit in you."

David's use of "B" for "be," and "2" for "to," struck me as odd, and somewhat affected, but I didn't say anything. How petty of me to even think that when the message was so meaningful.

I told him I liked the card, and thanked him. He said he hoped I knew he didn't give cards to all his patients, and I said okay.

I was watching TV one day, when I saw a newsmagazine show, like *20/20* or something, about a therapist who turned out to be a brainwasher, sort of a David Koresh–type; and when I saw it I wondered briefly if David wasn't some sort of brainwasher.

At first I was scared to tell him because I thought he'd be angry and hate me for thinking that after he'd been so good to me. I'd had those thoughts about him being obsessed early on, but now I knew him better. How could I even think that, even for a second?

"I don't really think you're a brainwasher," I said, when I finally got up enough nerve to say something. "It just popped into my head when I saw it on TV, that what if you were?"

David smiled, and reassured me that he wasn't a brainwasher. But he asked me to really pay attention to why I might think that, even for a second. I thought about it and I came up with, "You're willing to do all you do for me, and you lowered your price, so there must be another motive."

I had told David a story once, about a boy named Brian whom I met my freshman year in college, and I had a huge crush on. He was blond and cute and sexy and I really liked him. We went out a couple of times, and then one night we got drunk. He ended up in my dorm room and spent the night there. We didn't do much, just made-out like crazy, but in the morning I felt really sick that I'd shown him I liked him.

That day was Valentine's Day, and Brian called me that afternoon, and told me he had something for me, a gift for Valentine's Day. And I don't remember what I said, but I decided he must be the biggest loser ever, and I told him I didn't want to see him again. And I never did.

David reminded me that my thinking he was a brainwasher or was obsessed with me was like me thinking there was something wrong with Brian and his gift for me.

And of course he was right. I smiled and said I knew he wasn't a brainwasher.

———

One day in session David said he wanted to talk to me about something. My first thought was, what had I done? Was he mad at me? "What's wrong?" I said. David smiled and said nothing was wrong.

"This is a good thing, Jennifer," he said. "I have something special I'd like to share with you."

David was writing a book, a thriller called *Enemy of Passion*, and wondered if I'd like to read the first seventy-five pages. I said, Of course. He'd debated asking me, he said, but ultimately decided that the beliefs espoused by the book (in other words by him) were ones that it would be good for me to see.

"It's about a serial killer, a passionless man who only targets people with passion," he told me. "Do you see why I think it might be good for you?" He said he would bring it in the next day.

I had brought David a copy of an adolescent psychiatry book my father had written several years earlier, and for which I'd done the cover illustration. David had wanted to read it. There was a dedication in the front, "To my wife, who has been both loving and patient."

David pointed out that my father hadn't even used my mother's name. He thought that was interesting. "I guess," I said. It had seemed fine to me. I joked, "Maybe it should have said, 'To my wife, who has been both loving and *a* patient'." (I'd told David many times that I thought my mother was not only depressed but crazy). We both laughed. David took the book home.

David brought in the first seventy-five pages of *Enemy of Passion*; but before he gave it to me, he said we needed to talk.

There was a dedication in the front of the book to his wife and children, and he wasn't sure if I wanted to see that. It was very different from the dedication my father had written to my mother. He wondered, should he give me the pages minus the dedication page?

My first reaction was that it was no big deal, so what? But then, looking at David, I remembered that I was supposed to pay attention. I thought about it, and admitted that it might be hard. I knew that David really loved his family, and I figured the dedication would probably portray the types of relationships that I had longed for, both with a father and a lover. Nonetheless, I told him I wanted him to include the page with the dedication.

"You've told me a million times," I told him, "difficult things aren't necessarily bad. If it causes me to be uncomfortable, then we'll talk about it."

David smiled. "That's really good, Jennifer," he said. He handed me the stack of pages, and I opened it to the dedication.

2: ROXANNA
My Dazzling, Irreplaceable
Guardian of Passion

and

2: DARIAN and VANESSA
The Ink Behind My Words

I handed him back the pages. David asked me what I was thinking.

"I suppose I wish someone in my life had felt that way about me, the way you feel about Roxanna and your kids," I told him.

David admitted that what he and Roxanna had was very special. But, he added, "You can have that same thing too, Jennifer."

"Yeah, well, let's not go down that path," I said. We'd already had innumerable discussions about the possibility of my ever finding love, and I didn't want to have another one. I knew that it would never happen for me. David disagreed. My argument was always the same— I'd always been alone, why would things change? I'd never *had* a relationship. I had no idea how to have one. I was too old. Too unattractive. All the good men were taken. And I didn't even want a relationship anyway.

David's argument was also standard—basically that all those beliefs were from the person I was before, not the person I was fighting to become.

I always had a rejoinder—"Okay, so it ends up that I *do* want a relationship. That'll be even worse. I'll be wanting one, and I'll be alone, and that'll hurt even more. Not that I hurt now," I quickly added. I would point out the odds—I would, of course, only want to meet one of the "Three," not one of the "One-ninety-seven." Of those three, if he's such a great guy, he's probably already married. If he's not already married, who's to say he lives in L.A.? And if he does, what are the chances of my meeting him? Maybe I already met him, and didn't even know it. Probably some guy in a car that I'd flipped off for cutting me off or something. Or some guy who had smiled at me, receiving in return a scowl. (I always believed that guys smiling at me meant they were ridiculing me or felt sorry for me. A pity smile.) The odds are one in a billion, I'd tell David vehemently.

"Maybe he's a guy like you, Jennifer," David would say. "His life wasn't great, he had no relationships, never got married, and now he's ready."

Tired of the argument, I would just scoff, insisting that we drop it. "This is a waste of our time," I'd say irritably. "We're never going to agree." And that's where the discussion would end.

Now I was looking at the words he'd written to his wife, and they shoved it home to me. I'd never have anyone love me that way.

Now I know your wife's name and your kids' names." I wondered if he minded. He said he wouldn't have given me the dedication to read if he'd had a problem with it. He reminded me that very few of his patients even knew he had a wife or kids, even fewer knew her name, and none knew his kids' names.

He was actually relieved I knew, he said. He hated having to refer to them as "my wife," or "my kids," when he was using them as an example. Now when he told me things about his family meant to illuminate a point, he'd be able to speak more freely.

Before I left the session, David told me that of course I realized I was the only patient he was letting read the book.

David told me he'd had a dream about me. He had gotten up in the night and typed it up on his computer, and asked if I'd like to read it. He said it was a great dream, and he thought I would love it.

DECEMBER 20, 1995

3:51 A.M.

My body feels heavy, cumbersome. I wonder why, quickly realizing that I'm wearing a chest protector, shin guards, and a face mask. Feels good to be protected.

My body feels precarious, a weird vestibular sensation, very off-balance. I wonder why, quickly realizing that I'm wearing skates, back on the ice. A hockey game is about to start. Excited to be playing again.

I look around, the stadium resembles the one I played in at the University of Maine. The crowd is hostile, screaming vulgar obscenities at me, belligerent. Identical to the crowd of immortals I described in Chapter 48 of *Enemy of Passion*.

Suddenly, during warm-ups, I get anxious—while the other team has dozens of members, I can't locate a single member of my team. Finally, Jennifer Miller emerges. I figure out that her petite frame has been hidden behind the very broad shoulders of all our competitors. I intuitively know that Jennifer is and will be my only teammate, in this battle against dozens and dozens of surly and rugged-looking men.

Shit! The puck has dropped. Jennifer and I have no time to prepare. The other team has ten players on the ice, including three goalies; we only have Jennifer on the ice and me protecting our net.

While Jennifer is skating, I observe our uniform: it is royal purple—with the Buddhist symbol for spiritual wealth (matching the color of the earring Roxanna bought for me: black jade with a gold outline) as our team logo. Jennifer has the number 1 on her back: I become curious, look at my sleeve, see that my number is 38. Both numbers please and inspire me.

Jennifer clears the puck, giving me a moment to relax—I use that moment to check out the uniforms of our opponents. They are totally grey, from top to bottom and from left to right, with each player only having a small letter p on their quad—I construe that to be the universal symbol for Pluto. They have no logo.

We're in trouble. Jennifer—not athletic and lacking any hockey skills or experience—skates back and forth, with virtual futility. The other team (Pluto) has ten players on the ice at all times—running well-orchestrated plays, passing exquisitely well—having Jennifer run around in circles. On one occasion, a Pluto player traps Jennifer by the boards and checks her violently into the glass. She falls, bangs her head on the ice, starts to bleed. Pluto changes shifts every two or three minutes, keeping their players fresh, while Jennifer and I do not have the luxury of a single substitution.

With Jennifer running around in circles, confused, Pluto is rocketing shots at me, shots of tremendous velocity; moreover, I am being screened during every shot. Regardless, I manage to save them all . . . not really sure how, since the puck travels so fast I can't even see it. I conclude that my success in defending the shots must be based on pure instinct. The third period ends; the score is deadlocked at zero.

Jennifer and I skate back to our bench. We have no coach. The referee, Mike Ember, skates over to tell us that we have five minutes to prepare for overtime. Feeling fortunate, I tell Jennifer that this is the opportunity we were deprived of at the beginning of the game. Time and space to organize a strategy. First, Jennifer tells me how tired she is: I tell her that we'll win if she can transfer energy from her mind into her legs. Second, Jennifer tells me how cold she is, that her extremities are losing their dexterity: I tell her that we'll win if she can transfer energy from her mind into her hypothalamus, to be used in the service of temperature regulation. She asks me how to do it—I am adamant, saying that every spirit must find the secret combination to her own transfer. Continuing, I say that she will only be able to break the combination by remaining in my company. Jennifer says she likes that, and that she understands. We sit together, on our antiquated bench. I change my mask, Jennifer says that she has an idea.

We never talk about her idea, but I know exactly what she arrived at, and manage—without words—to let her know I agree it's a great idea. We know that Pluto has perverted brilliance, so, to start overtime, we continue as before, with Jennifer skating around in circles and me stopping their fierce rockets. Suddenly— so theatrically that it didn't even appear as though she was acting— Jennifer seduces a Pluto player into the boards: he checks her; she screams, falls, holding on to her knee (maybe her ankle?), pretending to be hurt.

Pluto gets excited, seizes the opportunity that her alleged injury presents, and sends all ten players at me, on attack, for an all-out breakaway. They approach on my right: I consciously calculate their tight formation and decide to come out of my crease, trying my hardest to cut down their angle and give them the smallest amount of net to shoot at. They shoot, the hardest rocket of the game; still, I manage to make a kick save, ending up in a split. Fuck, I can't cover up, the puck bounces in front of me. Every Pluto player breaks on the puck, and I—totally contorted—extend my stick and succeed in just pushing the puck down the ice. Our plan works. Jennifer stands up, healthy and revitalized, approaching on her own breakaway. Even before crossing the red line, Jennifer cocks her stick and fires a slap shot. Their goalie is lazy, failing to come out of his crease and cut off her angle. Jennifer's shot lands in the upper-right corner of Pluto's net.

The crowd vaporizes, so do all of Pluto's players. We win: 1-0.

Jennifer skates, with renewed energy, back to me. We smile and congratulate each other. She tells me that the mystery of energy transfer was the key to our victory. I agree, adding that our endurance, our teamwork, and our ability to share inner hope while surrounded by outer chaos were also essential.

I ask when our game against Neptune is scheduled for. Jennifer says Thursday night, emphasizing, "But, David, I insist—we must practice before the next battle." I comment on how much wisdom she gained in the course of our war against Pluto.

I knew enough about psychiatry, both through my father and through common sense, to know that it was not commonplace for a therapist to reveal their dreams to a patient. The unusualness of it, even the inappropriateness of it, did flash through my mind for second. But I didn't care. No one had ever told me they'd dreamed about me before. I loved that he dreamed about me, and I loved the dream. Me winning my fight, David on my side. It was perfect.

———

Mark and I were sitting in the executive offices at NBC in Burbank. Tom Rhodes had loved our idea of a public defender, and Mark and I had written a script that Tom and his managers and his agent and our agent loved. Everyone loved it, the network too. They thought it was funny, and edgy, and the characters were well defined and interesting. They just had one problem with it. Did it have to be about a public defender?

They wanted a school show. Let's make Tom a longhaired teacher in a stuffy prep school. There were about eighty other school shows being written that season, and it wasn't really our cup of tea, but if that's what they really wanted . . .

Oh, there was one other thing. We'd be writing a whole new pilot, from scratch, with a new premise, new characters, new everything. There just wouldn't be a new paycheck. We'd been paid for the first pilot, we'd have to write this one for free. Of course, it was our choice.

In Hollywood, it's a generally accepted truth that among directors, producers, stars and writers, writers notoriously receive the least amount of respect, despite the fact that without them everyone else would be unemployed. There is even an old joke in Hollywood—"How did the Polish girl try to get ahead in show business? She slept with the writer."

It would be inconceivable for an actor to be asked to perform in another version of a sitcom for no pay, yet for a writer this was pretty much par for the course.

Well, obviously Mark and I could choose to walk away, and we'd end up with no show. Or we could bite the bullet, and write it again. Mark and I were really frustrated, but eventually agreed, we had a shot, we had to take it. We told NBC we'd think about some ideas for the school show, and meet with Tom and tell him.

———

Please just don't let me have to be something lame, like a teacher," Tom said, pacing his apartment. Uh oh. Mark and I looked at each other. Okay, we said cheerfully, how about something else, like a teacher?

Tom couldn't believe the network didn't want to make the public defender script, which he had just loved. Even more, how could they want him to do this? A school show? Working with kids? He just didn't want to do it.

Mark and I told him it was the only way to go, and that NBC seemed really committed to making the pilot. Like us, Tom had the choice of saying no way, but at what cost? Finally, reluctantly, he agreed. He said he trusted us to write it to his sensibilities. "I know you guys'll make cool, man," he said.

The network approved our outline, and Mark and I started writing the Tom Rhodes pilot for the second time.

———

It was just days before Christmas, which my family always celebrated in spite of being Jewish. We simply called the tree a big Chanukah bush. We would always have an enormous mass of gifts under the tree, knee-deep piles, spreading out into the living room. It would take hours to unwrap them all, even longer to discard all the wrappings. As a kid, what could be better? As an adult, I wondered what all these presents were compensating for.

David told me he was going to buy me a gift. So of course I was going to buy him one too.

We acknowledged that this was rather unconventional, for a therapist and patient to exchange gifts. My father would have been hor-rified. Even though his patients frequently sent him bottles of liquor for Christmas (despite the fact that he didn't drink) I didn't believe he would ever buy them a gift in return.

But I didn't care. I told David, "You know what, I don't give a fuck about unconventionality because this is helping me."

I had tried conventional therapy five times and gotten nowhere. My life was not like everyone else's. I'd gone through life as a ghost, and here was someone who was finally breaking through. Who was I to argue with it? If exchanging gifts was so unconventional, then maybe the conventions were wrong.

We agreed to exchange gifts on the twenty-second, the day before I left for Chicago to spend Christmas with my parents. I didn't want to go, but David felt it might actually be beneficial, that I'd be able to see things I'd never seen before. Grist for the mill.

Since I was heading back to Pluto, and it'd be very easy for me to slip back into oblivion, to shut down, to disappear, he made me prom-ise that I'd write him a letter every day, not to be mailed, just to keep me attentive.

We also arranged a phone schedule, that I would call him every night on his pager after my parents went to sleep, and he would call me back.

Before David gave me my gift, he presented me with something that Roxanna had sent—a tin of Christmas cookies that she had baked herself.

He was very excited about his gift to me, and couldn't wait to give it to me. He handed me the card. I was excited to read it, David's enthusiasm was infectious.

I opened the envelope and pulled out the card. The outside was a painting of angels. I opened it.

Dear Jennifer:

A few weeks ago, U asked me about the death penalty. I ex-pressed my ambivalence on the subject.

Similarly, when it comes 2 angels, I'm not sure where I stand, although I'd like 2 B on the side that believes both in their existence and in their inherent benevolence. But, in spite of that equivocation,

I strongly believe in one thing: that, if angels do exist, their olfactory sense would B extremely sensitive 2 the sweet smell of a soulful spirit. In fact, 2, take it one step further, I imagine angels 2 B addicted 2 that smell as compulsively as an alcoholic might B addicted 2 gin (albeit wonderfully, and not detrimentally).

U, Jennifer, exude that smell, the soulful odor that would make you a treasure 4 any angel. U R kind, depthful, devoted 2 truth, dedicated 2 light (while understanding that all light must possess some darkness), fighting 4 the noble triad of awareness, attentiveness, and authenticity, and—most of all—U R a warrior against history. 4 all those reasons—plus many, many more—U deserve the angel you always dreamed about. That is why I've chosen an angel as your gift 4 our 1st Christmas as a team.

Out of all the available angels, I selected the one with the most pained expression. It seemed appropriate. After all the anguish U have absorbed from others, it seemed only logical 2 expect that your angel would B committed 2 absorb most or all of your pain, excited 2 help U exorcise the vampires of Pluto from your blood.

I hope, when U look at her—your private angel—U feel the solace she wants 2 provide & that she helps introduce U 2 the angel inside yourself.

Namaste.
David

I opened the gift, and it was a Baccarat crystal angel. Kneeling, its hands clasped together. It was beautiful. David had asked Roxanna where he could buy one, then gone with her to pick it out.

As I had gotten older, frequently for my birthday or Christmas I'd actually gone to Neiman Marcus or whatever and bought things for myself and had my parents pay me back; or gone through a catalog and said to my mother, "Look at the Horchow catalog, page eight, there's a candlestick that I'd really like," and she'd order things for me. She couldn't be bothered to go shopping, or she was too tired, or she simply had no idea what I liked. Although there were mounds of presents under the tree, I usually knew what they all were ahead of time. My father would usually give me a check instead of a gift, or when I was a teenager, he'd buy me expensive gold jewelry, exactly the opposite of anything I'd ever wear. He was very, very generous; there was no expense spared. But I'd almost always exchange my father's gifts; or keep them, not wanting to hurt his feelings, and never use them.

My mother would rarely buy gifts for her grandchildren throughout the year, but when Jane would show her a new outfit she'd bought for one of her girls, my mother would offer to pay for it. Wanting to look like a good grandmother, she could say to her friends, "Look what I bought Emma." Jane later found out that my mother would mark down these gift amounts in a notebook, and list them on her tax return.

I'd always been very thoughtful about gifts I'd buy people. I could spend literally days finding something absolutely perfect; something meaningful; something I thought they'd really like, not just something I liked.

For the first time in therapy I started to tear up. I felt myself choking up. I had to bite it back because I didn't want David to see me. "What's going on, Jennifer?" he asked.

"Nothing," I said.

I gave him his gift. It was a piece of art I'd made a special trip down to Laguna to buy—a spirit stick. It was a figure made of fabric and clay and feathers, on a branch of wood. It was called "Passion." David loved it. He pointed out that essentially we'd both bought each other the same gift.

I was depressed about leaving for Christmas, and depressed that I wouldn't be seeing David for eight days. As always, I realized there'd be no one special to share the holiday with. I despaired that things were ever going to change.

"This is the last Christmas you're going to feel that way, Jennifer," David said. "Next year your Christmas is going to be different. I promise."

As promised, over Christmas I wrote a letter to David every day, to keep me paying attention instead of shutting down. One day I wrote only, "I don't feel like writing anything." Not exactly deep, but at least I was fulfilling my commitment.

We talked every night, after my parents had gone to bed. Clandestine calls. It was like a secret relationship, only with my doctor. My parents still didn't know I was in therapy, nor did I have any plans to tell them.

David had asked me to try to be more aware of my relationship with my parents. I started watching their behavior more carefully. Things I'd never noticed before, or just dismissed, became glaringly obvious, particularly when I contrasted them with David's attentiveness.

I collect miniatures—dollhouses, filled with perfect replicas of real furniture. Very detailed, very exact. I'd taken two rolls of photos of a completed house to show my parents. I had built it myself, decorated it, adding shingles, siding, individual strips of wood flooring, wallpaper, curtains, everything.

I gave my father this large stack of photos, pleased with how the house had turned out. It had taken me two years to complete. He glanced through the first few pictures, it couldn't have taken him more than about twenty seconds in total. "Very nice," he said, and handed the stack back to me.

I had shown the same photos to David before I left. He spent probably ten minutes examining every one, pointing to little things that amazed him. I brought in a miniature perfume bottle, no more than a quarter of an inch high, and he held it in awe, fascinated.

Previously I would've just shrugged off my father's reaction, or very possibly not even noticed what to me was normal behavior. Now I stepped back and looked at it. That couldn't be how a father is supposed to act. Is that what it had been like my whole life? Not remembering my early childhood, I could only surmise that his disinterest, dismissiveness and boredom, which was certainly evident later in my life when I would try to talk with him, was probably an old and very typical behavior.

I did know that I didn't remember ever doing things with my father;

playing with him, taking walks with him, sitting on his lap, having him read to me. I never ran to the door to greet him when he got home, never had him kiss a cut finger. We never built things together, never played sports; he rarely came to see me ride my pony, or later my horses.

I imagined that being a little girl, and having someone take that little interest in you, could only be devastating.

The first time I cried during the period I was going through therapy, I was driving home one evening on the 405 freeway through Santa Monica. It was dark. Out of nowhere suddenly an image came to me. A little girl, it didn't seem like me, just a girl, two or three years old, alone in a dark, empty room. She was turning slowly in a circle, searching for someone, looking, looking, but no one came.

I burst into tears, sobbing, almost unable to drive. My tears horrified me, disgusted me, stunned me. Where were they coming from?

Until that moment, I had been completely unaware that I even had the capacity for sadness. Things only pissed me off, or angered me, or frustrated me.

As a teenager, my sister Jane had written a poem.

THUNDERSTORMS
(For my sister)
...but I am not
always as I seem...
my wounds are internal
and unhealed
and I bruise
too easily...

So
listen carefully
to the words
I never say...
please read
between the lines...

unexpected noises
scare me

and I only cry
in dreams.

Jane didn't show it to me until 1997, many years later. Reading it, I said I felt sad that that was her experience, and I wished I could've been there to help her. "Jennifer," she said, "I wrote it about you."

David had often said he felt my desolate existence started almost at birth, that right from the start I had never been loved properly. And I would always protest, "I'm sure when I was a baby my mother held me and played with me."

"But how did she hold you?" David wanted to know. With attention, focus, joy at doing so? Or with resentment—Jennifer's crying again. "She would hold you and play with you," David said, "but it had to be on her schedule. When she was bored or feeling lonely."

My mother had often told me that as an infant I'd suffered from persistent colic and had to be continuously carried around to stop me from crying. This constant carrying me, on one side, had affected her hip, which had never gotten well and still plagued her. When I was older and we would go shopping together for clothes, she'd often look in the mirror and point out how to this day one hip was higher than the other. That I had done this to her.

David believed that even as a tiny baby I took care of my mother— cheered her up, entertained her, eased her depression, distracted her, kept her company, helped her avoid the fact that my father was never there and rarely spoke. I was important to her, but only for what I could do for her. And, as always, she expended only the minimum effort in taking care of me in return.

As a child my parents had collected dolls for me from all over Europe, a wonderful collection. They were beautifully dressed; some were porcelain, with delicately carved faces and real hair. My parents would bring them back from their trips, and I had amassed quite a number. There was a flood in our house one day and the dolls got wet. Rather than dry them out, or send them to be cleaned, my mother simply threw them away. There was no thought that these dolls were my memories, pieces of my childhood, beloved toys, or that I might someday want to pass them on to my children. They were in my mother's way, they would be a bother to repair, and so they were gone.

When I was older and I would come to visit, despite my being a vegetarian, my mother would often forget to have something in the house for me to eat. Her grocery store delivered, yet she couldn't even call in an order. My parents would sit eating their dinner and I would eat cereal or a bagel.

As a child, my father never *was* around. He worked six days a week, seeing patients from early in the morning until late at night, frequently lecturing out of town. When he *was* home, my strongest memories are of him on the couch reading or fast asleep. Sometimes he'd nod off at dinner, even in restaurants. He enjoyed gardening, but I never remember him inviting me to join him.

My mother would always be furious with my father's absences and lateness. One of the things David and I had talked about was that my mother spewed her poisonous feelings into me with her negativity and anxiety about so many things. If my father was late coming home, she'd first be angry and tell me how terrible he was, how dinner was ruined, etc. As the hour grew later, she'd then become crazy with panic. She'd tell me—a little girl—"Something's happened." She'd feel better having told me, and I would feel scared and have nowhere to go with it.

She often made Jane and me wait for his arrival before we could eat. That way she could be more angry at him because he'd kept his hungry children waiting. She would serve him first, and he would eat so fast that he was frequently done before Jane and I had barely sat down. Then he'd leave the table and go read or write. There was hardly any conversation at all, almost total silence, watching my father eat.

Sometimes my mother would tell me that she should never have married him, that he should never have had kids, that she'd made a big mistake. I had no idea these were not things you tell your children.

I remember the one and only time my sister and I tried to have a meaningful conversation with my parents. I was in my twenties. We told them we always felt caught between them, defending one to the other. That we didn't want to hear "Your mother's impossible" or "Can you believe what your father did this time?" My father's furious response was to tell us that we were wrong, and we were selfish, spoiled girls.

Jane tried to talk to him once on her own. She told him she felt he and my mother were overly protective of her. She was, for example, not allowed to go to concerts because, according to my father, "I know what goes on there." She told my father she believed their over-protectiveness stemmed from the time she was a little girl and almost died from pneumonia. My father screamed at her, "Don't give me any of your psychological bullshit!" It was devastating to her, and she never tried again.

My father moved his family back and forth across the Atlantic three times. He first took my mother to Canada shortly after their marriage, separating her from the place she had lived all her life, which was Yorkshire, in the north of England. She was born in Bradford, a neigh-boring town to Sheffield, where *The Full Monty* took place. (In one Monty Python film Bradford is referred to as "the armpit of the world.")

My brother Jonathan was born during their years in the desolate wasteland of Weyburn, Saskatchewan. My parents then moved to To-peka, Kansas, where I was born, while my father trained at the Men-ninger Clinic, a famous psychiatric hospital. When I was five (although I have no recollection of my life in Kansas and until recently believed I had only lived there a year) he moved my mother, brother, and me back to London, where Jane was born. When I was thirteen we all moved again, this time back to the States.

As an adult, I watched my sister and her husband move their three girls from Illinois to Ohio and back because of job-related issues. But they did it with preparation. The girls were encouraged to participate in the moves, to go looking at new houses, to learn about their new schools. They were invited to talk about missing their old friends and their worries about finding new ones. They were enrolled in activities in order to help them expand their social group. Jane made a particular effort to spend even more time with them than normal, understanding that they might feel scared or anxious.

When Jane and I later talked about our own experiences, we real-ized we were simply packed up and moved with almost no warning. And the results were horrible. The second move was when I was thirteen, an age when boys are merciless. Every time I'd open my mouth, they'd tease me and imitate my English accent, so I quickly learned not to speak. Throughout the entire eighth grade I barely spoke a word, which, for anyone who knew me at all, would be a sign that something was terribly wrong.

I was just entering adolescence in a new country, at a new school, in classes three times larger than what I was used to. I knew no teachers, had no friends, and was completely isolated. And my parents never did anything to help me. They simply couldn't, or didn't want, to see it.

My sister told me a story once which stunned me. I was twenty years old at the time it happened, yet had no idea this had occurred. True, I had moved to New York, but even so it just hammered home how far apart my sister and I really were.

When Jane was sixteen, my family was living in Ann Arbor, Michigan, where my father had been teaching at the University of Michigan. He had recently been offered a new job at Northwestern University in Chicago running the adolescent psychiatry program.

He had been commuting back and forth on the weekends, deciding whether to take the position, and finally decided that he would. Jane was a junior in high school at the time with only a few weeks until the end of the school year. Rather than waiting those few weeks, my mother left for Chicago to join my father, and Jane was sent to live with some friends of our parents, people she didn't even know. My painfully shy, sixteen-year-old sister lived with strangers, barely speaking to them, for almost two months. A junior in high school, abandoned by her parents. They simply gave her a checkbook (which she had no idea how to use and became hopelessly overdrawn) and left her.

Jane told me another story. She had come home one night, at the age of fifteen, totally plastered. She was so drunk that as she crossed the living room she actually fell into the wall. My mother looked up and asked if she was okay.

"I'm just tired," Jane said, seeing double.

"Okay, well, good night then," said my mother.

It seemed they were blind. It was as if they thought if they took care of the basics—our food, our shelter, our school, a few ballet classes—we would be okay.

One day I had told David that I had no concept of what the word "love" meant. He thought about it for a while, and wrote down his definition on a piece of paper. He suggested I copy it into my journal. The last of the six things I wrote down was:

(Love) views the satiation of (another's) basic needs as the absolute **minimum** of caretaking, as opposed to the location where caretaking stops.

Certainly my brother and sister and I were cared for financially. I went to private school in England; I had a pony. In America, I had two horses. My father bought me my first two cars and paid my college tuition. When I was struggling to make a living, he helped me with my rent. But more often than not, after weeks of no contact, our entire conversations consisted of "How are you for money?" and me answering "Fine," or "A little short."

Despite my growing awareness that something was very wrong in my family, I still continued to defend my parents.

My father's parents, though incredibly wealthy, millionaires in fact, had been miserably tight with money. My brother told me a story about my father, who had returned from a six-month stint in the army. "I was this little boy," Jonathan said, "desperate to see his daddy, so happy he was home."

My father took Jonathan out to the store and bought him a book. It cost maybe the equivalent of a couple of dollars. "I showed Grandma the book," Jonathan told me, "and she screamed at Dad, literally screamed at him at what a waste of money it was and how stupid he was."

I knew my father had vowed over and over to never be stingy with his children.

It was easy for me to understood his lack of emotion, his distance from his children, his disinterest—he had known so much grief, how could he afford to get close to anyone?

I continued to excuse my mother because of her depression, and because she was never properly loved and so never knew how to love her children. It wasn't her fault.

David said fault was irrelevant; what was important was the impact on me. I could forgive all I wanted, but it didn't change the damage their unmeaning neglect had wrought.

David pointed out that I was never properly loved, yet he'd never seen anyone take such loving care and pay such close attention to their animals. "People like you, deprived the way you were deprived, usually end up being the kind of people who torture animals," he said. More evidence, he added, of the goodness and strength of my spirit.

Had I been a weaker person, he said, my desolate existence would probably have killed me. Either I would've turned to drugs, alcohol, or promiscuity; and perhaps AIDS, madness, homelessness, or suicide would have been the result. Instead I became a comedian.

Even as a little girl, I learned to shut down all emotion, to protect myself from the most vast loneliness.

One of the letters I wrote to David during my Christmas visit to my parents, was of an image that had come to me in the night.

"I feel like I've been lying on the bed of a frozen lake," I wrote. "No one knows I'm there. And you've come to rescue me, and you're the only one. And you're walking across the frozen lake with an ice pick, and you're digging and chopping at the ice to rescue me. And it's black, black, black under the lake. And I'm going to make it because you're going to pull me out of the lake, and because I've been frozen I'm still alive. My body shut down and being frozen helped me live."

11

January 1996

Mark and I were working on Tom's pilot for NBC. Since Mark had a wife and a young son who were sort of a distraction to writing, we'd always work at my apartment. Even though it was Mark's decision as much as mine, he'd get very resentful at having to come over to my place, frequently arriving up to fifty minutes late.

"Wendy wanted me to vacuum the living room," was his excuse one time. What?

"Are you nuts? You're making money, hire a fucking maid," I wanted to tell him. But I said nothing. Instead I'd ask him over and over, could you please at least call if you're going to be late? Then he'd yell at me that I was bossy.

Mark was not at his best under stress, and now that we were writing this pilot for the second time, it just added to his irritation.

"We already wrote this fucking thing!" he'd shout, pacing around my apartment. "Fuck this, I'm not fucking doing it!"

I'd want to shout back at him, but I was scared to. I didn't know how he'd react. He could just as easily decide to quit the project as to finish it. If he quit, the project would probably pretty much go down the toilet, seeing as it was both of ours.

Livid inside, my heart pounding, I'd slowly ask him to please calm down, we had to finish it, that we'd made our choice, that we owed it to Tom, et cetera, et cetera. Anything to finish the script. And it would usually work. Mark would snap out of his mood, make some joke, and we'd go on. He'd apologize; sometimes he'd hug me. "I can't believe you put up with me," he once told me, "I've never been able to work with a partner before you."

When he was in a good mood, he could be great—funny, sweet—but I never knew when he was going to get angry. I told my agent that although Mark was never physically violent toward me, during his outbursts sometimes I felt like a battered wife—everything could be going along fine, suddenly I make the wrong thing for dinner, and Bham!

David asked if I was afraid that Mark would ever hit me, and I said no. But sometimes, when he lost his temper, the yelling affected me almost as much as a blow could.

Out of nowhere, I suddenly got the urge to start painting. Acrylic on canvas. It was a whim—I was driving past an art store and just turned in.

My first painting was small, sloppy, a mishmash of different images. A window symbolizing my look into my future; candles symbolizing David lighting the way; a rope hauling me to safety; an empty picture frame; a dog; a dark cave; a cat; sunglasses to hide vision; a clock ticking away; the word PASSION half covered over; and a small, white ghost, peering around in fear. I titled it "Your Soul Doesn't Know It's Saturday."

It was amateurish and childlike. David loved it. Raved about it. He thought it was brilliant. "You're like a mother, looking at her kids' refrigerator drawings," I told him.

David denied it; he said he really thought it was good. "But it's funny you should say that," he said, "because I actually feel very maternal toward you. Paternal *and* maternal." He told me he would do anything to protect me.

He did indeed make me feel very safe. Not only emotionally, but even financially, I felt support.

When I had read the first pages of *Enemy of Passion*, I had loved it. It was a thriller about a serial killer who targets people with passion. I walked in the next day and handed David a dollar and said, "I'm buying the film rights to this book."

I sort of meant it as a joke at first, but then David said okay. "Really?" I said, "for a dollar?" He reminded me that he didn't care about money, and if I really wanted the film rights, I could have them.

He told me that if the book sold and I really was going to produce it into a movie, we'd have to talk very seriously about it. "I would never let anything interfere with our therapy," he said. "Do you believe me?"

I wondered why he was always asking me that question. I assumed that he figured I'd never been close enough to anyone to really trust them before, and so needed the reassurance.

"David, you're the one person in the world I trust completely," I told him. "You don't need to ask me that. When you say things I believe you." He laughed and agreed that he'd try not to ask me the question again.

He said if we could work out the therapy versus producing situation, he'd love to have me produce his book into a film. In fact, he said, he was writing the sequel to that book, called *Guardian of Passion*, and he had yet another book in the works. He said I could have the film rights to *any* of his books.

"Jennifer, I want to do this for you," he said. "You can produce all my books into movies because I know you'll do a great job with them."

He was like a father, bringing his kid into the family business.

I still worried about my future in the entertainment industry. Even though it looked like I might get a pilot made, and maybe even a series on the air, I wasn't really happy writing, and had no idea what else I would do. I brought back the old joke about ending up living in David's basement.

"You won't have to live in my basement, Jennifer," he said smiling. "You can stay in the guest house."

A guest house? He must've been serious when he said he and Roxanna had money. I said, "Better not make that offer, I just might take you up on it."

David looked at me very seriously. "Jennifer," he said, "if you were ever in trouble, don't you know that I'd take care of you?" He went on, "I'm very serious about the guest house. If you needed it, you could stay there for as long as you wanted. And remember, Jennifer, I don't say things I don't mean."

———

Notwithstanding the discussions of the guest house, I had started looking to buy my own house, my first. I was very excited by the prospect, I had always wanted a home of my own: to decorate it, to have a garden. A full-size version of my perfect, miniature world.

I found a really old house that I fell in love with. Built in 1925, it had stained-glass windows, gabled ceilings, a wine cellar, a beautiful curved old wooden staircase. But it was small, only a one bedroom, and would need adding on.

I told my parents about it. My father's first response was that it was not practical, what was I doing buying a one-bedroom house? "How will the family come visit?" he said.

I thought that was ironic, considering that when I was living in New York, and my sister was in college, my parents moved from a house in the suburbs to a condo in Chicago. Despite having plenty of money, they bought a one-bedroom. Any of their children visiting would have to sleep in the den or at a hotel.

It was at that same time they got rid of our dog that we'd had for eleven years, ever since he was a puppy, a Great Dane who I adored. Never a word to me; he was just gone. There were plenty of beautiful houses in Chicago with gardens, but finding one was simply too inconvenient.

My father was critical of the age of the house I had found, fearing what condition it might be in. He wanted to know if the front door was sturdy. "Dad, it doesn't have a front door," I told him. "Just an big open gap and a sign saying PLEASE COME IN AND KILL ME."

"He's always so worried about everything, so negative," I told David. My parents were always fearful; there was always danger lurking.

A friend and I had once rescued some horribly abused cats from the backyard of two prostitutes who lived behind another friend of mine; basically stole them in the middle of the night, creeping around in the dark, peeling off in my car, with paper towels wrapped around the license plate so no one could trace me (clearly I was no expert at this). I paid to have the cats treated at the vet for all their many ailments—eye infections, cuts, fleas, scabs, bloody eyes; I had them spayed and neutered, and I found them all good homes.

Thrilled at what I done, I told my parents about my adventure. My father's response was, "Do you realize this could ruin your whole future? You're going to end up in prison, and if you do, don't call us."

David told me I should buy the house I wanted, that I could make it work. I could add on slowly. And if I wanted any of my family to visit, they could stay in a hotel. Whatever I wanted to do, he said he would support.

"Roxanna's pregnant," David said. He was grinning from ear to ear, leaning forward in his chair, obviously really happy and excited. It was close to the beginning of a session, and he'd said he had something to tell me in confidence. "And I'm only telling you, Jennifer, no one else," he added. He went on to tell me it wasn't just one baby, it was two! Twins again.

I was now seeing David five days a week, two hours at a time, and still talking to him on the phone when I needed. I liked all the contact, basked in it.

So I didn't know how to respond to what he was telling me. I knew what I was supposed to say, "Congratulations, blah, blah, blah," but all I could think was, What about me? How was he going to have time to take care of me with two more children? He was busy enough with two babies, now he'd have four?

Other people's self-interest makes me think I'm going to vaporize.

I'd written that in my journal. My belief that if anyone had to choose between taking care of themselves and the things they wanted, or taking care of me, I would come in a very distant second. It didn't occur to me that someone could do both.

"That's great," I said. "Congratulations."

He explained that Roxanna had a hard time getting pregnant and had to take fertility drugs. That was why she was having another multiple birth. "The pills made her feel shitty, but we both really wanted babies," David said, still smiling.

I really didn't want to hear about David and his happy, perfect family. I wanted to change the subject, move on to other things: my boring life, my wretched job. I knew I should tell him how I was feeling, but I was embarrassed. Was I so self-involved, so shallow, that I couldn't be happy for someone else? He was going to hate me.

Plus, admitting that I was worried would acknowledge my dependency. One part of me liked being taken care of, but another found it sickening. I finally threw out casually, "Well, how are you going to have time to see me, with all those diapers and stuff?"

"I knew that was going to come up, Jennifer," he said. "Did you think I didn't know that?" I shrugged. "I want you to know," he said, "I'm going to take just as good care of you."

I must have looked doubtful, because he said, "Perhaps this will explain it to you." He asked me to compare him having two more babies, to if I got two more kittens. "Would you take any less care of Lewis and Baby?

"I have plenty of energy, Jennifer," David said. "I think you know that." David slept only two or three hours a night. He saw patients, wrote his books, swam, worked out, sailed, ran, water-skied, sky-dived . . . I said congratulations again, and this time almost meant it.

I had talked to David a lot about my anger, that it had always concerned me that rage seemed to be my predominant emotion. It was never directed toward people close to me, only strangers—meter maids, parking lot attendants, a mailman. When my friends would point out or question my harshness, I'd always make an excuse—that the person I was yelling at was stupid, incompetent, rude; that I didn't care. Later I'd feel guilty for my meanness, and vow never to do it again.

I was also pretty much a control freak, although only over small, insignificant things that I could jokingly laugh off as me being a spoiled Jewish American Princess—*I* had to sit in the front seat, I had to see the movie *I* wanted to see, eat where *I* wanted to eat. Of course to tell someone I needed help, never.

Gradually I was starting to understand this anger and desire for control. I wanted people to listen to me, take care of me, to be responsible to me. To think that what I said, felt, wanted, had value.

When some clerk ignored me at a counter, or some fourteen-year-old ticket-taker at the movie theater wouldn't let me in early to use the rest room, I'd go crazy. Unable to tell my parents how they'd wronged me, I attacked the only targets I could.

There was only one time that I remember letting my anger at my parents get out of control. I was in Chicago visiting and was at home with my mother while my father was at his office seeing patients. As always my mother was being incredibly negative and pessimistic about everything, and it finally just got to me. I started screaming at her, just losing it. I was shaking with rage. I screamed at her that I was sick of her negativity, sick of the fact that her world was always black, that everything was always "no," that there was always a "but." I must have screamed for five minutes or more, raving, barely pausing to breathe. I think she was terrified by my rage, as I was. I wanted to kill her at that moment.

A week later, after I had gone back to L.A., I was feeling horribly guilty at how I had treated her. I felt worse and worse, and I finally steeled myself to write her a card. In it, I apologized for yelling at her, I said I was sorry and that I knew I was mean and that I just wanted her to be happy. It took everything I had to send that card, the first of its kind I had ever written. My mother never even acknowledged receiving it.

David promised me that the more attention I received from him, and the more I gave myself, the more value I believed I had, the more my anger would disappear.

I wondered what would be left in its place.

———

I had found another house, this one with more bedrooms, and made an offer, which was accepted. I had been saving money for years, and was at last feeling I could afford a down payment.

I was excited about the idea of my own home, but the pleasure was tainted. Like everything else I ever did in my life, I was doing it alone.

David still believed it was just a matter of time before I found someone. In fact, he confided in me one day, he secretly had a guy for me. His best friend, Angelo DiCecco, who lived in Boston. They had known each other since college; had been roommates and closest friends ever since. "Angelo's one of the three," David said, referring to the "three and the one-ninety-seven."

He thought Angelo and I would make a great couple. It was just a glimmer in the back of his mind, he said, but how great it would be.

I thought what he was saying was off-the-wall, and I had no interest in getting involved with anyone, least of all someone who lived on the other side of the country, but at the same time I was flattered. David would like to see me with his best friend.

"How am I supposed to meet this Mr. Right?" I asked him. It's not like most people hang out with their therapist's friends. "Hi, I'm insane. Canapé?"

"I was thinking, Jennifer," David said, "not yet, but sometime, when we think it's right, you can come to one of our parties."

He told me that almost every weekend he and Roxanna had these great parties by their pool, that I would love their friends, and they would love me. "Our pool looks out over the ocean," David said. "It's really beautiful." He said Angelo often came in from Boston to visit them, and I could meet him then.

"You're inviting me to your house?" I said. "My dad would love that."

"Your dad didn't do such a great job taking care of you, Jennifer," David pointed out. "Do you really care what he'd think?"

"I'd meet Roxanna and your babies," I said.

"Yes, you would," David said, smiling. "How do you feel about that?"

"I'm afraid she won't like me," I said. "She'll think I'm this pathetic loser. She'll wonder who is this person you've devoted so much time to, changed your schedule for; that you were crazy, what's wrong with you, how could you think this person is so special?"

David shook his head. "She's going to adore you, like I do. I've told her a little bit about you, is that okay? Nothing bad," he said quickly. He said that Roxanna picked up on people's spirit even better than he did, that she was very spiritual herself. "She's going to think you're wonderful. She already loves your paintings," he added.

I had been painting almost every night since I started, and would always bring the paintings in to show David. He loved all of them, each one more than the last. He'd asked if he could show them to Roxanna.

I had painted one called "David's Spirit." It was a big heart moving through space. Inside the heart were symbols of his wife, his twins, his dog Shadow, whom he had rescued from abuse, and his cat Puff.

David showed the painting to Roxanna, and told me she wanted to buy it. "It's not for sale," I said.

"She really wants it, Jennifer," he said. "You should think about it. You could name your price. Roxanna's very rich."

I wondered what kind of price he was talking about. He said he wasn't sure, maybe four or five thousand dollars.

That made me pause for a minute. She'd be willing to pay that much for what I considered a pretty amateurish painting? I knew she had money, but still. She must really love David a lot.

———

David continued to bring up the idea that my life was going to change; that I would find love; that everything was going to be different for me.

We were having one of our typical, "Will Jennifer ever have a relationship?" arguments. David said he'd make me a deal. If, when I was done with therapy, I didn't find myself in a great, loving relationship, he'd give me a hundred thousand dollars. "Now you're giving me an incentive to *not* want a relationship," I said. David told me he didn't feel worried, his money was safe.

I said that I was so sure of my position, that I'd give him a hundred thousand if I *did* find myself in a relationship. We decided that whoever this guy was, he better love me a lot—I didn't come cheap.

One day, again running in circles, David increased the figure to a hundred fifty thousand dollars. I countered back, two hundred thousand. We laughed. Then David told me that he wanted to be sure I understood, in all seriousness, that if I did win "the bet," he'd definitely pay up, but that he would not take money from me; I wouldn't have to pay. I argued, pretty halfheartedly, that that didn't seem fair. But, if he insisted.

Joking about the money aside, I continued to fight him. I knew how my life was going to be, and all David's wishing and prophesying otherwise wasn't going to make it any different.

In some ways I thought that what David and I were doing together was a mistake. Life was easy when I'd known I would be alone, but had learned not to care. Now I knew, and it was starting to hurt.

I had done a painting called "David Explains It to Me," which had three sections. One, of me being completely blank; then this chaotic mass of confusion; and then a part that was just peaceful. David had explained that in order to get to where I wanted, I was going to go through a lot of craziness and turmoil.

"That's how the process works, Jennifer," he said. "It's not going to be this easy journey: You just have to trust me to lead you through it."

And it was not easy. Before I had been strong, independent, stoic, a loner. Now, in the solitude of my private life, it was all breaking down. David was succeeding in waking this emotional Rip Van Winkle, but what a painful trip.

I felt shitty. Lonely. I had anxiety I'd never had before. I was crying more and more often, although never in front of David. The very idea of having him see or even hear me cry was humiliating, horrifying. He tried to tell me there was strength in vulnerability, but that was for others, not for me.

I could never really fully grasp why it was so revolting to me to have people see me weak or crying, why even now the thought of it sometimes makes me want to rip my skin. Was I rejected and rebuffed for some display of need, or totally smothered by my mother's fear? I don't know. It's elusive, like the thought of a smell, or a wisp of smoke that vanishes before I can even turn around. I search and search in my mind, feeling if I could just find the answer maybe my disgust would leave me, but I don't even know what I'm looking for.

I would not cry in front of David, but alone in my apartment, in my car, I would just sob, wracked with loneliness, aching with it. I felt it in my gut, despair, gnawing at me.

My gut, my chest, my inside is completely hollow. Like someone's taking their two hands, and slowly ripping my body, my heart, my space, an empty cavernous blank hole, cutting big chunks out of it with a spoon.

I knew I'd never have anyone the way David and Roxanna had each other.

My friend Deborah Swisher, one of the few people who knew I was in therapy, had asked me if I was physically attracted to David. I had told her he was young and athletic. She'd heard the stories about patients and therapists having sexual relationships, and wondered it that could happen here.

"You don't understand," I told her. "This guy's like a father, a mother, a big brother, all rolled into one." I explained that my relationship with David was about being a child again, or maybe for the first time.

"Believe me, Swish, this isn't about sex; I'm not planning on having sex with anyone. As far as I'm concerned the next person to see me naked will be a coroner."

Of course that wasn't strictly true. I did want love, and sex too. And yes, I wanted the sort of love David and Roxanna shared, but I didn't want it from David.

I had done a painting called "Olympic Love, I Can Dream." It was of two hearts (hearts were a theme in several of my paintings—I used them as a symbol for soul/spirit) intersecting like Olympic rings. The title was defensive: I longed for an Olympic-sized love, a huge love. I knew I couldn't have it, but even I, loser that I was, was allowed to dream it.

I was in a moment of rare anger with David. I told him, "Can't you just give up on this stupid notion of me ending up with someone? I don't know why you don't just face reality." I told him I was content to get better, to enjoy my life a little more, to be a little happier. If I was willing to accept that as enough, couldn't he be content with it also?

He said he wanted to share something with me. "This is really personal, Jennifer," he said, "but I think it will help you."

He took a deep breath; it was clearly hard for him to talk about it.

"Something happened to me when I was four years old," he said. He paused before going on. "I was sexually abused in nursery school. By satanic worshipers. Is it okay that I'm telling you this?"

I nodded. I really didn't know what to say.

"It was really horrible abuse, evil," he said, "with torture and threats and sticking things in me. They actually killed one kid."

I couldn't believe what he was telling me. It sounded terrible. I asked him what happened to the people who did it.

"They're still in jail," David said, "because of killing that one kid." He'd testified against them, and that was one reason he kept his life so private, in case they ever got out of jail.

He said all the children had suffered severe emotional problems because of what happened to them, and most still did, but through working hard David conquered his. He told me that he kept in touch with some of the other victims, and even now still paid for the therapy of one woman who couldn't afford treatment on her own.

"I'm telling you this, Jennifer," he said, "because this abuse was really terrible, and because of what they did—I'm not going to give you details—but I had some physical problems. I thought I'd never get married, and I'd never have children. I was totally alone, I lived alone, and I thought I was destined to be alone forever. Then I met Roxanna and my life changed, and I'm so happy with this wonderful wife and my beautiful kids."

He compared his abuse to mine. His was short-term but horrific; mine was outwardly less horrific but drawn out over my entire life. "My point is, there is still hope for you, Jennifer," he said.

I wanted to believe him. But the idea of believing it, and then being disappointed, was terrifying. I didn't know if I would be able to stand it.

Mark and I had just gotten another rewrite for Disney, on *Homeward Bound II, The Adventure Continues*. The movie had already been shot, and we were limited to giving the animals dialogue that would fit into the amount of time they were on screen. It's hard enough to come up with jokes, but to have to fit them into an allotted time slot is almost impossible. Still, we were happy for the assignment. Although it paid less money than the first, thirty-five thousand split between the two of us (netting us each about eighty-seven hundred), I was pleased. I had been worried about the down payment on my house, which would deplete my savings, so this extra money would come in useful.

Along with the Disney rewrite, the network had been happy with our first draft of the Tom Rhodes show, and it looked like they might want to go forward with it. Mark and I were now set up at Universal, which would be our studio. The way a studio functions in TV is that it's the place where you "lay the show off," which in general terms means that the studio puts up most of the money. The network pays the writer a relatively small sum for the pilot script, the studio adds a premium on top of that. They pay the salaries on the show—the crew, the writing staff, the production staff, et cetera. They pay for the sets and cameras and props and the actors, and everything else, and in return they own a large chunk of the profits. They also arrange and pay for the actual physical space (a soundstage, production offices, et cetera) where the show would be shot if it got picked up.

David was really happy for my success, both with the rewrites and my pilot, and he added that there was now a bidding war on *Enemy of Passion* from two different publishers. He didn't want to tell me which ones, or the price they were offering, for fear of jinxing the sale.

He had given me more of the book to read. I felt it was starting to change tone as it went along, which I didn't think was right, but I wanted to finish it before I gave David any comments. I didn't want to hurt his feelings or make him mad.

What I was learning about my childhood was coming out in my paintings, which I was bringing in to show David almost every week. "Look, We're Dancing" depicted a figure alone and sobbing, while a couple danced oblivious in the background, only aware and proud of how much fun they were having. "Prom Night" was a canvas divided in half—one half full of figures dancing, swirling, joyful; the other, a dark gray house. In one window a couple lies asleep; in another, a figure lies curled up, alone. "Fat House" was of a tiny, ghostly figure, desperately dodging being stepped on by the feet of unseeing giants.

I was starting to get a clearer picture of my parents, and an understanding of how the loneliness of my childhood had affected me. My father, this renowned adolescent psychiatrist who lectured all over the world about his use of breakthrough therapies—including holding therapies—had never touched me. Either physically or metaphorically. This man who preached that troubled kids should never be locked up or restrained, but should be loved and nurtured and comforted, had abdicated his responsibility to his children and left us in the hands of a chronically depressed and disinterested mother.

I suppose then I had a choice—to become terrified and paralyzed and totally incapable of taking care of myself, or to become coldly independent. And of course I chose the latter. My parents never touched me, so I became untouchable.

One evening David had taken a long time to call me back after I had paged him. "You know I counsel people who have cancer?" he reminded me when he finally called. I said I remembered. He had told me once that he worked at different hospitals, helping terminally ill patients live out their last months or weeks, still maintaining (as much as was physically possible) a passion for life. Even if you know you are dying, David felt, you shouldn't resign yourself to just waiting for it to happen. He was late calling me back that night, he explained, because one of his cancer patients, a thirteen-year-old girl, had died that day; and he'd spent her last hours with her.

That night I did a painting full of texture and depth and layers of color, with a body lying still in the middle of it. I called it "Dead at 13." I explained the title to David, that I would rather have died at thirteen and had a rich, full life than to have lived this long and felt nothing.

It seems I *had* wanted to feel something. I'd lived this long and never known it. More accurately, I had forgotten it, the possibility so remote. And now I was starting to remember.

Sometimes I'd show my paintings to David and he'd tear up. I would matter-of-factly describe the symbolism, explain the title, and I'd see a glisten in his eyes. He told me mine was the most desolate life he'd ever known.

"If I described your life to other therapists, they wouldn't believe it," he said.

I came into session one day, and David was smiling. He'd come up with an idea that he thought would be really interesting. He wanted to give me a Rorschach test. Not as a diagnostic tool for him to use, he explained, since at this point he already pretty well understood me, "but because I think it'll be helpful for you."

I was intrigued. I'd heard of the Rorschach of course, but never seen it. I thought it would be fun.

We agreed on a day for me to take the test—a Saturday, since as the last appointment of the day we could go long if we needed to. On the appointed day, before we got started, David explained that he was going to act differently than normal during the administration of the test. "I'll be more formal," he said, "less conversational, less friendly. I just ask you questions, I tell you when the time is up for your answer, we move on to the next question." He emphasized, "It doesn't mean I'm mad at you or don't like you anymore, Jennifer, it's just the way I have to give the test, do you believe me?"

We started the test. It was pretty much as I'd expected; David showed me the inkblots and asked me questions about what I saw. At the beginning I made jokes and said that every one was a huge penis, but then I took it more seriously and told David what I saw. Despite his warning of formality, he seemed like the same David to me.

A couple of days later he had the results. It had taken him a little longer than usual, he said, because of one thing I'd said about one of the inkblots. I had described seeing something as if viewed from above. David said he'd never had anyone do that before, and had had to look it up in several books and on the Internet before he could find out what it meant. "It's called a vista," he said. "It's so rare for people to describe seeing things from above that few books mention it." He said it showed that I felt completely alone, and that my total belief in life was that other people were of no use to me and could not possibly help me.

"It shows terrible, terrible isolation, Jennifer," he said. "It's so rare it's not even in most of the books. It just confirms everything we've learned."

———————

I was standing in my kitchen one day, cooking, when this flash came to me that I hated my parents. Hated them. It lasted a second, less, but it really disturbed me. I didn't want to hate them. Another thought traveled almost imperceptibly through my mind—this is what David does; he estranges people from their parents because he's mad at his parents for letting that abuse happen to him.

I didn't say anything to David. I knew I was just projecting; that it was only Pluto trying to wheedle his way back in.

———————

David had taken up painting. He was so compelled by my work, he said, that he wanted to try his hand at it. As I was doing, he'd bring his paintings in to show me. The first depicted a boy at the breakfast table, totally ignored by the rest of the family. David explained that his mother and father had liked him the least of their three children and had treated him very badly. They thought he was too independent and tried to squash his spirit. He said his brother was a loser who in his thirties still lived at home and pumped gas for a living. His sister and he didn't get along at all and barely spoke to each other.

Clearly David had not had an ideal childhood. Plus he had suffered that terrible abuse, yet here he was, a happy, passionate, loving (and loved) person.

I liked seeing David's paintings. Although I knew about my parents' own unhappy lives, I had not heard the stories from them. I learned from things I overheard, things I figured out, sometimes things my brother or sister told me. Emotions were kept secret in my family; sharing problems was unheard of. Family flaws were kept hidden. Everything had to look perfect.

My parents used to reminisce and laugh over an incident that happened in our house once. It was sometime in the seventies and at the time my father had an office downstairs where he conducted therapy. My brother Jonathan, who at the time had long black hair, dressed scruffily, and looked fairly unwashed (and admittedly was in all likelihood stoned), walked through the house while my mother was entertaining a guest. My mother's friend asked who that was. My mother told her, "Oh, that's one of Derek's patients."

A few years ago, when my father developed Parkinson's disease, my mother used to become angry with him for his clumsiness, and annoyed when he wouldn't hide his shaking hand.

———

I was loving coming to therapy. Every day David bounded out of his office to greet me in the waiting room with the biggest smile, delighted to see me. In sessions, he laughed at my jokes, he thought I was funny, he told me I was sweet. He said I was pretty, although I thought he was insane. We laughed at the ugly pictures on the walls of his rented office, and at the cheap upholstery. He complimented me on my clothes; he thought I had great taste. I had a pair of blue velvet pants, and whenever I wore them he would tell me they were his favorite. Incredibly observant, if I wore a new pair of earrings, he would notice. He picked up on my bad moods, and could always shake me out of them. I talked to him about everything and anything; he never judged me, only supported me. We had many of the same interests, and he shared my love of animals.

I was, and still am, a member of PETA—People for the Ethical Treatment of Animals; David belonged to a similar group—Psychologists for the Ethical Treatment for Animals. When he was doing his thesis for his Ph.D., and against his adviser's recommendation, he had actually refused to experiment on animals, and had had to come up with another way to prove his theories. It took him much longer, he said, but it was worth it.

He had told me earlier about his dog, Shadow, whom he adored. Shadow had been abused, and David had rescued him. It had taken hours and hours of patience, just sitting quietly, waiting for Shadow to approach him without growling or biting. And it had taken months for Shadow to finally trust David completely. "Kind of like you, Jennifer," he laughed.

We believed in the same things, liked the same music, read the same books. I had bought the Counting Crows CD, *August and Everything After*, and told David how much I liked it. The next day, he went out and bought it. "I'm already driving Roxanna crazy playing it over and over," he said. My favorite song was "Murder of One," whose lyrics I could relate to. In part they spoke of a girl whose life was a shame, and her love merely a dream; and went on to say that if she looked at herself she would be able to see "the flames of [her] wasted life." David admitted it was his favorite song too.

I shared my ideas for films I wanted to write, and David thought they were brilliant; really clever, imaginative.

One of the ideas was for a romantic comedy about a therapist who knows that two of his patients are perfect for each other. Realizing it would be unethical to put them together in a conventional way, he chooses instead to disappear, to vanish without a trace. Understanding his patients as well as he does, the therapist knows they will come looking for him, and in the course of their search, will find each other. David loved it.

Like me, David also loved going to the movies, and we shared similar views on what we liked. I went to see *The Usual Suspects* one day, and thought it was great. I came into session and raved about it to David. Two days later he told me he and Roxanna had been to see it.

"It was amazing, Jennifer," David said, "I think it's my favorite movie ever."

He liked that the truth was in the last place you'd look, and that nothing was as it seemed.

———

One day, out of curiosity, I asked David what kind of car he drove. I just wanted to know. I'd tried to guess what someone who dressed in goofy surfer pants and a mismatched T-shirt would drive, but hadn't been able to see it. Maybe an old Volvo? A VW Bug?

He didn't answer right away. He smiled a kind of funny smile and I said, "What?" He said he'd have to think about it.

"What do you mean, you have to think about it? Don't you know what kind of car you drive?"

He explained, "I need to think about this, and I'll tell you tomorrow. We'll talk about it tomorrow." I thought it was weird, but he was adamant. He'd tell me tomorrow.

The next day the first thing I said was, "Well, what kind of car?" He'd made such a big deal about it that I was dying of curiosity. What could he possibly have to tell me that took thinking about?

"I hesitate to tell you," David said, "because I think that you're going to get an image of me from what I tell you that isn't really me, and I wanted to think about whether I wanted you to know. It might bring up things.

"Okay," he said, taking a deep breath. "First of all, I have several cars." He seemed embarrassed, hesitant. "One of them is a Ferrari." He looked at me, waiting for my reaction.

Well, he was right. When I thought Ferrari, I thought flashy. Obnoxious. Loser guy with a gold chain, shirt unbuttoned to his navel, hairy chest, blond bimbo at his side. It certainly didn't seem like the right kind of car for David.

"That's why I didn't want to tell you," he said, "because that's not me. I mean, you know that's not me, right?" I reassured him I didn't think he was obnoxious and flashy.

He drove a Honda to work, he said, in case any patients saw him in his car. He didn't want them to know he was rich. "I don't drive it to show I have money," he said. "I don't like to dress like I have money, I don't like to flash things around. I have a Ferrari for the same reason I like to sky-dive, ski, water-ski, bungee jump. I like to go fast. On the weekends I take it out on country roads and just drive fast. No one sees me." He added that sometimes when he and Roxanna went out to dinner, they'd take the Ferrari, but mostly they didn't. They'd take one of their other cars. Roxanna had a Chevy Suburban for the kids, he drove the Honda to work, he had a motorcycle, and Roxanna also had a Bentley, which she rarely drove.

"A Ferrari and a Bentley? That's like two hundred thousand dollars' worth of cars," I said, shocked.

"I told you we were rich," he said, "really rich." He explained that Roxanna was a multimillionaire. She had inherited a fortune from her father, who was a mob lawyer.

"A what?" I said.

"Her father worked for the mob in New York," David said. He'd made a huge number of investments, and when he died he left it all to Roxanna.

"He worked for the mob? Are you serious? Wouldn't that money be sort of tainted?" I wondered.

"No, no, no," David said, very emphatic. He was very concerned that I not think badly of the guy, emphasizing several times that he was not what I pictured. He told me Roxanna's father fought really hard to keep his bosses' business interests honest, and basically ended up turning them on to more legitimate pursuits. "I met him many times before he died, Jennifer, and he was a really good guy," David told me.

I was very skeptical about that, but I didn't want to say anything. If that's what Roxanna's father wanted them to believe, that he was an "honest mob lawyer," and that's what David and Roxanna believed, who was I to say, "Oh come on, any shmuck knows the guy had to be a complete crook"? I had no proof David was wrong, why spoil his delusion?

David said this was not something he talked about, that it was another reason he kept his life so private, and that it was the one thing I could not repeat to anyone, ever. I promised to keep the information a secret.

I asked what Roxanna's last name was and David told me some Italian name like Anatello or something.

He said that having money was great, but not for the sake of having it, or to show people how much you had. It should be used to enjoy life. He added that he'd still enjoy life if he had no money, but having money certainly helped.

"I drive the Ferrari for pleasure," he said. "That's why we live in a big house and have a pool and a guest house, and everything else, because those things give us pleasure."

He said I deserved to have enjoyed my life the way he did, and it was terrible that I never got to. "It's a sin, Jennifer," he said, disgust in his voice. "It's sinful that no one took care of you."

"How are we doing today, Jennifer?" David asked. I was curled up in the corner of the couch, David a couple of feet away in the swivel chair in front of me, playing, as always, with his MontBlanc pen. It had become his standard question at the beginning and end of almost every session, checking how I felt about our relationship. Whether I felt close to him or distant or angry about something or ambivalent.

Sometimes I'd know the answer right away, sometimes I'd have to think hard to figure it out. Which was okay. David continued to stress that I should pay attention to my feelings.

This day I answered right away. "We're doing good," I said.

"I'm glad," he said, "I think we're doing really good, too." He went on, "But something's really bothering me, Jennifer." That scared me. Whenever he would say, "I have to tell you something," or "We need to talk about something," I would always think, he's going to cut back on our sessions, or he was mad at me, or he was going to quit being a therapist and I was going to be left. I always assumed the worst.

I thought about joining the Optimist's Club. But then I thought, "How much fun could that be?"

So when David said something was bothering him, I didn't say anything, but my heart started pounding.

He must've seen it in my face, because he said, "Don't worry, it's nothing bad.

"There's something you don't know about me," he said, "because you don't know me that well, but I let very few people into my life, and I tell very few people about my life." He paused, then went on, "But you're one of those people, Jennifer."

There were only about six people in his life who were really, really important to him, he said. His wife, his twins, his best friends Angelo and Janet, and me. He'd told me before that I was important; now he was telling me I was one of the top six people in his life.

"I feel like you're part of my family," David said. "And I love that.

Do you believe me? So it's really bothering me that we'll have to exchange money again at some point in our future."

I actually thought he was going to say he wouldn't take any more money from me. I couldn't believe it. I thought, Oh my God, he's so wonderful and he thinks of me as family and he's going to tell me that he's not going to take any more money from me.

He was quiet for several moments, closing his eyes to think. He'd come up with a really good idea, he said. He wanted to get money totally out of the way, and the idea he'd come up with was for me to pay for a lifetime of therapy in advance.

He said this would mean therapy for as long as it took. It could be four years, it could be eight years. It could be therapy until I'm ninety if necessary. "We'll know each other when we're ninety, Jennifer," he said, smiling. "Won't that be great?"

But now he wanted to get the money out of the way, and he'd come up with a figure. And he assured me he'd thought really hard about the amount, and knew that *I* knew he'd be fair.

I asked if maybe we couldn't talk about this in September. I'd paid in advance for a year already, September of 1995 through September of 1996. And this was only March of 1996.

He said, "Jennifer, you don't understand. I *hate* taking money from you. I don't even like *talking* about money with you. The very thought of it sickens me. I feel sick. It makes me physically sick!" And he got this look on his face like he was going to throw up; he looked just horrified. "Every time I think about you walking in here with a check, it disgusts me," he said. "I want to get money out of the way so we don't have to worry about that any more."

I didn't think it was fair to be bringing up money when I hadn't even finished the year, but I just said, "Well, it may sicken you, but it doesn't bother me. Really."

"I want money out of the way," David said again. "It's detrimental to our therapy. It's not good for you. I can't be as good a therapist. It colors everything that I know you have to pay me money." He was adamant.

I asked what kind of money was he talking about. I was hoping it would be some small amount. I already knew that he was incredibly wealthy, that he cared about me, and he knew I was worried about money, and I thought he would come up with something like a couple of thousand dollars. So I was shocked when he said, "I've come up with two plans." That didn't sound good to me.

"One is if you pay all at once, and one is if you pay in monthly installments." And I said okay. But I got very nervous. Because he'd been really generous with me in the past in terms of money, the sessions running over, the free phone calls, and I was scared that whatever he brought up, I wouldn't be able to argue it, because I'd be slapping his generosity in the face. Then I thought, Come on, this is David, why are you worrying?

He said, "If you pay me all at once, one lump sum, it'll be fifty thousand dollars. If you pay me over six months, it'll be ten thousand dollars a month, sixty thousand dollars."

I was shocked, just stunned. Even though I'd had word a couple of weeks earlier that my sitcom pilot was probably going to get produced, and that would be bringing me in a good chunk of money, it wasn't sixty thousand dollars.

I didn't say anything right away. I wanted to say "You've got to be kidding," but I couldn't.

I have to make it easy and perfect and not make a mistake otherwise why would people stay around? I can't figure out why anyone would put up with anything from me.

I'd shown this journal entry to David. He called it my "psychological legacy." My fear that people in a position of taking care of me would abandon me for any indiscretion.

As I'd told David in the past, it was easy to fight with waitresses, bank tellers, and store clerks who offended me, but if someone I *needed*—a friend, a doctor, an agent—failed to meet my standards, I was sure that criticism from me would terminate the relationship.

Even a minor error on my part could potentially drive them away— an argument, telling them I think they're wrong, being abrupt, forgetting to call them. Their desire to be around me was so tenuous, I was sure they were looking for any excuse to leave.

I was not going to argue with David and jeopardize this fragile connection. If I lost him, where would I be? Who would look after me? I had tasted being cared for, and I liked it.

I once told David, when I was able to formulate such thoughts of weakness, that if he started me down the path of dependency he would create a monster—a grabbing, many-armed beast clawing and scrambling for contact.

So I was terrified to say no. He'd think I was selfish and money-hungry and a user. I'd ruin everything. Please don't take this away from me. Instead I just said, "But I don't have that kind of money."

David explained that's why he'd come up with this plan, to help me. I actually felt that the plan seemed to penalize me for not having all the money at once, but again I couldn't bring it up. And also because if I thought about it, he was actually being generous. Therapy was five days a week, two hours at a time, ten hours a week, at seventy-five dollars an hour. That was thirty-seven thousand, five hundred dollars a year, already half his normal fee. A fair amount of people go to therapy, analysis, five days a week at a hundred fifty dollars an hour, sixty thousand a year, and David was offering me sixty thousand dollars for life. It would be selfish and greedy to bring up the idea that he was penalizing me. But I still felt the timing was wrong, and it was a very unusual thing for him to do.

So I told him I just didn't think I could do it financially. I'd already paid him close to thirty-four thousand, which was only four thousand less than what I'd netted on my pilot and my two Disney rewrites. And I'd just bought a house.

He said, "We *have* to, Jennifer. We *have* to get money out of the way." Whether I recognized it or not, he said, it was damaging to our therapy and damaging to my feeling of being family. And I needed family. I needed to feel that he was my parent. It was the only way I was going to get well.

He said, "How can I take money from a daughter? And how can you give money to the father who's supposed to take care of you, and to be responsible to you and to love you? You shouldn't have to pay for that."

I said, "But won't I still be paying you?"

He explained that once we got money out of the way, we could then forget about it, and the benefits of therapy would increase by leaps and bounds. "I promise you, Jennifer," he said. "It'll be better for you emotionally, and better for you spiritually," he said. "You're just not seeing how detrimental money is."

David knew me really well. I had a habit of being in denial over things, and not seeing things clearly, so I started wondering if he was right. "I guess," I said.

He reminded me that in my family I'd always had to do something in order to be taken care of. I'd had to be entertaining or cheer up my parents, or be the well-behaved little girl, in order for my parents to pay attention to me. And he didn't want me to feel like I had to do something to be taken care of by him.

He just wanted to be able to take care of me like a daughter should be taken care of, and like I deserved to be taken care of.

I said I'd like to think about it overnight, and he said okay.

The next day we talked about it again, for almost the whole session. I kept trying to get out of it, without angering him. "Could we at least wait until September to talk about it? Maybe we could wait until I have the full fifty thousand?" But David wouldn't bend.

"I wish we could do therapy for free," he said, "but I know you're too moral a person to let me work for nothing. You wouldn't do that, and I wouldn't want you to do that because I know it would make you uncomfortable."

He said, "I know you realize how hard I work for you. And believe me, I love doing it."

And he was right, of course. I would never take something from him for free. And I wanted him to be proud of me, and think of me as a good person.

Maybe it *was* better to get money out of the way. And I knew David would only ever do what was best for me. He said, "I've never, ever lied to you, Jennifer. There's some things I tell you that I'm not sure about, and I tell you I'm not sure about them as I'm telling you. And there's some things I tell you that I know for a *fact*. This is something I know for a fact, that this will be better for you. To get this money out of the way, and really feel like you're family. This is something I know. It's not something I think, it's not something I'm ninety percent sure of, this is one hundred percent."

And finally I agreed with him. I didn't really want to, and his reasoning never really made sense to me, but I was scared. What would be the consequence if I said no? All the things you're supposed to get, David was giving me; I was terrified to lose that. And he was offering me this special deal, and no one had ever offered me anything before.

If I turned it down, I may never get offered anything again. And ultimately, of course, David was my therapist. He was telling me that it would be detrimental not to get money out of the way, and I couldn't disagree.

I had done a painting that month called "Leaving Dead Lake." It was of a murky, dark, desolate lake, with souls rising out of it. And the souls that are just rising out of the lake are very tenuous and ethereal, because they're just breaking the bounds of the lake. And they're still attached to the lake with a little tendril, a thread. But as they rise away from the lake, and get farther away from its surface, the souls become solid and textured and full. I felt I was breaking away from Dead Lake, that barren, flat, and empty place, and rising. My spirit was rising. And it was because of David and his support. So when he was talking about therapy for the rest of my life if necessary, I could only think of what a pleasure that would be. Of how well he took care of me, and how much he cared about me.

And it was so much more than therapy. It was having someone to turn to for the rest of my life. To talk to, to listen to me, to believe in me. A lifetime of love, attention, friendship, support, from this warm, kind, exuberant man, who lived this glorious life of adventure and excitement, and loved being alive. He would teach me so much, show me everything. For the rest of my life, every day, I would have the father I had always wanted.

I knew that the money I made on my pilot would be gone, but we were talking about saving my very spirit, giving me something I'd longed for. Changing my whole life. How was I going to put a price tag on that?

I also felt I could afford to pay the sixty thousand dollars, even though I didn't have it at the time, because of the film rights to David's books. He had finally admitted that the selling price on *Enemy of Passion* was now up to a million dollars. I felt the book had completely changed in the middle—becoming weirdly darker and more surreal than the beginning, with talking demons where previously every character had been real; and the bizarre, violent death of a character who I thought was the hero. But I figured, who am I to judge? I couldn't even get through *Atlas Shrugged*, and everyone says it's a masterpiece. If publishers were fighting over David's book to this extent, obviously my opinion of it had to be wrong.

I knew that when a book sells for that kind of money, everyone in Hollywood hears about it. People at studios, at agencies, scour the book market to see what's selling. And I felt like, here I have the film rights to a book that's already on the block for a million dollars. Maybe the film rights could bring me a few hundred thousand. And maybe a producer fee on top of that. Even a writing fee . . .

All that was holding up the sale of *Enemy of Passion* was negotiations over the sequel and his other book. David was going to be a big hot-shot writer, which was a dream of his. So even giving up the sixty thousand dollars, I knew I'd have money coming in. If it wasn't this book, it would be another book. He'd promised me the rights to all of them. I knew David would take care of me. If I all of a sudden become destitute somewhere down the road, David has money and he loves me and he'll take care of me. It was a huge amount of money, but somehow I'd make it.

One thing still bothered me, though. I'd always had this fear that David would die. Always. Traveling back and forth from Dana Point to Los Angeles, he'd get hit by a truck, or his boat would sink, or he'd have a parachuting or surfing accident—something dreadful would happen. I couldn't believe that something as good as David could be permanent.

I thought that even bringing up the topic could be tempting fate, but still I said, "Well, what if something happened to you, David, and I've given you all this money?"

He looked at me as if he couldn't believe the question. "Jennifer, don't you think that I would take care of you? It's going to be in my will that if something happens to me, you will get all the money back."

He said he'd made a promise to be my therapist until I was completely better, and if that promise wasn't kept, I shouldn't pay anything. "If something happens to me, Roxanna will give you all the money back. You are going to be completely taken care of."

So I had this choice of fifty thousand all at once, or sixty thousand spread out over six months. And I told David I couldn't even pay him over six months, I just didn't have the money, so he said he had a way to make it work. I would write six checks for ten thousand dollars apiece and postdate them. I'd give them to him, and he wouldn't deposit them until I told him to. Even if my pilot didn't go, he said, Mark and I would get on another show, and when I made enough money, I could let him know.

I said, well then you're still dealing with money, every time I tell you to deposit a check, you're still going to be facing that issue that you hate so much and is so bad for us.

He said he understood that. "But it'll be different. I won't have to ask, you'll just have to say, 'Go ahead'—those are the only words you have to say—and that's it. And then I deposit it and that's over with."

I didn't quite understand the difference between him not wanting to discuss money, and then me having to bring up money every time he could deposit a check. It seemed to defeat his purpose. But David assured me it was the best thing to do. So after three days of discussing this I came into the office and wrote him six checks for ten thousand each.

He promised me he wouldn't deposit them until I gave the okay. "Do you believe me?" he asked.

That same day I told him he could deposit the first check, since I had money in the bank from my savings and the balance of my second Disney rewrite. I knew David knew I had the money, and I didn't want him to think I was cheap. He tucked the checks into his Filofax, and said he'd never ask me whether he could deposit any of the others, but it would always be up to me to say when I was ready.

"I know you'll be honest and tell me when you have enough money to cover them," he said. "I totally trust you." And he smiled at me.

I had to meet with my accountant, Jan Krauss, and I told him about the ten thousand dollars. He said it seemed like a huge amount of money. I said, well actually it's going to be even more than that. I explained the deal David and I had made. Jan thought it was unusual. I said, "Yeah, I know, but this is for life. I'll never have to pay for therapy again."

Jan wanted me to at least defer part of the remaining fifty thousand until my next tax year. He said the IRS was going to take one look at this medical bill and go, What are you doing? I told him I can't, David wants it out of the way. "I've already asked him," I told Jan. "David thinks this is better for my therapy."

Jan tried to talk me out of it, but it was hard going. First of all, how could your accountant argue about your therapy with your therapist? And, secondly, because even he had noticed how much happier I seemed. He said, "Well, I guess I can't argue with success. You're doing really well, if this is really what he wants, I guess you have to do it. I just think you should ask David again."

I did ask. And David said no, we had to get the money out of the way. I felt like it was fine that my accountant wanted me to spread it out to the following year, but David knew what was right for me, and I was going to do what David wanted.

I was so glad and so relieved that this conflict was over, and that money would never have to come up again. We could just focus on therapy. So it was with a great sigh of relief that I gave him the checks and it was out of my mind forever.

About a week later, David told me we had to skip a couple of days, because he was going on a business trip. He wasn't sure his pager would work so he wanted to give me the number at his hotel in case I needed to reach him. He was always very aware that I could need to reach him, and was very open to being called and, as usual, to taking care of me. He asked if I had a pen, and he handed me a piece of paper, and I wrote down his hotel number in Las Vegas.

NBC wanted to go forward with our Tom Rhodes script, moving it from the page to film. This would bring Mark and me additional money. With the exception of lots of free rewrites, each step in the process of a pilot triggers a payment. Writers are paid for writing the pilot script; for their producing services if the pilot gets shot; and there's usually a pickup bonus if the show goes to series. On the series itself, the writers also earn a salary, which is paid per episode. (An episode takes about a week and a half on average.) This can range from a couple of thousand per episode, up to over fifty thousand for an experienced top-level executive producer (which Mark and I were not). There's no question that TV money is good.

The powers that be at NBC didn't think Mark or I was experienced enough at that point to run a show on our own, which we weren't, so one of their conditions was that we would bring on what's called a "show-runner."

The show-runner heads up the writer's room, gives final approval to stories, approves the editing (if they don't actually do it themselves), approves casting, music, titles, sets, wardrobe, everything. Except for the network, they are the final authority on how a show turns out (unless the show has a huge star who takes over and starts making those decisions themselves; or at least tells everyone they do.)

Universal had a development deal with a guy named Peter Noah, a typical TV executive-producer—average looks, mid-forties, Jewish. A development deal is where a studio pays someone a ton of money to hang out in a very nice office on the lot. They try to think of pilot ideas, and then try to sell those to the networks. It's the easiest job in Hollywood. Since Universal was already paying Peter a huge amount of money, and he hadn't sold anything else recently, they asked him to come on board and run *Mr. Rhodes* if it got picked up to series. Peter agreed to do it, but it was still Mark's and my decision whether we wanted to work with him, or meet other show-runners. We met Peter at his office on the Universal lot. He seemed to have the same vision of the show as we did, he seemed like a nice guy, and we said fine.

The network had some notes that needed addressing before the show went in front of the cameras, and Mark, Peter, and I got together in his office over the course of several days for a rewrite. Mark and I had had this love interest for Tom's character in the original version (of the school show, not the public defender show), a hometown girl named Nikki that the character Tom knew from high school. She was a cool, independent, feisty woman.

Peter had just the actress in mind, Farrah Forke, a woman he'd worked with before. That was fine with Mark and me, as long as she could act (which she could). The only problem was, Peter wanted her character to go from our cool, feisty chick to a completely unbelievable, over-the-top, chain-smoking neurotic.

I hated the character, Mark hated the character. Where was the vision that Peter had shared with us, to make this show as real as possible? But he was now technically the show-runner. His decision was final.

In the room with Peter, Mark was pretty much fine. Going along, making jokes. Outside the room, my abusive husband was back. "Fucking Peter fucking Noah! Fucking hack! Can't fucking write worth shit!"

I didn't disagree. And I really wished our TV agents at William Morris had notified us that Peter was known to have more than one flop under his belt before they set us up with him. But right now I really didn't want Mark taking it out on me. I just wanted to shoot our pilot and have fun and get a TV show. Please, please, please let this go easy.

David was troubled by Mark's temper. He seemed really concerned that one day Mark could haul off and hit me. And I'd say no, no, it's fine, he'd never do that, Mark's not that bad; and then I'd spend hours of my therapy talking about how Mark would yell at me and how angry and frustrated he made me.

I asked my agent to talk to Mark, and he did. And for a brief while, Mark would calm down. But I was always on tenterhooks, never knowing when his anger might erupt. And trying not to let Peter see how pissed I was, while trying to tell Mark there was nothing to be pissed about.

David kept telling me to focus on what was important. I was going to have a pilot made. Forget that Peter seemed to be taking over the show, forget that Mark was volatile, forget that Universal was starting to treat Mark and me like we didn't exist. (They gave us parking spaces miles from the office; they set Peter up to interview a potential casting director without telling us; they told the trade paper *Variety* that they'd be shooting the "Peter Noah" project, not even mentioning Mark's or my name). There were a lot of other little and not so little things that were an attempt slowly, but surely, to push us out; and to justify the big money they were spending on Peter.

In my eight years in television, I'd found little support for the problems I'd encountered along the way; either from my agents or anyone else. It seemed women in particular were frequently looked down upon, and no one did anything about it.

My first job on *Roseanne* was as a term-writer, which is the lowest level on a writing staff, and until recently was not even credited on screen; even though you're there until four A.M. just like everyone else. One of the producers on the show, who went on to create several female-driven sitcoms and is thought to be a sensitive "woman's producer," announced one day in the writer's room that women should be frozen in ice and a blow dryer used to thaw out their vaginas because that was the only part of them that was any good.

He also suggested having a video camera that you could call a "clam-corder" that you could use to videotape young girls' vaginas. (This was a man with a young daughter.) No one thought this was weird or horrible, just comedy business as usual.

When no one among the other eleven writers spoke up, I knew then, so this is how it's going to be.

Obviously a lot of kids grow up without fathers, because of divorce, abandonment, or death, and I'm sure most pay a price for that absence. But, as I was learning, you don't have to be physically without a father to be without a father. The (emotional) absence of a male in my life affected a lot more than my dating. I had no clue how to relate to men; how to read them, flirt with them, be vulnerable with them, or how to stand up to them in appropriate ways.

A lot of women handle the sexism in Hollywood really well. They don't notice or they don't care, or they care but they're much smarter than me in handling it. Because of my own background, I reacted only in self-destructive ways. I thought this particular producer was a pig, and instead of keeping that to myself, I'm sure he saw my disdain. And with my problem of not knowing (a) how to handle my anger, or (b) how to handle men, I'd end up angry at basically all men, which predictably rather pissed them off. Not a very good move when you're starting out in a very competitive business run by those same men.

But this time around I'd have David. He was going to help me take whatever was thrown at me. I was bound and determined that this was going to be a great experience. And, God willing, I was going to have my own TV show.

For the first time, David was late to a session. In the entire time I'd been coming, every time I showed up, no matter how early in the day, he'd always been there ahead of me. This was really unusual but I tried not to worry. I was not going to react like my mother, panicking when someone is two seconds late.

I waited about ten minutes, then went to my car to use my phone. I paged David's number and waited. Nothing. I checked my home machine; there were no messages. Okay, something was definitely wrong. He had to know I'd be waiting for him, that I'd be worried. I knew he had a phone in his car. Why wasn't he calling me back?

I tried paging him again, adding "911" after my number, something he'd told me to do in case of an emergency. I'd never used it before. Still, he didn't call.

As the minutes ticked by, I became more and more convinced, absolutely certain that something had happened to him. There was only one reason he wouldn't call me. Only one. He was dead. My prediction had come true. My belief that I couldn't be lucky enough to have someone like David in my life. I knew it.

I'd written in my journal:

"God," whatever force controls the universe, has enjoyed watching me suffer. I was selected, it was a challenge, let's see if we can destroy her. When he saw that I was no longer (outwardly) suffering, that I had become small and hard, he sent me you, to tease me, lure me, show me what might have been. He and his pals are watching, laughing, waiting in anticipation of the fall. "Now, shall we do it now?" "Nah, she's not ready." He rubs his hands in glee, watching me get sucked in, melting, liking. "Look at her, she's so stupid, she's a fool, she has no idea." There will be a perfect moment, when he's bored, or angry, or sees me liking it too much, that he'll go, "now," and take away. "See, and you thought you were gonna get something, you stupid idiot bitch." And they laugh and giggle and clap like monkeys, but only for a minute. It's already boring, and they turn to poker and cigarettes. And I'm stabbed in the gut, bleeding to death, and they've forgotten I even existed.

I'd had such a fear of something happening to David that he felt it was getting in the way of me getting emotionally attached to him. "You need to learn to be attached to someone, Jennifer," he told me. "You've never experienced that."

I thought I was overly dependent on David already, but he explained that being completely dependent was crucial, at least temporarily; that only that way could the pendulum then swing back in the other direction.

He felt I was holding back, and so that I would feel safe, he told me one day that he'd asked Roxanna to step in if anything should happen to him.

"She's loving and motherly and nurturing and smart," he said. He'd asked that if something should ever happen to him, would she still talk to me and help me? And she'd said, of course, she wouldn't take money, but she'd do it as a friend.

But now I was outside his office, and I didn't know what to do, who to call. I didn't have Roxanna's number. I had no number other than his pager. He was now almost thirty minutes late. It was my fault. David was dead and it was my fault because I was cursed. My life was cursed, and the curse touched everyone around me.

Until this moment, I had not realized just how dependent I was on David. Now I knew. What was I going to do? What would become of me if he's dead? My heart was pounding.

Suddenly I heard footsteps behind me. I turned, and it was David. I blurted out, "God, I was so worried!" and instantly hated myself.

He'd been in a car accident. A guy had run a stop sign, plowing right into him. Although David was fine, just a few bruises, his car was totaled. Roxanna had brought him another car, then taken a taxi home.

"But I paged you twice. Why didn't you call me?" I was trying to act casual. Now that I knew he was safe, I could pretend it wasn't that big a deal.

He was surprised to hear I'd paged him twice. He never got the first page, and the second time, the number cut off. "If it'd been your home number, of course I have that memorized," he said. "But I've never called your car phone."

Unbelievable. First the accident, then the pager doesn't work, then it cuts off in the middle. I said, joking, that maybe Pluto was fucking with me, just to keep me on my toes.

I asked David, "Don't you think this is a little too much? I mean, I totally thought the worst. I don't like being that dependent, David." He reminded me that those thoughts were Pluto trying to take back control, to pull me away from him.

David tore a piece of paper out of his Filofax. As with many of his accessories, the paper was purple, his favorite color. Many of his clothes were purple or had purple in them, and anytime he'd bring in a notebook or folder, it was always purple.

He wrote down his cell phone number, and handed me the folded page. If anything like that ever happened again, he wanted me to call him in his car. "Don't give this number to anyone else," he added, obviously meaning Paul, since I knew none of his patients.

He felt terrible that I'd been so scared, and reminded me that we were going to defeat Pluto. "Nothing's going to happen to me," David said, "I promise."

———

It was five minutes before the end of a session, and David suddenly had something to tell me. He was going to Australia on vacation for two weeks.

I was totally freaked. How was I going to go for two weeks without seeing him? I couldn't imagine it. It was one of the few times I'd ever been angry with David. How could he tell me this just as the session was ending?

"You had to know this would upset me and I'd want to talk about it," I said. He apologized, and admitted that he probably hadn't told me earlier because he hadn't wanted to upset me and interrupt the session. I thought that was a really stupid excuse, but I didn't say anything. He promised me we'd talk more about the trip tomorrow. I left the session still angry.

The next day for once I knew instantly what to talk about. Without any preamble I sat down on the couch and asked, "Why do you have to go now? What am I going to do for two weeks?" I felt he was completely abandoning me. All this stuff was going on regarding my pilot, and he'd be leaving. At the same time I hated myself for even caring.

He said the trip had been planned for a long time, before he even met me, and that he was going with Roxanna, Darian, Vanessa, and their nanny. They'd be leaving in about seven days.

"But Jennifer," he said, "do you really think I wouldn't take care of you?" He said he'd thought about this a lot, and decided that we would work out a phone schedule so I could talk to him as often as I wanted. I would never be out of contact. He wanted me to think about how often I felt I wanted to talk to him, and he would think about what *he* felt I needed, and we would come to an agreement.

Part of me wanted to say I needed to talk to him every day, and part of me wanted to say Sayonara, have a good trip, I could care less. I told him I would think about it.

Eventually we decided to talk every two days. Now that I'd gotten used to the idea he was going, I felt that was too much, but David said there was a risk I'd start to get distant if too many days went by. He said he'd give me the hotel phone numbers as soon as he had them. I could only imagine what my phone bill was going to be.

———

It's not twins, it's triplets!" David was ecstatic. He and Roxanna had gone for an ultrasound. Tucked behind the two babies they knew about was another. My face must've shown total shock, because the first thing David said after telling me was that having three babies was going to be no different than having two. "I'm still going to have enough energy and passion for you, Jennifer," he said. "Everything will stay the same between us."

I couldn't believe this thirty-four-year-old man was going to have five babies. David laughed, and agreed it was crazy. He was almost giddy with the idea.

The only change, he said, was that for the next few months he might be a little less accessible on the phone. Roxanna was having a difficult pregnancy and after they got back from Australia, the doctors wanted her to stay in bed. Three babies meant more of a chance that she could lose one. "Of course, she doesn't want to stay in bed." He smiled. "She's very feisty." She wanted to take care of the twins, and was frustrated that she wouldn't be able to be as attentive to them. Even though they had a nanny; with Roxanna forced to be in bed, he'd be spending a lot more time with Darian and Vanessa.

He always loved spending time with them, he said, but now it was even more important to him. Once the triplets were born, Darian and Vanessa were no longer going to be the only children.

"I want to give them these last few months where they feel really special, and I can explain what's happening," he said. "And I'm not going to stop making you feel special, but I may need to spend a little more time with them."

When my sister Jane was born I had no recollection of even knowing about her arrival ahead of time. I suspect I was told, but I don't remember it. I can't remember her coming home from the hospital, but I believe it was at that time, so that I wouldn't feel bad, that my parents bought me a dollhouse.

On March 19 David left for Australia. We spoke every two days. I'd call him at the hotel at times when he had arranged for Roxanna and the twins to be gone, and we would talk.

He told me about the Great Barrier Reef and how beautiful it was. He'd been hang gliding and parasailing and bungee jumping. Although Roxanna normally loved to do those things, obviously this time she couldn't.

He told me he and Roxanna took the twins out on a glass-bottom boat, and how they laughed and loved it. I thought about vacations I'd been on with my parents. I remember them mostly through photographs or home movies, without those it's as if they never happened. I recall that once, at around age five, I mistakenly locked myself in a hotel room and had to be rescued by the fire department; I remember that I was once hit in the face with a golf ball near a golf course in Greece; and was told that my brother once (presumably by accident) almost drowned me in the ocean when he let the air out of our dinghy. My only other memory was that I was always carsick. The joke in our family was that I had vomited all over Europe. I always vomited, and yet we always took car trips.

I was jealous of how David's twins would grow up with more pleasant memories.

There had been a triathlon in Sydney, and at the last minute David had decided to enter. I knew he ran, but not that he was a triathlete. I asked how he did.

"I won," he said. I was really impressed, proud of him. The race had been run for charity, with the entry fees going to build or refurbish a new public pool. But when David won, he donated his prize money to the charity as well. "I don't need the money," he said. I thought that was so typical of David, to always do the right thing. I would've kept the money, but then David was a much better person than I was.

April 1, 1996

David had insisted on seeing me, even though he had just flown in from Australia that morning.

When I walked in I saw a wrapped package next to his chair. A few days earlier he'd told me he'd brought me the most perfect gift and couldn't wait to give it to me.

I told him I wasn't really in the mood for a gift. The night before David came back I had spoken to my father on the phone. Since my attempt more than ten years ago, when Jane and I had tried to explain, without success, that we felt caught in between our parents, this was the first time I'd had a real conversation with him.

I don't know how we got there, but at one point I said I felt he'd never showed me any love, except by giving me money and material things. I said I felt no love from him. He said that wasn't true, that of course he loved me. He was sorry I felt that way, but there was nothing he could do about it. "It must've been terribly sad to feel unloved your whole life," he said. It was like he was talking to one of his patients.

"Well, tell me how else has your love manifested itself?" I asked.

"You can't quantify it," he said.

"How else besides money, Dad?"

"I'm sorry you feel that way," he said.

My mother, obviously hearing his side of the conversation, got on the phone. She had heard him say that I didn't feel they ever loved me.

"Well, I'm sure that makes you feel bad," she said, "but how do you think that makes *me* feel? You have to realize what that does to me, hearing that."

So instead of opening the gift, I came into the session in a foul mood, bursting to tell David about this conversation. How frustrating it had been, how pathetic my father's attempt to deflect me, how predictable my mother's self-involvement, how foolish of me to have expected anything different.

David was listening to me ranting, but I felt bad that I'd spoiled his gift-giving, which he had been so looking forward to. I apologized. "Let's drop this," I said, "there's no point."

David asked if I was sure I didn't want to talk about it anymore, and I said I didn't even care. David smiled and handed me a greeting card, and the wrapped gift. I opened them both up.

Inside the box was a piece of ancient rock from the Raintree Rain Forest in Queensland, carved by an Aborigine artist.

In the card David explained that the carved piece showed two sides, symbolizing one spirit taking care of the other. The second spirit, David said, gains its identity because of the nurturing relationship. "Just like you and me," he smiled.

"Let's resume our art"—David wrote in the card—*"Your spirit, strong, rich and loving—is waiting 2 emerge!"*

One day David asked if I'd like to see a picture of Vanessa. He pulled a photo from his wallet, and handed it to me. It showed a beautiful little girl, smiling. I felt tears forming, and fought to keep them back. "What are you thinking, Jennifer?" David asked.

"I'm jealous of her," I said. "Seeing her makes me sad I guess." I added that my jealousy didn't mean I wanted to take anything away from Vanessa, only that I wished I could've had a father like David. I hoped she would grow up knowing how lucky she was.

"You didn't even need to say that," he said, referring to the jealousy. He knew that I didn't mean any harm to her; it went without saying. "Your spirit is too good," he told me.

I needed to talk to David one night, something was troubling me. I tried his pager, and there was a recorded message from PageNet that the system was down. I tried again over the course of several hours, and then decided to try the cell phone number David had written down for me. A machine picked up, with what sounded like an Indian or Pakistani voice. It was clearly not David. I tried again, getting the same recording.

Later that evening David called me. He'd found out the paging system was down, and just wanted to check if I called. I told him about the foreign voice on the machine.

He told me he'd canceled that cell phone a couple of weeks ago. "I was spending too much time in the car talking to people, returning patients calls," he said. "I just needed a little more private time." He added that of course I was not one of those patients who was an intrusion.

I couldn't understand why he hadn't told me. "You gave me this number in case of emergencies," I told him, "and you didn't think to tell me it no longer existed?"

He said he'd completely forgotten. Roxanna had actually been the one to call and cancel it, and he guessed it had just slipped his mind. I felt it was pretty irresponsible and I told him, "But you never forget anything. How could you forget?"

I'd never met anyone with a better memory than David. He could recall minute details of things I'd said months ago, sometimes things that I didn't remember telling him even when he reminded me.

David could tell I was upset and gently reminded me, "I'm calling you now, Jennifer," he said. "I had a feeling you might've tried to call me, and I was right. You don't need to worry, I'll always be there for you, I promise."

I calmed down. He was right. He'd just made a simple mistake, and he'd apologized for it. I had to learn to let this kind of unimportant stuff go.

May 1996

One of the biggest concerns Mark and I had had going into this pilot was, could Tom Rhodes act? The whole show hinged upon this stand-up comic, and we had no idea of his acting ability. As it turned out, to put it politely, he had very, very little. He was a sweet guy, but just way out of his league in terms of acting experience.

When trying to cast the love-interest (even though Peter had pretty much decided it was going to be Farrah Forke, we still went through the motions of holding auditions), we decided we needed Tom in on the casting sessions, to see if there was any chemistry between him and the actress.

We whittled the actresses down to our favorites, and arranged for Tom to be there for the call-backs. It was painful. These poor women were trying desperately to react and stay in character across from Tom, and he was just dreadful. Wooden and stiff and not funny. They were getting better chemistry with the female casting director.

We were all very discouraged—Peter, Megan (our casting director), Mark, and I. How were we going to get Tom ready to shoot this pilot? If the network saw that he was this bad, they would abandon our show. There'd be no pilot, never mind no series. There was only one thing to do. Not tell them.

We brought three actresses in to read for NBC; Farrah, and two others. When an actor or actress is going to be a lead on a series, the network has to approve them, and makes the ultimate choice.

We ended up in Warren Littlefield's office, the head of NBC Entertainment. Peter, Mark, me, Megan, several network executives from Universal, and Tom's manager, Michael Rotenberg, from 3 Arts Entertainment, who had heard the worst from us about his client.

The first actress came in. It's a very nerve-wracking time for any actor at this point, everything hinges on this moment. She started reading with Megan, and suddenly Warren goes, "Stop, stop, what is this?" And he sends the actress out of the room.

The poor woman leaves, having no idea what's going on.

"Where's Tom?" Warren wanted to know. "We're casting the love-interest, where's our star? She should be acting with our star."

There was total silence. Peter, Mark, and I couldn't look at each other. Couldn't look at Megan. Or Michael Rotenberg.

Michael fumbled around for several seconds, and then stuttered some excuse about Tom not being available or something.

"It's his fucking TV show," Warren said. "I want him here to read with the actors."

We rescheduled the casting session, and Peter, Mark, Michael, and I gathered in the parking lot outside the main entrance at NBC. This was a disaster. We had warned Tom that it was best he not perform in front of Warren until he'd had more rehearsal. Now he was going to totally freak out.

"What are we gonna do!" Michael Rotenberg said. It was clear that Tom now had to be at the casting session. He grabbed Mark by the arm, "You're gonna have to tell him!"

"What, are you nuts? You're his fucking manager," Mark said.

I like Michael Rotenberg a lot. He's a really sweet and nice guy, and smart, but the reality was, as Tom's manager, and like most managers who attach themselves as executive producers to a TV show, he was going to be making a substantial amount of money for doing virtually nothing on the pilot, other than watching the filming from a comfy director's chair, and spending time at the snack table. (Being a manager/executive producer on a TV show is an even better job than having a developmental deal, because you don't actually have to do *anything*.)

Michael reluctantly agreed that he should probably be the one to tell his client the bad news. Still, if any of us wanted to volunteer . . . ? We were all standing there laughing and trying not to freak out at the same time as we thought about what this could do to us. We'd been hoping somehow to dodge this bullet, to get Tom ready by the time we shot the pilot. Now he had to learn to act by tomorrow. We were screwed.

I'd told David he could deposit the second of the ten-thousand-dollar checks. Now I was starting to get nervous. I wasn't sure, but I believed the studio would still have to pay Mark and me for the pilot, even if it got canceled at this point; but it certainly looked like we wouldn't be going to series. All my sitcom dreams going up in smoke because this damn guy's as stiff as a post. Maybe we could hire someone else? Put a wig on someone? Shit, Tom's hair and mine were almost the same . . .

Even if we did make it to series, financially I still felt a little shaky. I was going through hell with my house, with one unexpected, and costly, problem after another.

When I took the wallpaper out of the kitchen, there was mold all over the walls. When we removed the old tiles, the floor underneath was falling apart. I ended up having to rip out the floor and the drywall, and rebuild the kitchen from the ground up.

One of the fireplaces was found to have been damaged in the 1994 earthquake. The home inspector had missed it, because the damage was inside the walls. It had to be torn down, destroying the wall in the process. Everything I'd fix would expose something else. I went through periods where I literally hated the house and was totally miserable. I didn't want to live there; the house felt cursed. I burned sage to ward off bad karma, secretly hoping it might catch the house on fire and I could collect the insurance. The down payment was starting to pale in comparison; this was costing me thousands and thousands more than I had planned or budgeted for. I had no idea how I was going to pay for it.

Please let Tom not suck tomorrow.

I was sweating like crazy, hoping no one from NBC could see the pools of moisture accumulating under my armpits. We were in the outer office, waiting to go in and watch Tom audition. A little two-page scene. Nothing. Piece of cake. He was funny in Montreal, please let him be funny again.

There was Peter, Mark, Michael, me, and a bunch of NBC personnel—executives, casting people, secretaries—milling in and out. We kept looking at each other, not wanting to say anything in case we were overheard. But we were all thinking the same thing—How disastrous was this going to be?

"Warren's ready." Oh, God. We trooped into his office, and arranged ourselves on various couches, chairs, and windowsills. There was a bowl of M&Ms sitting on a coffee table, and I kept shoveling them in my mouth. I think I ate about ninety of them. I don't even like M&Ms.

I must have been in a daze for the rest of the audition, because I don't remember anything else beyond being full of chocolate. But I do remember it being over, and Warren saying he liked Farrah the best, and us all agreeing, nodding vehemently. "Tom seemed a little stiff," Warren added. Which was fine with me—a little stiff was a lot better than what I'd expected. Stiff we could fix. Farrah was picked as the actress of choice, and Warren suggested that maybe Peter (who is also a director) could work with Tom before filming. Peter said absolutely, and reassured Warren he could get Tom where he needed to be.

We gathered again in the NBC parking lot. "Good luck," Mark and I teased Peter.

"Yeah, thanks," he said, "thanks a lot."

David was grimacing, clearly uncomfortable. "Something I said?" I joked. He asked what I meant. "You were making this weird face, like you were in pain," I said.

He was surprised, unaware that he'd been showing his discomfort on his face. He hesitated for a moment. "You remember I told you about being abused?" he said. I said of course. He explained that the abuse caused internal scarring, which he had to have surgically removed every few years. Typically, it had returned. "I'm fine, Jennifer. I'm really sorry I let you see that," he said.

He seemed to be really in pain, although he was obviously trying to hide it. For him to show any kind of discomfort was unusual. I knew he rarely got sick, and when he did he refused to let it affect him.

I had come in one day complaining of a cold and grumbling about how shitty I felt. David was very sympathetic, but wondered if I was really going to let it get to me.

He was always impressing upon me to look at what was really important. To understand that thinking about what's *unimportant* interferes with what *is* important. My cats Lewis and Baby were important to me, being honest was important; being true to my spirit; fulfilling what I was capable of; living in the present . . . Some guy in a parking garage giving me the wrong change was not. At least that's what David was trying to get me to believe. I still thought the guy should learn to count.

Still, being stoic about pain was one thing, having damaged insides was another. I asked if he was sure he was okay, and he said he was. "Let's talk about what's going on with you, Jennifer," he said. Always wanting to control everything, I told him he should see a doctor, and he promised he would.

———

I went to the movies one night with my friend Larry Silverman, and seated in front of us was an interesting group of people who I started talking to. There was a woman in her fifties, with two of her children; a daughter, fifteen, from her most recent marriage (she'd had four, none of which lasted); and her son, in his early twenties, from her first marriage. Her first ex-husband, also in his fifties, sat on one side of her; and on the other, her boyfriend, who was nineteen.

Waiting for the movie to start we were all laughing, making fun of this woman's many husbands and the fact that she had a boyfriend younger than her son. We got along so well that they said they wanted to adopt me. Even though it was a joke, I was flattered that these total strangers found me so appealing.

The next day I told David. "I'm jealous, Jennifer," he said, laughing lightly. "I thought *I* was your family."

I told him that of course he was, and he said that if anyone tried to steal me away, he'd beat them up.

———

David's office was on Sawtelle, in West Los Angeles, between Pico and Olympic. Since our sessions frequently ran long, parking at a two-hour meter could be risky, so I would park a little farther away, where the meters went for four hours. One day as I was walking to my appointment, I noticed David's car. When he had told me about the cars that he and Roxanna drove, he'd mentioned that they all shared a similar license plate—the letters SHIH, and then a number.

"Shih," David told me, was a Buddhist word. Although he wasn't a Buddhist, he believed in many of Buddhism's principals. The word *shih* meant "nothing comes between." He and Roxanna had that license plate on all their cars because nothing could come between him and Roxanna.

So when I saw this Honda with the license plate SHIH 38 I knew it had to be David's. Thirty-eight was the number on his football jersey in college; it was his favorite number.

It struck me as weird because I thought this was the car he'd told me got totaled in the car accident the day he was late. Maybe I had misunderstood him.

I went into session and I didn't say anything. I didn't want him to think I was questioning him or doubting him. It weighed on my mind, though, for several days, and finally I had to speak up.

"David, I have to tell you something," I said. I was very hesitant, nervous, my voice was almost cracking.

"What's up, Jennifer?" he said.

"Well, uh, I got it into my head that you lied to me about your car accident, because I saw your car outside the office, and you told me it got totaled."

David explained. The car he was in did get totaled, but it had been Roxanna's car. He'd borrowed it that day because his was out of gas. His car, the Honda, was the one she had brought to replace the totaled one.

"Oh," I said, "I thought you said it was your car."

"I think I just said the car. I'd never lie to you, Jennifer," he said, "But I can see where you'd be confused."

"I didn't really think you lied to me," I said. "I just wanted to tell you I had that thought." David said it was fine, I was allowed to think anything I wanted. He wasn't mad, wasn't offended, I didn't need to worry.

"We're doing really good, Jennifer," he said.

I was relieved to hear his explanation of what happened, because actually for a brief moment I *had* thought he lied. I felt guilty for even thinking it.

One day in session David and I heard loud chanting and weird noises and groans coming from the therapist's office next door. We started laughing, making jokes and theorizing what could possibly be going on. We heard only one voice, so we were pretty sure it was the therapist in there by himself. "But he sounds insane," I said. David said I'd be surprised at how crazy some therapists were.

He said that one time during a session, he heard screams coming from the women's bathroom. He and his patient went to investigate. They found a woman on the floor, beaten up and covered in blood. The patient went to call 911, then the woman's boyfriend showed up, screaming at David to mind his own business, that he could beat up whomever he wanted. He was a psychologist who worked in an adjoining office.

He told another tale of a very attractive female patient he had at his old offices in Beverly Hills. While she was waiting for her session one day, a therapist from an office in the same suite, a lesbian, talked this patient into coming into her office, telling her that sometimes a person needs two therapists.

Yet another tale was of a female therapist who had an obsessive crush on an actor, and gave up her marriage and successful practice to pursue him around the country. The crush lasted until she, a Democrat, found out he was a Republican, which caused her to have a nervous breakdown.

David had many similar stories, so many that he thought maybe he should turn them into a book. "And then maybe you could write a movie about it," David said, smiling. We thought that everyone would want to hear about crazy therapists.

June 1996

Somehow Peter had dragged Tom through the pilot, but it had been really touch and go for a while. We'd had what's called a "table-read," which is where the writers and the actors and the director sit around a big table, and the actors read the script. It went really badly, so badly that the network wanted a major rewrite.

We got through that, staying up until four in the morning; then it was on to rehearsals. Typically a sitcom rehearses for four days, then shoots on the fifth. Much as I was angry with Peter for taking over, and being basically totally dismissive of me, I had to commend him for how he hauled Tom through the rehearsal process. The director pretty much gave up on Tom, focusing on the other actors, the camera moves, the lighting, etc. Peter took Tom aside and rehearsed with him for hours at a time, trying to get something out of him.

We had our run-throughs, which are rehearsals without wardrobe, makeup, etc. The actors go through each scene, standing in their right positions for the cameras, delivering their lines, while the writer/producers see which jokes work, which don't, what lines don't make sense.

Tom actually seemed to be getting better. Sometimes. And then sometimes he'd just be terrible again. We hoped the actual night of filming would hit the up cycle.

Of course first we had to get through the dreaded Network Runthrough. A full complement of executives from NBC, including the comedy-development executives, publicity, casting, promotional department, and of course Warren Littlefield, would watch a rehearsal from beginning to end. It is the network's last chance for final notes, thoughts, or to back out.

The cast ran through the entire show, and except for an occasional forced laugh from one of the crew, or from Peter, Mark, or myself, there was not a laugh to be had in any scene Tom was in. (The crew, of course, had an interest in the show going to series, so they tried desperately to laugh where they could. But they were only human.)

The actors were dismissed for the day, and Warren said he thought we all needed a meeting. With the Universal and NBC executives in tow, everyone headed into the bar set, where Tom had one of his most awkward scenes.

There was a long silence, while Warren obviously tried to think how to put this. Finally he turned to Peter.

"Do we really think this guy can do this?" he asked. Peter didn't want to lie; he would like to work with Warren again.

"I don't know," he said, "I really don't."

We told Warren we'd seen better, and we thought that Tom could probably pull it off. Maybe. I was praying, Oh, God, please let Warren not pull the plug.

Finally Warren suggested we put off the filming until Monday, giving Tom the extra weekend days to rehearse. This would cost Universal more money, but it was that or sink the pilot.

Universal agreed, and we set the filming for Monday night.

Warren must've really wanted to give Tom a shot, and he clearly had a lot more faith than I did, because if it was me I would've pulled the plug.

———

My friend Paul Avery, who had introduced me to David, made a living doing audience warm-up on the set of several of television's highest-rated sitcoms, and I had asked if he'd do warm-up for our pilot. He's the best in the business at standing in those bleachers, telling jokes and keeping an audience alert, happy, and laughing. I suspected we'd really need him. He agreed to do it, and, as always, was great. The energy level in the audience and on the stage that night was terrific.

Tom was a stand-up comic, and clearly fed off the audience reaction. He was the best I'd seen him, but the night was still a little rough. Of course all pilots are hard—there's a lot at stake, an enormous amount of pressure. Even during the regular season it's not uncommon to shoot scenes or portions of scenes over and over, sometimes going so late that the audience members are let go even before seeing the end of the show.

Sometimes lines that are funny on the page, and hysterically funny in the writer's room at three A.M., don't come out of an actor's mouth that way. It can be the fault of the writing, the acting, the directing, even the audience. It doesn't matter. When you're on the floor of the stage, in the middle of filming, you have to replace the line. There is a huddle as the writers gather and feverishly pitch replacement lines. Finally one hits, or comes close enough, and the actor rushes off to learn it.

On the other hand, some actors will take a nothing line and turn it into gold, surprising everyone. Tom was far, far away from that level, but God bless him, he was trying. Peter would take him aside and guide him through the scenes until he got them right, and then send him in front of the camera. There was a normal amount of re-writing of jokes, not only for Tom, although for him more than others. Ron Glass (from *Barney Miller*), for instance, hit gold with almost every line. But even for our seasoned cast there were jokes they had trouble with, or that simply weren't funny enough to begin with, or jokes which the audience just didn't get.

A large portion of our audience that night was from a drug-rehab group, which is not abnormal. Neither is paying an audience, whose members usually get around five dollars an hour. It's hard to get people to come to tapings, particularly for unknown shows, because the process can be very tedious. Almost all shows shoot on Fridays or Tuesdays, so the audience pool is limited, and tourists in particular prefer to go to shows they've heard of. A typical explanation for being at a lesser-known show is that they couldn't get into *Frasier* or *The Price Is Right*.

The rest of the cast was great, energetic and funny, and their experience and professionalism helped pull Tom through. A surprise to us was that Tom remembered all his lines, and didn't flub once. No blooper reel here. He had clearly worked very hard to give this his best. At the end of the night, we were giddy. We had done it.

Now on to the editing process, and then the worst part of all. The waiting. Would we be picked up to series or not?

———

After several weeks of being in obvious pain, David had had surgery to once again repair the damage inflicted on him as a child. He was obviously in terrible pain, but insisted we meet.

He'd hobble into the waiting room to get me like an old man, walking really slowly. He made jokes about it, saying that I could kick his ass. "I could always kick your ass," I joked back.

Of course that wasn't even remotely true. David was in great shape. Besides being a runner, he worked out with weights every day. Roxanna had been a physical therapist before she quit to have children, and in fact still did occasional therapy on some professional athletes from the Lakers and the Raiders. They had a full gym in their house, with Nautilus machines, weights, treadmill, a StairMaster.

I, on the other hand, never worked out, ran only as far as I needed to get to my car. I was a vegetarian, didn't cook, and I probably got only half the amount of protein I should have.

About seven months into therapy I'd come into session one day on crutches, having torn a ligament in my vegetable-weakened ankle. While writing the pilot, Mark and I had gone to grab takeout. Leaving the restaurant with bags of Thai food, I stepped off a curb into a hole, and went flying. I ended up sprawled facedown on Sunset Boulevard, barely avoiding getting flattened by speeding cars (none of which stopped). I was having trouble using the crutches, which were causing shooting pain under my arms.

After my session with David was over, he called Roxanna on the phone. For more than half an hour she painstakingly passed along information to David. David would ask questions like, how does she go up stairs, Roxanna would tell him, and he'd pass it on to me—the crutches should be this long, this is how you hold them, this is where you keep your elbows.

Later she wrote me a two-page letter telling me she hoped my foot was okay.

David had been showing Roxanna almost all my paintings. She wrote me a letter one day to tell me how much she enjoyed them, that she was shocked at the talent, that they looked like the work of a seasoned professional. Along with the letter, she'd sent a gift; a potted plant, a hyacinth, which came from their garden. David had told me she loved gardening. Roxanna wrote me a letter explaining that hyacinths were "for your soul."

> . . . Keep fighting, soul is the only thing worth fighting for. And from what David tells me, you're well on your way to winning the fight!

There had been rumors about *Mr. Rhodes*, and the possibilities of a pickup. Rumors that NBC was thinking about it; it was on the short list; it was a definite maybe. I was calling my agent every day, "What have you heard?" "What are the chances?" "Can't William Morris pull some strings?"

Finally the call came. NBC had picked up the show. We were going to series.

———

Because of my preproduction schedule on the show, I had to be at the studio, which was an hour away from David's office, at ten every morning. Preproduction is the time prior to shooting, where the newly hired writing staff comes in every day to come up with story ideas for the upcoming season, to get a jump on writing scripts, and to take really long lunches. Since once you're in production you usually work through lunch, this is the only time you're going to get that opportunity. You might as well take it.

In order for me to make it to the Universal lot, we had to change my appointments to seven A.M. As always, David was happy to do it. I was no longer so awed at the things he'd do for me, they were almost becoming expected.

"That's how it should be," David said. "You should expect your family to want to do things for you. That's normal."

I was not having a great time on the show. Peter was not making it easy. After the pilot was shot, I'd really been looking forward to learning about the editing process, and getting involved in the titles and the music, etc. If I was going to be in this business, and stay in this business, I really wanted, and needed, to learn how to run my own show.

Except Peter had other ideas. "I don't want you there when I'm editing," he told me.

I explained, I wouldn't make comments or anything, I just wanted to observe. "I just want to watch, so I can learn," I said. Remember, this was *my own pilot*.

"Sorry, you can't be there."

I was stunned. Why? What was the possible reason for this? As far as I was concerned, it was just mean-spirited, plain and simple. I told my agent, who did nothing. This was a "package" through William Morris, meaning they owned part of the show. It seemed to me they could've stepped in and backed me up.

In addition, Universal decided they were going to pay for Peter alone to go to New York for the network announcements. Each year, sometime in May, the four major networks head to New York to announce their upcoming fall schedules. Everyone from the press is there, every major and minor newspaper, *TV Guide, Entertainment Tonight, Access Hollywood,* everyone. Foreign press, local press, print and TV. Agents, actors, managers, publicity people. It's a big, big deal, very exciting; a thrill for any first-time show creator.

For the first time, William Morris stepped in. Finally disgusted by Universal's behavior, they offered to have the agency pay for Mark and me to go. Perhaps shamed, Universal agreed to foot the bill, and Mark and I went to New York. Still, Universal's treatment of us continued to taint the whole experience.

I kept trying to remind myself: It doesn't matter, your pilot got shot; look at the bigger picture. But it did matter. I was hurt, I was offended, I was angry. Universal completely backed Peter. Their attitude was that it was his show; Mark and I barely existed.

Mark vacillated between outrage and not caring at all. "I don't even want to go to fucking New York. I don't even want to be in on the fucking editing, I'd rather be with my family," he would say in one breath, and "Fuck that asshole" in another.

Sometime after it was edited, the pilot went out for testing, which is where a test audience views the show and then the members are interviewed about what they do and don't like.

Each year, the majority of shows that are put on the air fail, even though those shows presumably tested well. And shows that test terribly (the classic example being *Seinfeld*) can become huge hits. Year after year testing continues to be relied on heavily by the networks, and no one understands why.

I wanted to sit in on one of the testing sessions. I'd be behind a two-way mirror, secretly listening in to the comments. There's a TV in the viewing room which can be seen from behind the mirror. They put the tape in, the show began, the credits rolled. They read, in effect:

MR. RHODES

starring **TOM RHODES**

created by

PETER NOAH

and

MARK BRAZILL & JENNIFER HEATH

Unbelievable. Peter had his name put first, on a show Mark and I had brought to *him*, that we had written *twice*. Not only was I convinced that this was completely contrary to Writer's Guild rules, it was just low.

I was pretty sure that if it wasn't for David, I would've completely lost it over this, especially when William Morris didn't want to get involved. Of course what could they do? They were only one of the largest, most powerful agencies in the world.

I ended up fighting it myself. I told the executives at Universal that what they did was totally inappropriate (although I used the words "fucking assholes"), and I went to the Writer's Guild. According to the Guild, the created-by credit should go only to the original writers, unless it could be proved that Peter wrote parts of the final version of the pilot script *by himself*. Mark and I were unaware of anything Peter had written on his own. As far as I knew, Mark and he and I had all done the rewrites together.

David kept telling me, Peter's not important. He's nothing to you. And he was right and he was wrong. I didn't care about Peter, but he was going to be running my show. I wanted desperately for it to be a good experience, I didn't want to make an enemy of him, more than he already was. It seemed that for some unknown reason he had resented Mark and me from the start. Mark and I talked about it, and after long discussions and advice from the Writer's Guild, we agreed to give Peter a "created-by" credit on the show, although his name would follow ours.

David's message was sinking in. A name on a screen wasn't that important. If sharing credit would make things go smoother, make my life easier, more peaceful, I was more than willing to do it.

————

David's birthday would be coming up in September; he was going to be thirty-four. I had seen another spirit stick at an art show, this one by a different artist. It was titled "The Healer." How perfect. Even though it was only June, I had to have it. Now I couldn't wait to give it to him. I teased him about it, telling him I'd found him the greatest gift. He kept asking me to give it to him early, that he couldn't wait, but of course I refused.

I arrived at session one day to find David bundled in a sweatshirt, in spite of the heat. I asked him why. I'd never seen him in anything but a short-sleeved T-shirt. He explained that because of his surgery, he was still a little woozy on his feet. Coming downstairs at his house, he'd tripped and fallen and was covered in bruises. "They're really ugly," he said, showing me just a glimpse of them. "I didn't want you to have to look at them for the whole session."

————

David told me they were very close to finalizing the deal on his book. The publisher had asked him to do some rewriting, but just the beginning of the opening chapter and some small things in the middle. David was very excited; they were also making him a deal for yet another book. His dream of becoming a novelist was coming true, and with it, David reminded me, my dreams of becoming a film producer.

————

As therapy continued, I was becoming increasingly aware of my desolation. More wracked with loneliness. More filled with despair at the utter waste of my life. It was too late for me. I'd missed too much. My life had gone by. I had touched no one, and no one had touched me.

I had done a painting called "The Emptiness." A body lies spread-eagled on an ice-cold black wasteland, a trail of blood leading to where it finally comes to rest. Ice swirls around it in a violent wind. Later, when my parents visited me and were looking around my new house, my mother said she liked the painting. She asked if the figure in the painting was a bird.

"It's a person," I told her.

"Oh," she said, and moved on to look at something else.

I toyed with the notion of wanting to meet someone. There was one other woman on the *Mr. Rhodes* writing staff, a writer/producer named Michele Wolff. Michele and I spent more than a fair amount of time on the stage scoping out the crew for romantic possibilities. Since almost all of them were either a lot older or married or gay or female, our choices were limited. Our only hope lay with Ted and Andrew, our two cute story editors. The fact that they each had girl-friends and were about to get engaged, only made them cuter, and Michele and I would have fake fights over who would get who.

Joking aside, I felt open to the possibility of a boyfriend, although, like a dog chasing a car, I wasn't sure what I'd do if I caught one. And of course I don't know where I thought this boyfriend was going to come from, since I didn't go to bars, I didn't go to parties, I didn't go to temple. I stayed at home on Saturday nights in the hope that some cute, sweet guy, maybe lost, would come knocking at my door.

The reality of meeting someone seemed impossible, and it seemed also that the fear I'd expressed to David was coming true: that I would finally be in the right place emotionally to meet someone, and wanting to meet someone, and there would be no one there. I was terrified to feel that loneliness.

The only thing that gave me any hope for my future was knowing that I would always have David.

I hadn't finished paying him the balance of the sixty thousand dol-lars, which I was giving him in ten-thousand-dollar increments. One day he brought up that he was in no rush for it, but just wondered when I might give him the next payment.

"We have so much money coming in each month," he told me, "from Roxanna's trust, from my patients, my consulting jobs, that it's hard to keep track."

I told him I didn't know exactly. Universal was holding back on paying us, since, per our lawyers' instructions, Mark and I wouldn't sign our contract, which was now different from what we had agreed to. I needed to get that resolved and then I'd be able to pay him.

I told David he was being pretty thoughtless—telling me about all his money, so much that he couldn't even keep track of it—when he knew that money, and not having enough of it, was a big issue for me.

I reminded him that the point of our arrangement was so he'd never have to talk to me again about money, and here he was bringing it up.

"I'm sorry," he said. "You're absolutely right, we did make that deal, I just forgot."

I said, Okay, but again, I was surprised that David, with his impeccable memory and attention to detail, would have forgotten. "But you remember everything," I said.

"I do remember everything, Jennifer, especially when it comes to you," he said, but added that he'd recently been through very traumatic surgery, and maybe his mind had been other places. Surely I could understand that? He was very gentle with what he was saying, but it was clear he was reminding me that I was finding the unimportant important.

He promised he wouldn't bring up the money again, and I told him I'd pay when I could.

A few weeks later I got paid part of what Universal owed me, and I told David he could deposit two of the checks. I'd now made the third and fourth payments, making it forty thousand of the sixty thousand dollars I owed him.

20

July 1996

David had decided to put his second dream into motion, which was of opening a clinic so he could train other therapists.

He had decided to open not one clinic but two—one in Orange County, one in Los Angeles. He and Roxanna were looking for spaces, and his top choice so far was the Water Garden—a luxurious office complex in West L.A. It was an expensive place to set up a clinic, but he said the money didn't matter. Roxanna knew this was his dream, and she was going to help fund it. He asked if I'd do some paintings to hang in the waiting room, that he would like to buy some. I was touched and flattered, and said that I would love to.

David told me he had to take a trip to Washington, D.C. He had to meet with this panel of psychologists to apply for credentials to open his clinics. But he'd only be gone a few days, he assured me, and he'd scheduled it so I'd only miss one appointment.

———

David had terrible laryngitis, he could barely speak. Except for his surgery, it was the first time in almost a year that I'd seen him sick. For over a week he spoke in barely a whisper, straining to be heard. I told him we didn't need to meet, that he should rest his voice, but he insisted.

"I want to see you, Jennifer; you're my family," he said. "Not *like* family, but really family." He said that to me so often, but sometimes I wondered what it really meant.

I had done a painting, called "Touch with Your Eyes, Baby." It was about the idea of parents taking their kids through stores, and the kids want to pick up everything, and the parents tell them, "Look but don't touch." That was how David's words felt to me. That he was telling me about his beautiful family, and telling me *I* was family, but I was only allowed to look in from the outside.

I was having a rough day in therapy, just really sad. In a year I had still never cried in front of David, but it was obvious to him that something was up.

"What's wrong, Jennifer? What can I do to help you?" he asked.

"Make me three again," I said. Whispered. I wanted my life back, the life I never had. I wanted to live it over.

David was very quiet. He just sat there. And I just sat there trying not to cry, and I finally said, "Can you do that, David? Can you?" And of course I knew he couldn't.

"I want to do something for you, Jennifer," he said. "I just need to think about it for a minute." He sat quietly for another few minutes, closing his eyes as he often did when he was really concentrating.

"You know how we've joked about you coming to live in the guest house if you ever lost all your money or became destitute?" he said finally, and I said, Yes. He went on, "I said you'd always have a place to stay, for security, for safety until you got back on your feet." I nodded. He'd said it many times.

"But that's not how a family operates," he said, "only being there in time of emergencies. I've told you you're family, and I want to treat you like family and have you *become* family. I want to give you the guest house."

I didn't understand what he meant.

"I want to give it to you, I want it to be yours, for you to live in, for the rest of your life. Give it to you."

I still couldn't comprehend it. "Give it to me? How can you do that?"

"I haven't asked Roxanna yet and I need to ask her, but I know she'll say yes." He said they never used it, just for occasional visitors. It was sitting there, empty.

I was speechless. I couldn't believe what I was hearing. "You mean I'd live there?"

"You could live there whenever you want, Jennifer," he said. "You could come down for the weekend. You'll have a place to stay if you just want to get away from L.A."

I just kept staring at him, stunned.

"We'll give you your own key to the main house as well," he said, "like a real family member." He was getting more and more enthusiastic, as if the idea was becoming bigger and bigger in his head. "You could come and you don't even have to tell us you're coming. Like a daughter. A daughter doesn't have to tell her father she's coming, she just comes. The only thing is if you're coming for dinner you might tell us so the cook can make enough food."

"David, this is insane," I said.

"No, what's insane is your life, Jennifer," he said. "That's what's insane. I want to do this, Jennifer. You deserve it. You can come and tell us you're there; you can come and not tell us you're there. You'll eat with us; we'll all eat together, the whole family. You can come and paint, you can write, we can hang out in my painting studio and paint together. And you can drive my Ferrari; we'll take it out. It's so fast, Jennifer, you can drive it as fast as you like."

I tried to interrupt, but he was so excited by this notion. And I was thinking, could he really mean this? Could it really happen?

"And when we move out of our house with all the kids, when we buy a new house, we'll even buy one with a guest house so you'll always be part of our family."

I had to fight to keep from crying, I couldn't even look at him. It seemed too generous, too kind. I wanted to say, "That's impossible; it wouldn't be right." But a bigger part of me was thinking, *Please, yes, I deserve something, and here it is.*

I would never have asked for this. It was so bizarre it wouldn't have even occurred to me. But once it was offered, it was so enticing. I had this idea that ethically this couldn't be right, to take so much from someone who really *isn't* your family. But stronger was this need I had, and my feeling, finally, that I *did* deserve it. I was greedy, I *wanted* it.

David said again that he'd have to ask Roxanna, but he knew she'd say yes.

"But what if she doesn't?" I said. She was the one with the money; it was technically her guest house.

David reassured me. He was positive she'd love the idea. "I'll ask her tonight," he said. "But, Jennifer, I know she'll want to do this."

I was nervous that whole evening, and of course David knew it. He called me to tell me Roxanna was thrilled with the idea. That she knew what I meant to David, that through my paintings I'd become important to her, that it would be great to add me to their family.

I felt as if I was dreaming the whole thing. This couldn't be happening. Good things happened to other people, not to me. I had always said, only half-jokingly, that in another life I must have been Hitler. How else could I explain my terrible karma?

So when David was offering me this miracle, it bewildered me. I also knew it was beyond unconventional; we had left unconventional far behind. But I didn't care. I reveled in the idea of a family.

I had had the most minimal of relationships with my grandparents, and virtually none at all with my aunts and uncles and cousins. I saw them rarely, years apart, and felt completely unknown to them. They meant nothing to me. I didn't know them, didn't care about them, barely knew their names. And I'm sure the feeling was mutual. At least I had no reason to think otherwise.

I had a friend named George in New York, who every year travels to Iowa for a family reunion. Each year more than three hundred people show up. He would tell me about his insane uncles and crazy cousins, his sisters and brothers and great-aunts and nephews and nieces. Three hundred people connected by blood or marriage—all knowing each other, reminiscing over past stories, talking about their futures.

My parents seemed totally isolated from their roots. Part of this was due to physical distance—most remaining relatives still lived in England, while we were in the United States—but it was more than that. Even as a child living in England, I remember almost nothing of spending time with family members.

Even my brother and sister were distant from me when we were young. There were almost ten years between Jane and Jonathan, and I was in the middle. I remember as a child building forts in the living room with my brother; and that one time he slashed the roof on my doll carriage. Those are almost the only things I remember connecting us.

I don't recall Jane and I ever playing together, although I assume we must have. I recall only that I thought she was a crybaby and that I didn't much care for her.

As adults, the three of us continued to be distant. Jane and I talked occasionally but were not close, although we were working on it. Sometimes I'd look at other people and their relationships with their siblings, and wonder how it came to this.

My sister's three girls scrap and fight as all kids do, but they love each other. They love to play together and sleep in the same room. They hug and kiss, they look out for each other, they say "I love you." I had never told my sister, my brother, my mother or my father that I loved them. I had said those words to no one. Nor do I recall ever hearing them spoken to me.

David was offering me instant family. A chance to do it again.

———

In the middle of July I received more of my salary from Universal, and I told David he could deposit the last two checks. I was set. Safe. Therapy, David, for life.

———

Roxanna and I want to go back to Australia, and we want you to come with us." David was living up to his promise to make me part of his family. As soon as I was finished with *Mr. Rhodes*, he wanted to go. I only knew it would be sometime in early 1997, and depended on how many episodes we ended up doing.

NBC had ordered the standard thirteen episodes, but there was always hope that good ratings would lead to a pickup for an additional nine, making a typical season of twenty-two episodes. Of course it was still only July. We hadn't aired even the pilot, and had no idea if audiences would think Tom, or the show, was funny.

The critics, however, *had* seen the pilot, and had definite and none-too-gentle opinions. Every day copies of reviews would arrive at the production office, courtesy of the publicity departments at NBC and Universal. About thirty percent liked the show, leaving a substantial majority disliking it, sometimes violently. The most common criticism was that Tom couldn't act, that he was wooden, stiff, not funny, and that his hair was too big. But they also criticized the premise, the writing, the jokes, the producers. No one was spared. Still, we'd already had one miracle, which was getting the pickup at all, so we knew anything could happen.

David said of course I would be their guest on the Australia trip. They would pay for everything. He said he couldn't wait to take me to the Great Barrier Reef, which he thought was the most beautiful place in the world. I told him I didn't know how to scuba dive.

"I'm going to teach you," he said. "Did I tell you we have two pools?" He had told me. They had a lap pool, and a regular pool. David had described the guest house to me, which was small but very pretty, like a cottage. Close by it was the regular pool, which had a waterfall next to it that spilled into the pool and then recycled. "The waterfall's kind of loud," David said, "but you can turn the pressure down if you want. You'll just hear a trickle of water if you want, and that's what you can go to sleep by."

He knew I loved to decorate, and he told me I could decorate the guest house any way I wanted. "It's your house," he reminded me.

David had scuba diving equipment, and he wanted to teach me. He didn't want me spending money on classes, but he explained I'd still have to get certified. "And I want to teach you to hang glide, Jennifer," he said. I wasn't sure about that. I didn't believe people were supposed to fly around in the air unless it was First Class with a nice reclining seat. David asked me to think about it. "I won't ask you to bungee jump, I know you'd never do that, but maybe you'll hang glide or water-ski or windsurf."

I promised to think about it, and I meant it. I'd never done anything like that before. Never done anything. I'd been taught that there was risk in everything. If I drove too fast, I was going to get killed. If I rode horses, I could break my neck. If I rescued cats, I'd be arrested. If I bought a house, someone might break down my door. But now David was offering me this chance to literally soar, and I was going to try to do honor to that gift.

———

David asked if he could show me a painting he'd done. I said, Of course, I liked to see all his paintings. "This one's a little disturbing," he said. "Are you sure you want to see it?"

I said sure. How disturbing could it be?

The next morning when I walked in a large canvas was leaning against the wall, the back side facing out. David didn't want to turn it around until he'd explained a little more about it.

"It's about the sexual abuse I had as a kid," he said, still concerned I might not want to see it.

By now of course I was dying of curiosity. David got out of his chair, went over and turned the painting around. The canvas was largely in purples, with a large penis taking up almost the entire canvas, with safety pins and other objects stuck into it. In the corner of the painting was a yellow section, almost like a patch of sunlight. As I did with my paintings, David had written his title on the front. He called it "Roxanna's Shelter."

"It's about my abuse, and how Roxanna supports me," David said.

I was completely speechless. Honestly I thought the painting was disgusting. Just bizarre and way too intimate. But at the same time, David was sharing something with me. He trusted me that much. And he had no shame in admitting that this had happened to him, which amazed me. I looked at the painting, and I didn't say anything, trying to convince myself, "Come on, Jennifer, grow up, art is *supposed* to be personal."

Finally I spoke, digging deep for something good to say. "Well, it's really nice you have Roxanna."

———

I didn't feel ready to go to the guest house, to meet Roxanna and the twins. It still seemed too strange of an idea. David and I decided that the perfect time would be for me to spend Christmas with them. I would meet the whole family, I could spend Christmas night in the guest house. Just kind of ease into it.

The triplets would be born by then, and I was really excited that there'd be this big family for me to be a part of. I knew I didn't want to spend another Christmas with my parents, and I'd been wondering what I was going to do. It would be the first Christmas I'd spent without them.

I told only two people about the guest house, recognizing that most people would think I was totally demented. Without me even going into much detail, I'd already heard some doubts from people about the unconventionality of my relationship with my therapist. They thought it was unusual, or at the very least not the way their own therapist behaved. Whatever concerns were expressed, I pushed aside. "I know it sounds crazy, but you don't know David. If it was anyone else but him . . ."

One in particular who questioned the relationship was a friend in Albuquerque named Joan Parrich, who happens to be a social worker. She's known me and my family since I was about ten years old. I was a bridesmaid at her wedding. I told her about David, going on and on about how great he was, and she became concerned that I was getting too dependent; and that his behavior seemed to be pushing the ethical envelope.

"But he's helping me, Joan," I told her. "Just the fact that I'm telling you I'm seeing a shrink proves he's helping me."

Joan admitted that I did seem more open, that she'd never heard me like this, so enthusiastic. In all the years she'd known me, she'd never seen me really care about anything. Still, it didn't sound quite right to her. I told her, "Look, he's a nice Jewish doctor. Don't worry."

"He's Jewish?" Joan said. "Well, okay, I guess." She was still reluctant. "Just be careful."

I told her I would, but that believe me, she had nothing to worry about. David was wonderful. Joan finally seemed to accept that David was not an ax murderer, but I still knew the guest house idea would probably not impress her. I decided to keep quiet.

I told Larry, my friend who had been at the movies with me the night that crazy family offered to adopt me (making David jealous). Larry's fairly unconventional himself, and didn't seem to find the idea of the guest house that strange. He had told me that his own relationship with his father was very strained, and I think he could understand my desire for a loving family.

I also told my sister. Jane thought it was unusual to say the least, even peculiar, which didn't surprise me; but she too couldn't help admitting that I had changed dramatically since meeting David. We had been talking even more about our parents, about our faint memories of our childhood, and the experiences we shared and didn't share.

She was disappointed that I wouldn't be seeing her and her children for Christmas. She was hurt. She felt that she was losing me to David and his family. "You don't understand," I told her. "David wants to meet you. You can come to the guest house any time. You can stay there with me."

David had told me I could bring whoever I wanted down to Dana Point. Whenever I wanted. My friends could meet his friends.

"You're going to meet great people, Jennifer," he said. "Our friends are wonderful, all part of the three." There were parties all the time. Every weekend their friends came over, staying late into the night, eating, talking, swimming. I'd have to lose weight.

I'd asked David to make me three years old, and of course that was impossible. But as he'd promised me in my birthday card, he was going to help me squeeze fifty years of life into my next decade.

———

I have an idea, Jennifer," David said. It was almost the end of a session, and he was smiling at me. "This is going to be really good for you."

I couldn't imagine what it could be. He'd done everything for me already, what could possibly be left? But everything he'd come up with so far had been so warm, so loving, so helpful. I couldn't wait to hear what it was.

I'd been seeing David five days a week, every day but Thursday and Sunday. He wanted to add a phone session on those two days, a formal arrangement where we'd talk for two hours each day.

I didn't like the idea at all. What was he talking about? It was true that in the past I'd always craved more contact with him, that I loved talking to him. But now I felt like what we were doing was fine. Any more felt like too much. I said I didn't want to do it.

He said he thought it'd be really beneficial to me. There must be a reason I was trying to avoid contact, he said. "There is a reason. The reason is that I think we talk enough," I told him. I really felt uncomfortable with the idea.

David reminded me that I couldn't always rely on myself, that Pluto still fought to win back control. To make me distant, pay less attention. "I've never, ever suggested anything that wasn't good for you, have I?" he asked. "Why do you think I would suggest this if I didn't think it would help you?"

He had a point, but still I was very reluctant. We went round and round about it for over an hour. I kept saying, No, he kept saying, "That's not you, that's Pluto, that's your defense mechanisms." He was relentless. "Don't you trust me, Jennifer, to know what's best for you?" He wasn't specific about why it was best, just that I really needed this. He was gentle, but he seemed really frustrated with me.

Finally I said, "Okay, look, if you really think it'll be better for me, I'll do it, even though it feels like too much." He was happy that we'd come to a decision, and reassured me that I was doing the right thing. We arranged our first conversation for the following Sunday, nine A.M.

When I walked into the next session, I told him I'd changed my mind and I didn't want to do it. It was the first time I'd seen David angry. He was silent for a moment, then he said I'd made a commitment, and a warrior doesn't go back on her commitment. He had never gone back on *his* word. His voice was unexpectedly cold. "I've rearranged everything to accommodate these phone calls," he told me.

With Roxanna in bed because of the pregnancy, David and the nanny were doing most of the duties when it came to Darian and Vanessa. David had worked out a complete change in the nanny's schedule to allow him these four hours of phone time.

"I'm very honest with you, Jennifer," he said. "I've always told you when I think you're wrong or you're making a mistake. And I'm telling you, what you're doing now is wrong." He told me I was being inconsiderate, that I had gone back on my word, and that I was obviously scared of the intimacy of everyday contact.

He was so upset and disappointed in me, it was obvious I'd made a big error. It scared me. If I make him mad, maybe he'll change his mind about the guest house. Why would he want someone so inconsiderate in his life? Someone who couldn't even stick to a commitment? It didn't occur to me that if David backed out of the guest house deal, he'd be doing the exact same thing to me. I told him that I would add the hours and that I was sorry. He softened, and said, No, he was sorry. "I shouldn't have gotten upset, Jennifer, I made a mistake," he said. "Because you're doing so well, and you've come so far, I forget that even a warrior is allowed to slip back sometimes."

I said it was okay. I was just happy he was back to the David I knew, and that this was settled. We would add our four hours of contact a week, and I promised I wouldn't change my mind again.

David suggested twelve thousand dollars as a figure to cover it. I was floored. I wanted to say something but I couldn't. I'd just assumed this would be part of the lifetime payment. Part of me was thinking, I don't want to pay this; it's wrong. But the bigger part, that scared part, was thinking, Don't say anything, don't say anything—you'll lose it all. I have to make him like me again, or I'll have no one. He'll think I'm greedy and selfish and petty. *I have to make things easy.* And the more I thought about it, the more I thought, How could I have been so presumptuous? Especially after David had been so generous in the past. I realized that I had misunderstood—the lifetime of therapy had been intended for five days a week, not seven. Of course I should pay for it.

I think David could see I was a little taken aback, because he joked, "This has to be the last payment, Jennifer, there are no more days in the week."

I nodded, and I said that next time I came in I'd bring him a check for twelve thousand dollars.

David was swiveling back and forth in his chair, using his foot to push off against the couch where I was sitting. There was a weird smile on his face. I asked him what was going on.

"Nothing's going on, Jennifer. What do you mean?" he said.

I told him he'd had this look on his face for the last ten minutes, that I knew him well enough to know something was up. He denied it again, and I said, "David, come on."

"Okay," he said, "there's something I need to tell you, but I'm really nervous about telling you this."

He was really hesitant, so I started guessing. I asked if it was something with his children and he said, Yes. It wasn't the twins so it had to be the triplets. They hadn't been born yet, but I wondered if something was wrong with one of them. "Is one of the triplets going to be deformed or something?" I asked.

He said, No, it wasn't about the triplets. I said, "Well, I don't understand. It's not about the twins and it's not about the triplets, but it's about one of your children?" And he nodded and said yes. I was confused.

"I have another child, Jennifer," he said. He seemed almost ashamed of what he was saying. I think my eyes almost popped out of my head, and he said, "I know, it's crazy, but I have another child. A daughter. She's seventeen."

That *was* crazy. He was not even thirty-four himself.

David explained that in his freshman year in college he'd gotten his girlfriend pregnant. "Her name was Julie, and I loved her, but she was totally irresponsible," David said. "She didn't want to take care of this baby and I did, so I took the baby and raised her myself." At the same time as he was getting his undergraduate degree and playing football in college, he raised the baby; and then continued when he went on to get his Ph.D. in psychology at Pepperdine.

"Are you disappointed in me?" he asked.

I asked him why he thought I would be disappointed. He said because it's totally irresponsible to get someone pregnant when you're seventeen, and he was ashamed of it. "I love my daughter," he said. "I'm not ashamed of her. I'm ashamed of how irresponsible I was."

I thought it was really commendable that he raised his baby. "You probably did a great job," I said. I was picturing David at seventeen, loving and caring for this little baby.

I asked her name, and he told me it was Selena, and that she'd just been accepted to the University of Miami to study marine biology. "We have a great relationship," he said. "We're best friends. I'm still her dad but we're best friends."

"So she was in Australia with you," I said. I felt weird that he'd talked about his whole trip, his whole life, and left out this huge part. David said, Yes, Selena was there.

"I'm sorry I never told you about her," he said. "I never tell anyone about her. I mean, of course my friends know, but I don't tell strangers because I'm still sort of ashamed of what I did."

I said I thought it was odd to not tell people about your children, and he reminded me that he was very secretive about his whole family. Being abused as a child had made him incredibly protective. He asked if I understood that, and of course I did.

"Once I knew you were coming to the guest house, of course I had to tell you about Selena," David said. "It would be hard to hide her every time you came." He smiled.

It bothered me that he'd kept this big secret from me. After almost a year, after inviting me into his family, and he hadn't told me this? He apologized again, and said he hoped I understood how embarrassed he was that he'd been so stupid at seventeen.

"Hey, David, it was seventeen years ago, time to get over it," I said.

"You're probably right," he said.

It occurred to me there was an inconsistency about what he was saying. When David had told me about being abused, he'd said that until he met Roxanna he thought he'd never meet anyone, and he'd be alone his whole life. Yet he'd obviously had this girlfriend, and had a daughter. How could he be alone if he had Selena?

"I meant that I had this child, this beautiful little girl, but I thought I'd have no one to share her with," he explained. "My physical problems started after Selena was born, when all the scarring started to build up. I thought I wouldn't be able to have any more kids, and no one would want to marry me, and I'd spend my life alone, just me and my little girl."

I didn't consider that having a daughter exactly fit the definition of being alone. I thought that "alone" was what my life was. But I could see how he'd felt that he wanted more.

So, not even thirty-four and you're going to have six children," I said.

"Actually, seven, Jennifer," David said, and he smiled at me.

July 22, 1996

It was the one-year anniversary of the day we met, and David had suggested we exchange gifts. He had been teasing me for days about what a perfect gift he had for me. I tried to guess what it was—large, small? Wood, fabric, stone? Finally I guessed correctly—it was metal. After quizzing him more, I decided I knew what it was. Metal, the perfect gift, pointed at one end . . . it was the key to the guest house. David agreed that that would've been a cool gift, but that wasn't what it was. I would just have to wait.

I had bought him a framed photograph. The title was "Resurrection Door." It was a juxtaposition of two images—a large tree in the middle of a clearing, covered in ferns, with an old door superimposed into the trunk. I had liked the photo and the title had intrigued me, and the photographer explained it to me. The fern was found in the South, she said, it was called a Resurrection fern. These ferns could lie seemingly dead for years—wilted, brittle, faded—but when you water them, they spring back to life.

David's gift to me was hidden by the side of the couch. He hadn't been able to wrap it because of its shape. "Go get it, Jennifer," he said. He was smiling, leaning forward in his chair, excited.

It was a sword, in a scabbard. The handle was wrapped in what looked like embroidered silk. "It's a Samurai sword," David said. "Open the card."

7.22.96

7 AM
Dear Jennifer,
    Although I relentlessly hunt joy & peace, I love anniversaries because they represent the dedication & commitment it takes 2 conquer the conflicts bound 2 arise in every dynamic relationship. In

spite of how rich & soulful our relationship is, it has not been without conflict—projections, miscommunications, details in contention, things that we may never agree upon. But what the fuck . . . here we R . . . 357 days after I called you Heather and exactly one year after U told me that U have no needs . . . conquering/annihilating/absolutely dominating all of the adversity that has attempted to bruise our trail. For this, Jennifer, I salute your spirit. Given the paucity of love & guidance in your past, it is amazing and awe-inspiring that U have been asked to stand in the ring with adversity and match him punch for punch.

For that reason, plus many-many others, U, Jennifer, embody the indomitable spirit of a warrior. U R strong, although only using your strength in the service of goodness; tough, although not in the way U previously believed, courageous, swift, agile.

I have recently become addicted 2 using the word warrior when describing U, so a symbol of a warrior seems like the perfect gift for our 1st anniversary. Whenever U look at your authentic warrior sword, I implore U 2 think of the psychological symbolism & spiritual significance & know exactly how I C U.

Anniversaries, Jennifer, R my favorite thing 2 celebrate. Everything else—from birthdays 2 Thanksgiving—R more or less arbitrary. Our anniversary, on the other hand, is the antithesis of arbitrary—it is the product of a profound partnership that can & will alter the orbit of your destiny. Above all, Jennifer, I want U 2 know that I view your soul with reverence, our work with reverence, our relationship with reverence. Namaste. David

It was a lovely gift. It was not aesthetically my style, but symbolically it was perfect.

I gave David his photo, and a card explaining its significance. It was still hard for me to get too sentimental in my cards, but I thanked him for the past year, for his support, insight, generosity, belief in me, and for loving me.

I had told David months ago that I didn't know the meaning of the word love, and he'd had me copy down his definition into my journal.

LOVE . . .

1. Never suggests that self-importance is synonymous with selfishness.

2. A generous willingness to extend yourself without expecting anything in return.
3. Being willing and/or happy to experience discomfort if it means it will help the object of your love prosper.
4. Never asks or even covertly suggests that the beloved swallow or hide an aspect of her soul.
5. Passionately cares about what the beloved passionately cares about.

I thought about those things, and what his criteria for love was, and I came into session one day and said, "I want to tell you something." I was really nervous, shaking. He asked me what I wanted to say, and I said, "Sometimes I feel like you feel love for me." I couldn't even look at him, it seemed presumptuous even to suggest it.

David said, "I do feel love for you, Jennifer."

I got really nervous, and really embarrassed. It was the closest thing I could remember to someone telling me they loved me. I quickly changed the subject, and we went on to talk about other things.

David loved his photograph. He was excited by the notion of all the anniversaries we'd be sharing together, and we wondered how we were going to keep coming up with the perfect gifts.

———

We talked on the phone, as planned, on Thursday and Sunday, the twenty-fifth and the twenty-eighth. Two hours each time. David had scheduled the calls for very early in the morning, and I was sort of irritated that I had to get up so much earlier, particularly on Sunday, but I didn't say anything. We'd already had our argument about this decision and I didn't want to rock the boat.

Mr. Rhodes was about to start shooting, and it was a pretty stressful time. The staff was busy writing scripts, which consequently meant there was a lot of rewriting.

One of the most common questions I get as a sitcom writer is "How do you write all those scripts?" (At least that's the question from people who don't think the actors make it all up as they go along.)

It's really pretty simple, although very high-pressure and always exhausting. A writer comes in with a story idea, such as: "Let's have everyone stuck in an elevator," and pitches the basic premise to the room. Once it's determined by the executive producer/show-runner to be a good idea, the writing staff "breaks" the story as a group. Everyone sits around, throwing out suggestions, arcs for the story, scene endings, jokes, plot twists; and a writer's assistant writes them all down.

The writer's assistant's job is completely insane. A room can consist of ten or more writers, all jumping in with suggestions, arguing, all talking at the same time, often punctuating things with loud laughter. The assistant has to determine which comments were thrown out seriously, which were just asides, which are really valuable, which are just funny anecdotes about the writers' personal lives. At the same time the assistant has to write it all down at lightning speed, as the writers continue to talk.

Once the story is broken, the writer of that particular script is given the notes that were taken by the assistant, and shapes them into a full outline: Act One, Act Two, scene breaks, etc. That outline goes through a final pass in the room, and after approval by the executive producer, the writer is sent off to write "The Elevator" episode.

Once that script is written, every staff member reads it, and comes back into the room to "table" it. Everyone sits around, either around a literal table, or on couches and chairs; and the script is rewritten page by page, top to bottom. This can take place over several days, and go until the wee hours of the morning. Even though the original writer is credited on screen, the script has had input from the entire staff, and sometimes bears little or no resemblance to the writer's original draft. (This "table" is different from the "table-read," where the actors sit around the table on the stage, and read the script aloud for the writers to hear.)

Along with breaking stories and writing, there was still some worry about Tom's ability. Could he pull off the stuff we were writing for him, particularly the emotional relationship with his love interest? I prayed that he could. As a co-creator, with so much at stake, I really wanted and needed the show to go well. To be a hit, to go on to syndication, to make me rich.

I'd been trying to be as pleasant as possible to Peter Noah, so much so that Michele, the other female writer/producer on the show, had noticed and commented on how nice I was to him. In spite of that, he was still very dismissive of me.

It's always been interesting to me that Hollywood, this supposedly liberal place, run by educated men in their twenties and thirties, is still such a misogynistic world. I can't speak for the feature film side of the business, but in sitcoms women are frequently ignored, their opinions dismissed, they are thought to be not funny (or at least not as funny as men) and are considered to be troublesome, moody, or bitchy if they demand things (Roseanne vs. Cosby—both notoriously difficult and nasty to work for, but who have you heard of as being impossible?).

The female show-runners with the most power are all partnered with men. Diane English (*Murphy Brown*) is partnered with her husband, Joel Shukovsky; Linda Bloodworth (*Designing Women*) is partnered with her husband, Harry Thomason; and Bonnie Turner (*Third Rock From the Sun*) works with her husband, Terry Turner. Maybe it's just coincidence.

Mark obviously felt the stress too, but he'd found a good stress reliever. He'd come into my office and yell at me. In one particular incident, when I was stuck on a story point in a script I was writing, I asked for help from Ted and Andrew, the two story editors who shared an office next to mine. Writing a sitcom is totally collaborative, and this was a totally normal thing to do. But Mark was furious. "Don't you know who you are," he screamed at me, leaning at me over my desk, pointing at me. "You're an executive producer! You don't ask for help from story editors! This is unacceptable!" I'm five feet tall, Mark's probably over six feet. I was so shocked, I was actually shaking, my hands were shaking. I squeaked out, "Please get out of my office."

Mark stormed off down the hall, and later Peter told me, "So, I hear you and Mark got into a shouting match."

Added to the stress of the show was the fact that I was moving. Finally all the construction was done. The renovation had cost me a fortune, more than twice what I had anticipated. My savings were almost decimated, but my house was finished. My first home.

I canceled my appointment with David on August 1, my moving day. I'd heard that moving was one of the most stressful times in a person's life, and I could believe it. The truck was four hours late;

when it did arrive, it was too small. This of course caused just a tiny little conflict with the dispatcher. When I told him to "get a fucking truck here, *now!*" he said I only used the word "fuck" so I could sound like a man, at which point I promptly told him to go fuck himself.

This, plus the idea that I was embarking on this whole new venture—a home, a mortgage—made for a pretty tension-filled day.

Still, I was in a surprisingly good mood. My own TV show, a new house—maybe my life had really taken a turn for the better.

On Thursday, during our phone conversation, David canceled our Friday appointment. A few days earlier I had paged him, needing to change an appointment time. Weirdly, at eleven o'clock at night, he'd been asleep. He normally slept only two or three hours a night, going to bed at one or two A.M., waking by five. His tiredness was starting to concern him, he'd been feeling lethargic ever since his laryngitis, and Roxanna was making him go to the doctor for a checkup. "She's very bossy," he laughed.

He called me Friday evening. His doctor wanted him to go into the hospital overnight for some tests. That sounded really serious to me. David reassured me, his doctor was a very good one, and just wanted to be thorough. "He's just being cautious, Jennifer," he said, "but I promise you, nothing's wrong."

Saturday night my phone rang. I knew it was David, I'd asked him to call me when he got the results.

His voice was shaking, cracking, he could barely get out the words. "Jennifer, I have to tell you something. Please don't be too upset. I have cancer."

I had a girlfriend once, Annie, who had a friend with AIDS. Annie called me one day, crying hysterically, to tell me her friend had died. She was distraught, devastated, could I come over?

I went to her house. When I walked in, she lunged at me, grabbing me, hugging me, sobbing. I made all the comforting noises I knew you were supposed to make, and halfheartedly hugged her back. But in truth I was embarrassed and disgusted by her grief, her need, her desperate clinging.

I had never been affected by human death. When my grandmother died, I felt nothing. When my cousin committed suicide by setting himself on fire, I thought it was horrible but I was not sad. Of course, I rationalized, I didn't really know these people, was not close to them, so how could I be expected to feel anything? But even when my best friend Larry's father died unexpectedly of a heart attack, I felt nothing for Larry. I felt no real sympathy, no empathy toward him. I saw that he was upset, and said the comforting words, but had no understanding of how he could be feeling. I was a supportive friend, and he thanked me for my caring, but to me it was all a show. I sort of knew that these reactions probably weren't normal, but I had no idea what the correct one would've been or what to do about it.

The only thing that moved me emotionally was animals. If I even heard a story of an animal suffering, it would make me cry. If I saw an animal abused or in pain, even on TV, it affected me for days. I couldn't watch *National Geographic* specials on animals, for fear one would die, or get caught in a trap, or a baby would be left without its mother.

When I ever thought about the inevitability of my parents dying, I was more or less unmoved. I supposed that I would miss them, and that it would be weird to be parentless, but I felt no fear or sadness at the idea. Again, the awareness of those (non) feelings had always seemed vaguely wrong to me—weren't you supposed to feel more for your parents?

I told David my concern about my lack of feelings for people. He said I identified with animals because of their innocence, their helplessness. Creatures who should be taken care of, being abused or ignored, devastated me. No one had cared for me, so I responded by caring for the weakest.

People didn't affect me, because people had never done anything for me. I did not connect with them, how could I be expected to relate to their sadness or mourn their passing?

Now David was telling me he was ill, and I was destroyed. Totally devastated. I flipped out, I was hysterical, crying. "I knew it, I knew it," I said. "I told you something was going to happen. I predicted it, I wrote in my journal!"

I was doomed, I was cursed. My curse had hit David. There was no way to correct my past; it could not be fixed. David was going to die.

David tried to reassure me. He had Hodgkin's, he explained. "If you're going to get cancer, it's the best kind to get," he said. I was still freaking out, I couldn't listen. David was dying. I'd killed him.

"Jennifer, Jennifer, it's not so bad," David said, trying to calm me down. "It's stage two Hodgkin's, it's ninety-five percent curable, and for me they're saying even higher because I'm an athlete and I'm really healthy. I'm really strong and I'm only thirty-three."

He was going to start radiation right away to shrink the cancer in his chest. "The doctors say that's what caused the laryngitis," David said. He was going to have radiation for four months and, concurrently, chemotherapy for three.

The chemo was an option, David explained, but the doctors believed it would be beneficial. David had seen his mother die slowly and painfully of brain cancer after choosing not to do chemotherapy, so he felt he had to do it.

"I'm going to do everything I can to live, Jennifer," he said, "so I can take care of Roxanna and my babies and Selena and you."

I felt terrible, filled with guilt. Here was David, who had just heard he had cancer, and all I could think about was myself.

"Can I do anything for you, can I help you, what can I do?" I said. David almost laughed.

"You don't have to do anything for me, Jennifer," he said. "I just want you to keep paying attention, and keep working hard, and meditate like I taught you, and we're going to be back to therapy in November. We're still going to do Christmas together, Jennifer, I promise."

I told him not to promise, that he had promised me he wasn't sick, and it was a lie.

"I did promise you that, Jennifer," he said, "and I'm sorry. But I'm going to get better, and we're going to have Christmas, you're going to have the guest house, and we're going to keep doing therapy, and all that is true. Do you forgive me?"

I said, Of course I did. I apologized for being so selfish, and David reminded me that I was allowed to feel whatever I wanted. "Whatever comes out of your mind is sacred and important," he told me. "Remember, a warrior doesn't confuse self-importance with selfishness."

Even with cancer, David was still teaching me.

I was going to be without therapy for four months. From seeing David five days a week, plus the two days we had been supposed to talk, to nothing. No winding down, no preparation. But worse than the abrupt withdrawal of contact was my conviction that David was not going to make it. The gods, Pluto, whoever, had finally made their move.

At work, I was a wreck. I didn't tell anyone what was wrong, and I think they believed I was having some sort of breakdown, which I suppose, at least part-time, I was.

Eventually I confided in Michele. She was sympathetic and tried to comfort me. I supposed it was evidence of David's teachings that I even let her try—before David, I couldn't bear for anyone to express sympathy or concern for me about anything, and would brush off or become hostile to anyone who tried.

David had my work number, and would call me frequently. Sometimes I'd page him, just to say I was thinking about him, or even just to hear his voice, and tell him he didn't need to call me back, but he always did. He was feeling good during the first few weeks of treatment, and said talking to me helped him.

Paul Avery and I had spoken rarely about David and therapy since the time he first suggested I see him. Occasionally Paul would ask, "Are you still seeing David?" and I'd say yes. I didn't tell him how extensive my therapy had become; just that I went a few days a week.

I knew that Paul's therapy, after almost six years, was starting to wind down. He'd told me several months earlier that he thought he was done, and it was time to move on.

Now both our therapies had come to an abrupt halt. Paul called me, shocked about David's situation. He couldn't believe this strong, healthy guy, who ate basically only fruits and vegetables and low-fat food, worked out daily, didn't smoke or drink, could get cancer.

"It just seems wrong," Paul said, with disbelief. "David of all people." We both agreed that nobody deserved cancer, but for David, so generous, loving, attentive, passionate about helping others, it seemed particularly unfair.

I didn't tell Paul that David was calling me all the time, because I thought it might hurt his feelings. He'd been David's patient for six years, yet David was calling him only very rarely. I loved hearing from David, I needed to hear from him. Working on the show, trying to be funny, trying to keep others from knowing anything was wrong, was the hardest thing I'd ever done. At what should've been one of the best times of my life, I was in a profound depression.

As the weeks went on, David called me less often, and would stay on the phone for a much shorter time. When we did speak, he sounded terrible—tired, weak. The radiation was starting to get to him, causing lesions in his chest and throat that made eating difficult. He'd started chemo, and was starting to feel sicker and sicker.

I got home from work one day and there was a message on my machine that David was canceling his pager. He had been getting so many calls from patients and felt obligated to return each call, but he was too exhausted to do so.

"I can't stand having patients calling me saying they need to talk to me, and then just ignoring them," he said. "I can't do it to them." Roxanna had finally persuaded him to disconnect his pager service. I couldn't call him, but he promised to call me.

I completely freaked. Now I had no way to reach him, this person I had talked to almost every day for a year. I had no home phone number. I didn't know where he lived. I felt completely abandoned.

He called me later that night, and I told him how flipped out I was that I couldn't contact him. What if I had an emergency, I wanted to know. I understood that he didn't want to talk, but couldn't I at least have a number to use in an emergency? "Please, please," I begged, "I have to know how to reach you."

David knew I was really upset, and he gently reminded me that he had a wife, twins, triplets on the way, a seventeen-year-old daughter, and cancer.

"I'm fighting for my life, Jennifer," he said. "I need to summon all my strength to heal my body." As an athlete, he really knew how to focus on his body and make his body work for him. That's what he was trying to do, and he wanted me to understand that.

He promised he'd call me whenever he could, that talking to me helped him. "We're still on track, Jennifer," he said. "We're still doing Christmas, still going to Australia. Nothing's changed. Do you believe me?"

I said I did. And I tried to think that it was true, that everything was going to be okay, but I still was filled with terror.

I wasn't eating, and I couldn't sleep, and it finally got so bad that one day I told David I needed help. Asking him sickened me, but I had become desperate.

David asked me what kind of help I meant, and I said, "Maybe I need some medication." David agreed that that might be a good idea. He called my doctor, Paul Geller, a very sweet and kind man, and they spoke about what would be best for me. Dr. Geller told David, "Look, you just work on getting better and I'll pick up the slack and take care of Jennifer."

He prescribed Prozac, and it just horrified me that I was going to be taking this medication. I don't drink or smoke, or eat meat, or take drugs of any kind except the occasional Advil. And here I was taking an antidepressant. There weren't words to describe how disgusted I felt with myself to have sunk so low. But I didn't know what else to do. I was finding it almost impossible to function at work. I never knew when David was going to call, the calls were short, and they weren't every day.

Anyone who ever knew me even a little would always have described me as the most together person. I presented myself as independent, tough, strong, which were all true. But those traits had obviously covered up a lot more underneath. And now I was a mess.

I took the Prozac but I still couldn't sleep. Dr. Geller prescribed six or seven different kinds of sleeping pills, but none helped. I'd be awake all night, and then at work I'd start to fall asleep during the rewrites.

Still, no one except Michele knew what was going on. I tried to hold it together, and certainly I wasn't a complete wreck every second of the day. Working on a sitcom can be a lot of fun. You probably laugh more on this job than on any other in the world. You sit around in a room all day with really funny people whose only goal basically is to make people laugh. So there'd be periods where I was laughing along with everyone else, and pitching jokes and being funny, and then David would pop into my mind and I'd go in my office and lie down on my couch and cry. Then I'd sneak into the bathroom, wash my face, put on masses of makeup, and start over.

I was hearing from David four or five times a week, but speaking to him much less often. Usually the message would be, "Hi, it's David. I'm doing okay but I'm really tired and I'm not going to be able to call you later."

That was fine with me, as long as I'd heard from him. His voice sounded very hoarse, the radiation was really affecting his throat. The steroids he was taking to reduce the lesions were making his face swell, and he was puffy and uncomfortable, he said.

On top of everything, Roxanna was getting closer to delivering, and was still supposed to be in bed. But she refused, insisting on going with David to the hospital for treatment. He tried to stop her, but she was determined. Her doctor told David it would probably cause her more stress to fight with her about it, so he eventually gave in.

We've got three new babies, Jennifer!" David said. He'd called me at work to tell me the good news. They had known ahead of time that they were having two girls and boy—Isabella, Holden, and Oteista. Oteista's name was originally going to be Jillian, but David really liked Oteista.

Even though David was going through radiation and chemotherapy, and feeling terrible, he didn't want to waste his time. He wanted to keep his mind active, and as much as possible keep doing the things he loved to do. With Roxanna's help, he had written another book. She, stuck in bed, helped with the typing as he dictated his thoughts. The book featured a heroine, and out of nowhere David had come up with the name Oteista. "What do you think, Jennifer?"

What I thought was that they should cut back on David's medication, he was clearly overdosing on *something*. What I *said* was, "I don't know, David. Oteista Cohen? It sounds a little . . . I dunno, African?" I warned David that she was probably going to catch a lot of shit in school, and he'd be paying for his choice. "She's going to hate you forever," I said.

David laughed, but he really felt the name had come to him as if in a message, that it was an omen. He really wanted to keep it.

All the babies were fine, he said, all healthy, thirty fingers and thirty toes. In spite of feeling weakened by his treatment, he had helped in the delivery.

I wanted to be able to get in touch with him. I wanted to send gifts, a congratulatory card, something. I asked him again for an address, a phone number. I begged him, please, please, why won't you let me contact you?

He was firm; he had to do this his way. He needed to be in control of when we talked. "If you call, I'm not going to be able to refuse to talk to you, Jennifer," he said. "I care too much about you."

I protested. "If you can't come to the phone, I'll understand. Just let me leave a message." I asked for his fax number, so I could at least write him. "You don't even have to reply," I said. "Just so I can feel there's someone out there."

"But I'd have to write you back," he said. "How could I not write you back?" It didn't really make sense to me. He was refusing me the ability to contact him; what would be the difference if I *did* contact him and he didn't call me back?

"Jennifer," he said, "you have to let me get through this the best way I can. I'm not going to be able to refuse to talk to you if you call, and sometimes I'm having a really shitty time from the chemotherapy—I'm vomiting all over the place, I can't eat, I can't swallow, I have diarrhea, I'm almost passing out. You have to understand."

But I didn't understand. "I'm supposed to be your family," I said. "I'm supposed to have the guest house, I'm supposed to have Christmas with you and go to Australia and you won't give me your fucking phone number." I asked him, what if something happened to me? What if I died in a car wreck? No one would even be able to call and tell you.

But nothing I said would change his mind. "Look," he said, "I've got three babies in the house. I've got the twins. Selena's freaking out. Roxanna's freaking out. This just isn't the right time. When it's all done you'll come to the house and be part of our family, I promise you. But now you're just going to have to be patient."

When David had told me about being abused in nursery school, he explained that the way he survived was to withdraw, that he went inside himself to get away from the horror of what was happening to him. And in his adult life when things went wrong he really needed to focus on internal stuff and not think about the outside world. He was asking me to let him do that.

Finally I realized, Oh, my God, I'm being so selfish. This man has cancer and he's calling me four or five times a week and I'm still complaining. I promised him I wouldn't ask for his phone number again.

———

David and I had spoken only three times as part of our phone schedule; in fact, I had given him the twelve-thousand-dollar check just days before he learned he had cancer. I wanted the money back, but I didn't know how to ask. I was afraid he would see it as addressing his mortality, as if I was thinking he wasn't going to make it, so give me back my money. Likewise the sixty thousand. I wanted it back, since we weren't even doing therapy, and I could repay it when we resumed, but I didn't want to ask.

I didn't want him to feel I didn't have faith in his recovery. In private, my thoughts were dark and desperate and filled with negativity; but David needed positive thoughts, and I was going to be there for him.

———

Michele was my lifesaver on the show. She's very funny (considering that she's a woman and everyone in Hollywood knows women aren't funny) and could always make me laugh. She saw how Peter treated me, and she totally got it. She'd gone through the same things herself: being in a writer's room, pitching something—a joke, or a fix for a scene—and it would be as if you'd never spoken. Except this time, rather than letting the fact that I was being ignored make me crazy, Michele and I would make jokes about it. One day in the writer's room, we carried on an entire conversation, normal volume, just feet from the rest of the staff, which consisted of one of us going, "I'm invisible, are you?" and the other one answering, "Not just invisible, not here at all." And then we'd laugh and just go on pitching and being ignored.

Michele and I are both vegetarians, and when we'd suggest a place to eat where we could at least get a choice of maybe two vegetables (as opposed to someplace like Micky's Sausage Heaven, where the closest thing to a vegetable was the paper plate), the rest of the staff would pay no attention. Instead of getting mad, which I might have done in the past, Michele and I would just send a production assistant out to a different restaurant. This of course earned us the labels "difficult" and "demanding."

September sixth. David's birthday. I had been looking forward to giving him his gift, "The Healer" spirit stick. I wished I could've mailed it to him, but I was not going to ask for his address or a way to contact him again. I had promised to give up that fight.

My backing off from that request clearly made David feel relieved, because one day he said he wanted to do something for me. He was going to give me his phone number. "It's for total, total emergencies, Jennifer," he said. "I mean, you have to be practically dying to use this."

He gave me the number, which had a 310 area code. It was the number at their Santa Monica condominium, now being forwarded down to the house in Dana Point. I wrote it in my address book. I swore I'd never call, never. Just having it was enough.

A few weeks had passed, and David was due for his first big checkup; to see how the cancer was responding; and to make sure his blood levels were okay, that he wasn't becoming too toxic from the chemotherapy. He explained that the point of chemo is to keep you pumped up with enough drugs to kill the cancer without killing you.

I asked if he was scared about the test, and he admitted that he was a little apprehensive. He had told me the day he was going in, and all day I thought about him. I was distracted, checking my messages every twenty minutes, trying not to panic.

He called me that night. He was upbeat, giddy. The results couldn't have been better. "The cancer's a lot smaller, Jennifer," he said, barely able to contain his excitement. "The doctors said they'd never seen anyone respond so well to radiation." His blood, too, was doing really, really well, which they believed was because he was so healthy going into the treatment.

I started to get a glimmer of hope. Maybe he was right, maybe he was going to make it. Everything he'd promised could come true.

I had asked Dr. Geller about Hodgkin's disease, and he had confirmed David's figure of a ninety-five percent recovery rate. With that information, plus what David was telling me, I almost felt like I could breathe again.

"I have to tell you something," David said. He told me he'd had a dream the night before the test, and in the dream the test results were bad, the cancer was growing. And David made a decision, in the dream, that he didn't want to live the rest of his life having treatment with radiation and chemotherapy and feeling shitty; that he wanted to spend his remaining time with his family and give them the best of himself. If it was six months or three months or a year, he wanted that time to be the best he could have. So he stopped treatment, and as time went on, he started to become sicker and sicker, and finally he was so sick he knew it was time to end his life and he asked me to help him. And I said I would. That was his dream.

And I said, "Well, David, if that ever really happened, you know that I will help you." He said he'd never really let me do that, and I said that I would if he wanted me to.

23

David asked again when I'd be done on *Mr. Rhodes*. If we got canceled before completing a whole season, I'd be done in January. If we finished twenty-two episodes, we'd go through March. The ratings indicated January. The critics for the most part still hated Tom, and the audiences clearly didn't feel much differently. (When we got beaten in the ratings by a show about pumas, I knew we were in trouble.) I asked David why he wanted to know.

He wanted to make our reservations for Australia. There'd be eleven people going: David, Roxanna, Vanessa, Darian, Selena, the triplets, Selena's boyfriend, Dominick, the nanny, and me. For that many people, flying first class, the reservations needed to be made well in advance.

We agreed that sometime toward the end of March would be safe. I was amazed that the trip was going to be arranged to suit my schedule.

The last trip I took with my parents was to Paris, several years ago. They had made reservations at a five-star hotel, which was their usual custom. In fact, they were so picky about their accommodations that frequently they'd take vacations and end up calling to notify us of a change in their hotel because they were dissatisfied with where they were staying. This time my father booked me into a different hotel than theirs. It wasn't even a hotel, it was more like a rooming house. It was small, dingy, dark; the room, with its twin bed, didn't even have a television; not that that would've made a difference, because I don't speak a word of French. It was down a narrow alley, a few blocks from where my parents were staying. I had gone to Paris with my parents on vacation, and I stayed alone in a dumpy hotel.

David wanted to know if the cities and places he and the others had selected to visit were all right with me. Along with Sydney and the Great Barrier Reef and other cities, they wanted to go to New Zealand.

"Is that okay, Jennifer?" David asked. "Because if you don't want to go there we don't have to."

I would've gone anywhere—probably to the Ralph's Market if that's where they were going. But we were going to Australia, eleven of us, living high off the hog. It sounded like a dream come true.

David almost always called me at around six in the morning. I am definitely not a morning person, but I was getting used to it, and I couldn't exactly complain.

One morning he called very excited. Although he often sounded hoarse and tired, this time his voice was strong. He'd had a great idea, a wonderful idea.

"Remember how I told you they had to keep an eye on my blood to make sure it wasn't getting too toxic?" he asked. "Well, first I want to tell you that the doctors say I'm doing great, just great, Jennifer, better than they ever expected, do you believe me?" He went on, "The only bad thing is my blood is just full of chemicals; it's gotten to that toxic point." He'd been feeling sicker and sicker, he explained, throwing up more and more frequently, losing more weight, feeling very weak. They had to stop the chemotherapy.

I said, "This is *good* news?" David said he wasn't finished. He was stopping temporarily; twelve days without chemotherapy, then back for three more weeks and he'd be done. He was ecstatic at the notion that he'd be finished soon, but more than that he was thrilled with his idea.

"I want to see you, Jennifer," he said. "I'm going to have twelve days off, and there's three people I want to see. I want to see a friend of mine in Arizona, I want to see Angelo, and I want to see you."

I asked if he was sure he was well enough. He assured me that he was great, and I suggested we should meet in Dana Point so he wouldn't have to drive.

"Well, I was thinking I could see you at your house, Jennifer," he said. "Would you like that?"

David had told me many times that he couldn't wait to see my new house, and how I'd decorated it; and we'd talk a lot about how after Christmas, he wanted to bring Roxanna and Selena up to see it also. "Selena's going to love your doll's house," he said. "I told her about it, she can't wait."

Still, I was surprised that he wanted to come to my house so soon.

Taken aback. I guess David could tell I was thrown, because he asked me if the idea made me uncomfortable. "I guess not," I said. "It's just kind of hard to picture you here, I guess. I thought we'd meet at the office or something."

"I thought we could spend a couple of days together," David said. I didn't understand, and I asked him what he meant.

"You know, stay in a hotel in your neighborhood, spend some time. I don't want to just see you for an hour, Jennifer."

I didn't answer. I was just kind of shocked.

"I could even, and this would be totally up to you, I could even stay at your house if you wanted," he said.

I asked if he didn't think that would be a little weird, and then I thought, Well, why not? I had a beautiful guest room; no one had used it yet. Who better than David to be the first? "You can hang out with my boys," I said, meaning my cats Lewis and Baby. "Maybe they'll sleep on the bed with you."

He said he would love that, and he couldn't wait to meet them. "I really want to see you, Jennifer," he said. "I can't tell you how much I want to do this."

We planned a date for his arrival, and with a little nervousness about the idea, I hung up.

October 30

David was flying in from Arizona, and I picked him up at LAX. After almost a year of therapy, I'd still felt uncomfortable if I saw David in the hallway as opposed to actually inside his office—he seemed strangely out of context, unfamiliar. Now, as he walked toward me from the gate, toting a small carry-on bag, I was embarrassed, at a total loss for words.

We walked through the terminal, barely speaking. "This is pretty weird, huh?" he said.

"I feel really awkward, David. I can't believe we're doing this," I told him.

He said he couldn't believe it either, then he laughed. "I'd probably lose my license if anyone found out." He had told me once that he'd still see me even if I lost all my money and couldn't afford to pay him. At the same time, he'd asked if I'd still see him if his license was ever taken away. "A piece of paper doesn't mean anything compared to how I treat you, right?" he said.

On the ride home, it gradually got more and more normal between us. David filled me in on his treatment, on his trip to Arizona, just small talk. I wondered what Paul would say if he knew that not only was I seeing David, whom he had only heard from occasionally, but that he was going to be staying at my house.

"He'd think we were crazy," laughed David. "I don't think you better tell him."

Paul wasn't the only one. My father would probably have had me committed had he known.

David got out of my car and retrieved his bag from the trunk. "Your neighbors will think I'm your boyfriend," he said, smiling. I thought that was kind of weird, but I didn't say so. I pointed out they could just as easily think he was a relative or friend, and he agreed that that was true.

I opened the door with a lot of expectation, and of course David didn't disappoint me. He loved my house. He went from room to room, examining everything in detail. "Oh, Jennifer, this is beautiful," he exclaimed over every painting, piece of ceramic, candlestick. He said he couldn't wait to see what I was going to do with the guest house. "Oh, that reminds me, Selena wants to help you decorate it," he said. "She wanted me to ask you if that's okay." I said of course it would be okay; it would be fun. "She's going to love having you there," David said, "and you'll be there by Christmas."

I'd expected David to look puffy when I saw him. He'd told me the steroids had made his face swell up, but I didn't really notice any change. He looked fine to me, still muscled in his arms, the same weight as I remembered. Maybe I was just so happy to see him. I did notice that his nails were bitten totally to the quick, which they never had been before.

"Oh, my God, David, look at your nails," I said, blurting it out. He looked kind of embarrassed, trying to hide his fingers.

"I guess I've been under a little stress lately," he said, smiling at me. "You can't blame me, right?" He wanted to stop biting them, but Roxanna had told him he had enough to worry about, to wait until after treatment. "If I quit biting them now, I'd probably just start something worse," he said, "smoking or drugs or alcohol." I knew he was kidding. David didn't put anything into his body that wasn't good for him.

It was the day before Halloween, and I was worried that David would not be home to take his twins for their first time trick-or-treating. He admitted he was sorry he was going to miss it, but that Roxanna had promised to fill him in on all the details, and he'd taken pictures of them in their costumes before he left. Darian was going to be a Ninja Turtle, and Vanessa a fairy princess. "They're so cute in their costumes, Jennifer," David said. From the photo I'd seen of Vanessa I could imagine her as a little princess. I agreed that she must look adorable.

I asked him how he was going to handle the candy problem, since he didn't let his kids eat junk of any kind. He explained that he and Roxanna had come up with a system—that each ten pieces of candy would equal a gift from the toy store. "Selena's probably going to get a shit load of candy and ask me for a new car," he joked.

Knowing David was such a health nut, I'd gone to Whole Foods, an organic grocery store in my neighborhood, and bought him an array of healthy food. He'd told me what he wanted; bananas, pasta, applesauce, vegetables. Plus he was under doctor's orders to drink cranberry juice three times a day to help flush the toxins out of his body, and I'd bought him an organic brand, made of a hundred percent pure cranberries. I didn't realize this made the juice really sour, and he hated it.

I felt terrible and offered to get him another kind, but he said it was okay. Still, I had to force him to drink it. He'd sit on the kitchen counter taking the smallest possible sips and making faces, while I'd encourage him and tell him how good it was for him. "You're just like Roxanna," he said. "She's a bossy nurse, too."

―――――

For some reason Baby was petrified of David. When David would approach him or even enter the room, Baby would flee in total fear, crouched low, ears back, his feet scrambling so fast he almost couldn't make purchase on the floor. The only time I'd ever seen even close to similar behavior was during the '94 Northridge earthquake, when he'd urinated on the floor in terror. (I couldn't be mad at him, I'd almost done the same thing.)

I couldn't understand it. Baby is usually exceptional with his affection, climbing on total strangers, kissing their noses, purring happily. He loves everyone, from the plumber to the UPS guy, to the really strange guy who came to my house once to catch and relocate a wild animal that had been digging in my yard—"I don't mind if skunks spray me," he'd told me.

I'd been looking forward to David meeting Baby (he'd already met Lewis when I'd once brought him to the office on the way to the vet), and had told him how sweet Baby was and how much they would love each other.

David spoke to Roxanna on the phone that night, and the next day offered an explanation for Baby's surprise reaction. Roxanna had told him that chemotherapy leaves a smell in the body, and Baby must be smelling the chemicals still in David's blood. I wondered why Lewis wasn't scared. David asked me which was the more intelligent cat and I said, "Don't tell Baby, but probably Lewis." David nodded, that made sense.

"The more intelligent an animal, the less he relies on his sense of smell," he said. "That's why humans don't have a great sense of smell compared to animals. If Baby's less intelligent, maybe he has a more sensitive sense of smell."

It was the only explanation that made sense, and David and I agreed that for the rest of his visit, we wouldn't try to get the two of them together.

David loved to go hiking, and wanted to take me to one of his favorite trails, in Will Rogers State Park. I had never gone hiking before, and he warned me that this was a fairly tough trail. It wound really high into the mountains, and it was very strenuous. I told him I'd beat his ass to the top, and he smiled. "You have a slight advantage over me, Jennifer," he reminded me. I told him chemotherapy was a lame excuse for getting your ass kicked by a girl.

The trail was beautiful and, as David had warned me, pretty steep. At least it seemed that way to me. Of course I never exercised, and had only recently bought some work-out equipment on David's recommendation, including a home StairMaster (its appearance was only improving as the layers of dust accumulated on it). I was really out of shape. I was breathing heavily before we were even halfway up, and I couldn't believe David used to run all the way to the top. It shocked me to realize what a change he must have gone through. He was wheezing, and having to take frequent breaks, and his chest was hurting from lesions caused by the radiation.

He was struggling to keep going, and I said that he better not pass out. "I'm not carrying you back down," I told him, "although I could roll you down." Joking aside, he looked terrible. Even though I had made up my mind that I was going to make it to the top, I told him I couldn't finish. He thanked me for letting him save face.

He sat on a rock for several minutes, getting his breath back, and then we headed back down. It worried me to see this strong, healthy man, this triathlete, so weak. David assured me this was normal in the circumstances, that in a matter of months he'd be back to his usual self. "We'll come back here, and I'll beat you to the top," he said.

When we got back to my house, David drew me a picture of the cancer lesions prior to treatment, and the one lesion remaining now. It was almost completely gone, tiny, less than a pinhead. "I'm going to totally recover, Jennifer," he said, "I absolutely promise you."

We had planned to go out to dinner, but David was too tired. I don't really cook, but I offered to make pasta, which he'd told me he liked and was able to stomach. He didn't want pasta, he said, he wanted pizza. From Domino's. I was stunned. Pizza? It's not exactly the healthiest of foods.

"I guess I'm feeling like if that's what I want, I should give it to myself," David said. "After what I've been through, if my body's craving pizza, I should let it have it." I was surprised but happy to oblige, and offered that I had Haagen-Dazs in the freezer too. I was kidding, but he jumped at it. "Pizza and ice cream," he said. "It's like we're in college together. Wouldn't that have been fun, to be in college together?"

I had bought a bunch of Halloween candy, which was sitting out in a bowl, and I noticed David had been eyeing it. "You want candy, too?" I asked.

He admitted he did, just one piece. He ended up eating about half the bowl. "Roxanna's going to kill me," he joked.

When we were planning David's visit we'd discussed eating at my local sushi restaurant, just a block away, since sushi was, for both of us, our favorite food. David had asked his doctor, who recommended against the idea. With David's lower resistance to infection, the threat of parasites from raw fish was even greater. Now I wondered why David was filling his body with junk when he was trying to stay as healthy as possible, but, like he said, he deserved to do whatever he wanted.

David had insisted that we schedule a regular therapy hour for the time that he'd be visiting. We sat in my living room and tried to have a formal session, but it was just too weird. I told him I didn't need therapy right now, having him there was therapy enough, and the conversation ended up just being about his visit, and the guest house and stuff. Still, David was anxious that my therapy not be forgotten. He got out his Filofax, and asked me to go get my DayRunner. "We're going to set our schedule," he said. "I'll be back in January, and I want us to get back on track."

We wrote down a date for early in January. I was starting to feel even more secure about his full recovery.

––––––––

Do me a favor, Jennifer," David said. I asked him what he wanted. "I want you to sign something for me." He pulled a deep purple folder out of his bag. "I like to have my closest friends' signatures," he said. "I collect them."

I thought it was kind of odd, but I took the folder. "What should I write?" I asked.

"Just your signature, and a date," David said, "That's all."

October 31

As I'd done the day before, I'd taken this day off from *Mr. Rhodes*, claiming to be sick. We went out to lunch, which David insisted on paying for, he took me to a sporting equipment store and bought me a weight bar (which I figured I could use as a doorstop); and we went to Neiman-Marcus. I'd heard about this MontBlanc pen which was going to be a collector's item. The company had planned to put on the signature of Alexandre Dumas, but had mistakenly put on the signature of his son. I thought David might want to add it to his collection. He did want it, but thought that Roxanna might like to buy it for him for Christmas. He had the clerk put it aside, and said Roxanna would call with their Neiman-Marcus charge account number. "That was really sweet of you to think about me, Jennifer," he said.

I wondered what I should get David's family for Christmas. I had already bought David his present, which was a painting on metal of a beautiful dovelike bird, swooping over a nest with an egg in it. It was titled "The Guardian." I knew that buying for the twins and the triplets would be easy, but couldn't imagine what to get for Roxanna and Selena. I didn't know either of them at all. David said he'd think about it, and let me know. "Also, Selena's boyfriend Dominick is going to be with us for Christmas," he told me. "You might want to get him something, too." I said I'd find something from the Gap or somewhere, and David thought that would be fine.

I still hadn't given David his birthday gift from September, I'd been waiting for the right moment. We knew kids would be starting to knock on the door soon, trick-or-treating, so we agreed that I'd give him the gift right after we ate dinner, which, at David's request, was pizza again.

He opened the wrapping, and pulled out the spirit stick "The Healer." I don't remember what I wrote on the card, but both the gift, and what I had written, brought tears to his eyes. "Thank you, Jennifer," he said. "I love you a lot."

David went to put the gift in his carry-on bag. He was going to Boston after he left L.A., and he wanted to show it to the man he had decided would be my future boyfriend or husband, his best friend, Angelo.

—————

I have some gifts for you, too," David said. He didn't have them with him, but he wanted to tell me about my Christmas presents. Good Jew that I am, I preferred to wait until Christmas, but David said he couldn't wait to tell me about them. "Please let me tell you."

The first gift was that of course he and Roxanna were going to pay completely for my trip to Australia. The second gift he wanted to keep a secret until Christmas, so I'd have a surprise to look forward to; and the third was this one that he just couldn't keep to himself.

"You know that Roxanna wanted me to keep my mind really active during treatment?" he said. I said I remembered, that that's why he wrote the book. "Not just the book," David said, "I've actually been doing something else while I've been sick.

"You know I love sports," he said, and I nodded. "Well, I've been betting on sporting events. I read up on each team, and each player, and what the weather's going to be like, and who's out sick, and I calculate all the odds. Jennifer, you won't believe this, but I've been like ninety percent accurate."

He explained that you can't bet on sporting events in California, but he'd been going down to Mexico. There was a building just on the other side of the San Diego border, run by the Mexican government. They taxed the winnings; it was totally legal. "And then each person can bring back ten thousand dollars at a time into the country," he said.

I asked if he had to declare that money, and he said he didn't think so. That didn't sound right to me, but David said even if you were supposed to, there was no way for anyone to find out. "The Mexican government doesn't tell anyone, as long as they get their taxes," he said.

"I'm best at football, but I've been good at everything," he said. "Jennifer, sometimes I hit eleven games out of twelve. It's unbelievable. Roxanna says I'm a freak."

He went on. "As a gift to you, Roxanna and I put in five thousand dollars in your name. Jennifer, it's worth thirteen thousand dollars now!"

"You gave me five thousand dollars?" I couldn't register it. "You can't do that."

"We did it, Jennifer. We wanted to do it, we can afford to do it, and we're both just so happy that we could do this for you."

David wanted to know if I wanted him to give me the money, or to keep going. "We can go get the money any time you want," he said. "If it's more than ten thousand, you just have to take more than one person." He explained that because they'd bring back the money in cash, these bodyguards that Roxanna's family knew would go with them.

I couldn't believe what he was telling me. It felt almost dreamlike that someone would be this nice to me. Even as rich as David and Roxanna were, who would do this? Only someone who really loved me.

I wondered if maybe I should give the five thousand dollars back, and just keep the winnings. David refused. The money was a gift; they wouldn't take it back. "So, do you want me to keep going?" he asked.

I wasn't sure. I could certainly use an extra thirteen thousand, but if his success rate was really so high . . . "You really win that often?" I asked him.

"Jennifer, it's scary," he said. "I'm like a savant. I don't know if it's because I'm analyzing the games and the players in a psychological way or what, but I can barely lose. I've been doing this for Angelo, and I've been doing this for Janet. Angelo gave me like twenty-five grand, and now it's worth over a hundred grand!"

It seemed unbelievable to me, yet really exciting. The idea of making that much, in cash.

"I'd like to make you more money," David said. "I'd like you to have thousands and thousands of dollars just sitting in safety-deposit boxes all over the place, so you never have to feel unsafe again."

"Are you sure this is legal?" I asked again.

"Come on, Jennifer, I would never do anything to hurt my family or put them in danger, do you believe me? I don't want to end up in prison. I asked my lawyer about it, and he looked into it, and he said it was fine."

I told him I would've thought the U.S. government would want to tax those winnings. "I guess because it's already taxed in Mexico, you don't have to," David said. "And like I said, no one knows anyway."

That seemed like contradictory issues—one, that it was legal; two, nobody knows about it if it isn't; but it was also so enticing. Was I going to turn it down because it *might* be on the shady side of the law? It wasn't like *I* had done the actual gambling. I knew I was splitting hairs, and if it did turn out to be illegal my feeble argument wouldn't do me a bit of good as I was becoming someone's girlfriend in prison (but hey, a relationship's a relationship), but still. David was positive no one could find out.

"If you wanted to add some more money to the pot," Davis said, "I could make it grow that much quicker."

That was an idea. If he'd already made five thousand into thirteen in a week . . . I was working on *Mr. Rhodes*, I was making good money. He'd turned Angelo's twenty-five thousand into a hundred . . .

"Just so you know, Jennifer," David said, "if something happened, and I lost any money that you put in, no matter what, no matter *what*, I'd give it back to you. If I stop winning, and lose every penny, I'll give you everything, including the thirteen thousand, 'cause that's your gift. I would never let you lose money, Jennifer."

That night after David had gone to bed, I called my friend Bill Fitzhugh, just to talk. During our conversation I couldn't help but spill the good news about this plan of David's. "That's crazy," Bill said. "No one can make that kind of money."

"You don't understand David," I told him, "he's brilliant." Bill wondered if it wasn't a scam of some kind, and I laughed. "You don't know David," I said.

November 1

David and I went down to the AFTRA-SAG Credit Union, which is the credit union for screen and television actors, where I had my personal bank account. I had wired twenty-five thousand dollars from my money market account, where I kept all my savings. David told me that he believed in a matter of weeks he could double that money, that I could take back the twenty-five thousand, and from then on everything else would be profit.

"We'll go down to Mexico and get you cash whenever you need it," David told me. "You'll put it in a safety-deposit box, and that's what you'll use to buy clothes, go grocery shopping. You never have to use your credit card or write checks unless it's for your mortgage or something."

David needed the money in cash, and I had to sign paperwork, required by the government on any cash withdrawals or deposits over ten thousand dollars. I guessed it was to stop the laundering of drug money or something, and David and I joked with the bank officer that we were drug dealers. She didn't find us very amusing.

We left the bank with twenty-five thousand dollars in cash, stuffed into my purse. I was really nervous, convinced that every street person in Hollywood knew, could see this big flashing sign above my head SHE'S GOT CASH!

We made it home without being robbed. David took the money and put it in different places in his jacket and in his carry-on bag, packing it carefully around the spirit stick. "Don't worry," he said, "even if I got mugged or something in Boston, and they took all my money, it doesn't matter, you're safe."

He couldn't stop talking about how excited he was, how happy that he was going to do this for me. His goal after he got back to Dana Point was to make me a hundred thousand dollars by Christmas. I told him I didn't want our relationship to become about him making this money for me, that I didn't want to hear about it every time we talked. He agreed, but he asked if he couldn't at least tell me how the first week of betting went. "Just the first week, I promise," he said.

We agreed that he could tell me about the first week, and from then on would only tell me how much my "account" was worth if I asked.

I took David to the airport, and we sat and waited for them to announce boarding. We were both very silent, and it seemed a distance had come between us. David explained that we knew we wouldn't be seeing each other for a while, and were separating psychologically from each other to make it easier. Once he'd explained it, the distance between us seemed to close, and I felt more at ease. They announced David's gate and we stood up. I was really nervous and hesitant, terrified to ask what I wanted to ask. Finally I just blurted it out. "Can I get a hug?"

David smiled at me. "I was just thinking the exact same thing, Jennifer," he said, and he hugged me. A father's hug. Warm, strong. Then he turned and walked toward the gate. In his bag he was carrying twenty-five thousand dollars in cash, and "The Healer."

"I made you ten thousand dollars! Your account's worth forty-eight thousand!" David was ecstatic; he could barely contain himself. "Jennifer, I'm going to make my goal for you, I know it!"

I couldn't believe he'd been that successful already. Ten thousand dollars in a matter of days. How could he be so accurate? Before he left my house we'd watched part of a football game together (even David couldn't get me to agree to watch the entire thing), and he had predicted the outcome correctly. The point-spread and everything. Of course it had taken him half-an-hour just to explain what point-spread meant, but once I understood it, I was amazed at his accuracy.

I knew people went to Vegas and made thousands at a time, using complicated formulas and counting cards. I supposed that figuring outcomes of sporting events using psychology was similar. Or maybe he really *was* a savant. Either way, it didn't matter. He was making me money, and it was very exciting.

"One more week and you can have your twenty-five grand back," David said. I was relieved. I told him to remember our agreement, that I didn't want our conversations to be all about money, and he said he knew. "But if I do really good I have to tell you, Jennifer, I won't be able to contain myself."

I had to admit that it was fun hearing how much money I was making, and I agreed that if he had a great weekend, he could tell me. I think we both knew that I'd probably be dying to know.

———

Somehow, miraculously, *Mr. Rhodes* had been picked up for an additional five episodes, meaning we now had a total of eighteen. We'd been hoping for nine, but were thrilled with the five. All along our ratings had been average at best. We had occasionally beaten some other shows (although not the puma show), but only by marginal amounts. NBC was taking a wait-and-see approach to see if we could get those numbers up.

I didn't have a lot of faith. Sometime during the fourth or fifth episode, Tom had really started to improve, and we thought we had a good shot. But it must have been just wishful thinking, because as time went on, he seemed to get worse again. We'd already eliminated the romantic relationship with the character of Nikki, which was meant to be a big part of the show, because Tom just couldn't connect with the emotion of it; now we were cutting back on his dialogue altogether, and giving jokes originally meant for him to other actors.

I wanted to think it was just me, that I had a bug in my ear about Tom's acting ability, and wasn't willing to see improvement even when there was some, but I was soon proved wrong.

We were down at the stage one night, watching the filming. It was an episode guest-starring Pauly Shore, who, like Tom, was a client of 3 Arts Entertainment; and Michael Rotenberg (Tom's manager). Shelley McCrory (from NBC), Michael, Michele, and I were sitting in a row of director's chairs. Tom was fumbling through a scene when Michael leaned across Michele and me to whisper in Shelley's ear, "How about the *Mr. Shore* show?"

He was teasing of course, but even this light-hearted joking reflected the general sense that the show was in trouble.

———

David was finishing up his last three weeks of chemotherapy, and again the treatment was making him feel terrible. The doctors were blasting him with extra-heavy doses to totally destroy any remnants of cancer. On the phone he sounded really tired and weak but happy it was almost over.

It wasn't necessary to go to Mexico to actually place the bets, and David was continuing to make money for me, placing bets by computer. I asked him when I could get my twenty-five thousand back, and he said Roxanna could go get it (since he was too weak), or I could wait until Christmas, when he'd be feeling better, and we could all go down to Mexico together.

It was already close to the end of November, and I decided I could wait. Roxanna had enough to think about with David, the kids, Christmas coming up; to be worrying about going to Mexico to get my money. I knew it was safe, and I'd get it in a matter of weeks.

David was continually thrilled at what he was doing for his friends. "Just to be able to make this money for you and Angelo and Janet makes me so happy," he said. "Roxanna and I don't even care if we don't make money for us; we just love helping you."

Angelo worked for a drug company, and made a decent living, so for him the money was more icing on the cake. But for Janet, David had a strong motive. "She's in a shitty marriage," he told me, "and I'm helping her to get out." She was planning to take her young daughter with her. Since she didn't work, and had no savings, David was making her money to use to get away. He had made forty thousand dollars for her so far, and she was almost ready to make the move. "She can move away, start her life over, without worrying about that creep," David said. "Can you imagine how happy that makes me?"

———

I was almost done with Christmas shopping. I had the painting "The Guardian" for David, and I had bought a doll for Vanessa, stuffed animals for the triplets, and a toy steering wheel for Darian, who David said loved to ride in the car with him. I'd even bought cat and dog treats for Puff and Shadow. I still didn't know what to get for Roxanna and Selena; as yet David hadn't come up with any ideas.

On *Mr. Rhodes*, as with all sitcoms, it's customary for the producers to buy the cast and crew (totaling about one hundred fifty to two hundred people) Christmas gifts. Typically it's T-shirts or sweatshirts with the name of the show; or if the show is a hit and making everyone a lot of money, letterman jackets. Our ratings continued to slide and we were looking more and more like we would probably be canceled, so jackets were out. A group of producers got together and ordered sweatshirts, and I arranged for some extras to be put aside; for my parents, my sister and brother-in-law, and for David, Roxanna, and Selena.

———

David had one more test to go, to reconfirm that all the cancer was gone, and then he'd be totally, completely done. The chemotherapy and radiation were finished, and David was really weak. The test involved a full day in the hospital, scanning all his organs and his blood, and the doctors recommended waiting a week until David felt a little better. He was anxious to get it over with, to move on with his life, but he reluctantly agreed to their suggestion.

He went in on a Monday, and he had promised to call me that night or the next morning. I was hoping it'd be Monday night, but he didn't call. I tried not to let my natural negativity take over—he *had* said it could be Tuesday.

The phone rang at six A.M, as always. These calls from David were causing me to get very little sleep; especially on days when our rewrites would go well past midnight, which was often; but David had explained that he always felt stronger in the mornings, more alert.

"Hi, David," I said, sleepily. It was very quiet on the other end of the phone, and I heard a sort of weird sigh, an odd gulp.

"It's bad, Jennifer," he said, almost whispering.

"What? What?" I sat up. My heart was pounding.

"It's in my bones," he said. "I have bone cancer."

Michele and I had a script due for *Mr. Rhodes*, one that had originally been assigned to Mark. Mark announced at the last minute that he couldn't turn the script in. Days before "The Italian Show" episode was due, he told us he had pneumonia.

Michele and I were told, here's Mark's outline, you've got four days. Writers are usually given a couple of weeks to write a first draft start to finish.

Michele offered to write it alone, but I wanted to go to work. There was no way I was going to be able to just sit home and think about this. I was a wreck. I lay for hours at a time in a fetal position on my couch. I wasn't sleeping at all, I couldn't eat, I lost five or six pounds in a matter of days. It was an effort to get up and feed my cats. If I stayed in the house, I would go insane.

We worked in my office, using my computer. I had told Jane much of what was going on, but at work only Michele knew, and she tried hard to keep my spirits up. There were moments during the writing of the script where I became lost in what we were doing; but frequently I would get very emotional and start crying and have to run into the bathroom as I thought about what was happening.

This time there was no optimistic "it's ninety-five percent curable." David was really sick. The bone cancer had been there the whole time, the Hodgkin's was in fact a secondary cancer. For four months the bone cancer had been allowed to continue to grow untreated.

David didn't know what he wanted to do. He didn't know if he could stand to go through treatment again. I told him he had family to think of, he had to get it. He was angry, distraught. "You don't know what chemotherapy is like, Jennifer," he said, almost shouting. "You can't imagine what I've been through."

He and Roxanna were going to take a few days and go to Arizona to a place called Camelback Mountain. It was David's favorite place, a spiritual place, and he wanted time to think. He was so depressed, it was frightening to hear him. Even when he'd told me had Hodgkin's, he'd had a positive attitude about it. This was a David I didn't recognize.

It occurred to me that the doctors must not be very optimistic about

David's chances, if he wasn't even sure he wanted treatment. As for me, I was convinced either way he was going to die. Treatment, no treatment, this was it.

David called me from Arizona, and told me he was going to go ahead with treatment. He sounded awful. Depressed, hopeless. "It's like a Nazi experiment, what they're going to do to me, Jennifer," he said, "a Nazi experiment."

The plan was to remove his bone marrow, radiate it for three days to get rid of the cancer, then put it back in. During the time his marrow was removed, he'd have to stay in what was basically a plastic bubble, to prevent infection. "No one can touch me, I can't touch anyone, I can't see Roxanna and my babies," David said. "It's horrible, Jennifer, just horrible."

It was a new, somewhat experimental procedure, and he'd be going to New York, taking his family with him. The treatment might have to be done up to five or six times to destroy the cancer, and between times he'd stay in the hospital a few days to recuperate, then go home to rest—home meaning someplace in Manhattan. "I won't be able to travel," David said. "I won't be able to do anything."

It could take up to four months or more, and Roxanna had already flown on to New York to start looking for a condo to rent.

I was terrified to ask, but finally I asked David what they thought the chances were. He said about seventy–thirty in his favor. He and Roxanna had done a lot of research during their time in Arizona; gone on the Internet, talked to a lot of doctors; and decided this was the best course of action.

"David, you have to tell me what hospital you'll be at," I begged him. "Please don't shut me out again."

He said he couldn't tell me, that I couldn't ask him again. "I don't want any cards, I don't want any phone calls, I don't want to see anyone," he said. "To be honest, I don't even want Roxanna and the kids there." He reminded me again how he needed to shut off during times of great stress. "I just want to disappear inside until this is all over," he said.

I asked if it wouldn't be better to focus on getting well, to pay attention to healing his body.

"I can't pay attention to this, Jennifer," he said, "I can't. I can't think about it. This treatment is awful. I'll be in agony. It's agonizing. I'm going to feel the worst I've ever felt."

How could he possibly feel worse than me? It would be impossible.

A few days later David and his family packed up and moved to New York. The five babies, Selena, Roxanna, and the nanny. He had to undergo a few days of tests, then his first treatment would begin.

He called me three days in a row, and on the last told me he wouldn't be talking to me again for at least seven or eight days. He'd be in this bubble thing for three, and the doctors were telling him to expect at least three days of recuperation before he'd be able to do much of anything.

Seven days. The longest period of time without talking to him since the day we'd met. "Are you going to be okay, Jennifer?" he asked. I wanted to say No, how can I possibly be okay? You're dying, and you're going to leave me and I'm going to be alone the rest of my life; but I didn't. I told him I'd be fine, that he should just stay strong, that he could do this. "It's really important to me that you're okay," David said. "I'm sorry I did this to you."

"Oh my God, that's crazy, David," I said. "You didn't *do* this to me, you didn't want this to happen."

"I didn't want it to happen, Jennifer," he said, "but I'm still sorry you're having to go through this."

I told him not to worry about me, that I'd be okay, that he should just focus on getting well. He said he'd call me in about seven days, and we hung up and I burst into tears.

———

Dr. Jeffrey Hutter was a former teacher of David's at Pepperdine University. I had gone to see him on David's recommendation.

"I have to see someone, David," I had told him a week or so earlier. "I'm so depressed, I can't do this alone."

After the seven days without talking to him, I realized I was going to have trouble functioning without more regular support, and I wanted a name of another therapist.

David seemed surprised and hurt that I would think of seeing someone else. "*I'm* your therapist, Jennifer," he told me. "I call you whenever I can, don't I?"

I said I knew that, but I just needed someone to help me until he got back. Someone to talk to on a more regular basis. David gave me Dr. Hutter's name, and told me he thought his office was in Santa Monica. "But you promise you'll come back to me, right?" he asked.

———

Dr. Hutter remembered David, and was startled to hear he was so ill. Even though David had told me his first treatment had gone remarkably well, and the prognosis had improved, I spent most of the hour curled up on the couch, sobbing, telling him I knew David was going to die. Dr. Hutter barely commented, just sat there watching. In contrast to my sessions with David, he seemed very cold to me, very distant. At the end of the session he asked if I wanted to see him again and I said no.

Before I left, Dr. Hutter said he'd had a friend who'd gone through successful bone cancer treatment. Since he'd never heard of this new procedure, he wondered if David might like to check out any other options. I grabbed eagerly at the idea of a cure for bone cancer, which I had thought was basically a death sentence; and told Dr. Hutter he should definitely tell David. But the only phone number I had was the one that transferred down to Dana Point, and David was in New York.

"There is someone coming by to take care of their animals," I remembered, "Maybe she'll get the message and pass it along to David."

Dr. Hutter asked me for the number, and I said I'd call his service when I got home and give it to him.

———

I checked my voice mail constantly at work, running back and forth from the writer's room to my office, hoping that David would call. He knew how to reach me in person through the secretary, but I'd often be on the stage, watching the rehearsals, and was hard to track down. Other times he didn't have the energy to talk, he just wanted to leave a message.

I checked my voice mail and heard I had one message. I was sure it was from David.

"Hello, Ms. Miller, this is Dr. Hutter. I think you must have given me the wrong area code for David because I called that number and they'd never heard of him. Please call and tell me if you have the right number."

That couldn't be right. Three-one-zero was the right area code for their Santa Monica condo, and it was supposed to transfer down to Dana Point. I called Dr. Hutter's office immediately. Maybe it's seven-one-four, I told him, which is the area code for Orange Country. He said he'd try it and call me back.

"Nope," he reported, "no such number." I didn't understand it. I said I'd ask David when I next spoke to him.

———

Why are you giving Dr. Hutter my phone number?" David wanted to know. He sounded irritated.

"He wanted to help you, David. He thought he could help you."

"I don't want to hear about some other treatment, Jennifer, I'm doing this treatment. It's none of his business."

He seemed unexpectedly angry, but I supposed that the idea he could have embarked on the wrong treatment would not be one he wanted to entertain. "I'm sorry," I said. "Dr. Hutter just wanted to help.

"Anyway, it wasn't even your number," I added. "I don't understand; that's the number you gave me for emergencies."

"That *was* my number, Jennifer," David said, "but Roxanna had it disconnected. We were getting so many calls transferring from Santa Monica, it was getting crazy. I just forgot to tell you. You can understand that, right? I've had a little bit going on."

What could I say? This was the second time he'd forgotten to tell me about changing his phone number, but under the circumstances did it really matter? Remember what's important, I reminded myself.

"David, it would really help me emotionally if I just had a number for you," I said. "I promise I won't use it, but I need just to have it. Knowing I had that other number made me feel better; now I don't have it. Please give me another number. Or let me visit. Please."

"Jennifer, no one has my number here," he said. "Not Janet, not Angelo, not my father. No one. I don't want anyone contacting me. I don't want anyone visiting me. Do you understand? I can't handle it. I call Angelo and he's crying on the phone; Janet's freaking out. Angelo's been my best friend since I'm seventeen, and I'm not letting him call me or visit me."

I couldn't understand why he was so adamant about not having his friends visit. Isn't that what friends are all about?

"Jennifer, you don't understand. I'm embarrassed to be ill. I don't want people to see me this way. I'm disgusted that I'm sick, that my body's betrayed me like this. Maybe it's related to my abuse, but I feel terrible when I'm ill. I feel embarrassed and humiliated and weak."

Those were words I certainly understood, but still. I was supposed to be family. Not *like* family, but family. I was not going to give up so easily. "David, family's not only for the good times," I pleaded. "I don't think you're weak; you're not disgusting. Please let me at least send you a card in the hospital, a way to contact you, something."

He told me I was being selfish, that he was going out of his way to call me, and finally I backed off and apologized.

———

Along with my everyday despair and panic over David's prognosis, I was still concerned about the money that he had. The twelve thousand dollars, the sixty thousand, the twenty-five thousand in Mexico. Again I wanted the money back, but realized that even more than before, David might see that as a very pessimistic view.

In the back of my mind I wondered that if something happened to David, would Roxanna know how to reach me? Then I would get angry at myself. What was I doing thinking about money when David might be dying? What was wrong with me?

December 24, 1996

Hi, Jennifer, it's David. Um, it's about a quarter to two. Um, I hope everything's going okay with you. Um, you have a really good Christmas. I thought you would, um, be home by now and not at work. I will try you at work. I'm doing okay . . . (BEEP)

Hi, Jennifer, it's David. Um, you, you're, I was right, you're not at um, work, um, I wanted to call again. Um, I hope you have a really great Christmas, if um, I'm, you know, cogent enough or whatever to talk I will call you back. Um, I'm doing okay, the prognosis and everything is good, just . . . (BEEP)

Jennifer, I'm sorry for being a nuisance, I just didn't get to finish, um, I miss you a lot, I've been thinking about you a lot, um, I hope you're taking really good care of yourself and, um, try not to worry about me, I'm doing okay, um, and um, I will um, try really hard . . . (BEEP)

...Everything's going, you know, as well as can be expected here...
(BEEP)

His voice was so weak, so hard to hear, that my phone machine kept cutting him off. I was happy he called, but upset that he was wishing me a great Christmas. Did that mean he wouldn't be calling me tomorrow? This was going to be my first Christmas without my family, the Christmas I had expected to spend with David. I'd invited a few friends to come by, but it was not going to be the Christmas David had promised me a year earlier.

December 25

I had been too depressed to buy a tree, and my house was hardly festive, but I did have a few friends over, maybe six or seven in all through the course of the day. I was trying to be upbeat for my guests, but I was sad. I missed David, I missed having a tree, the presents, a family, the festivities of Christmas that I'd looked forward to. My parents called to wish me Merry Christmas, as did my sister Jane and my nieces. But to me it really didn't feel like Christmas, just another day.

December 26

David was sorry he couldn't call me on Christmas, but he'd had a bad day. He assured me they were still saying the prognosis was much improved, but the treatment was just wearing on him.

"I have an idea," he said. "Let's have Christmas when I get back. Whether it's March, April, whenever, we'll have our own Christmas."

I said that would be great. "You promise me they're saying the prognosis is good?" I asked.

"Better than eighty percent, Jennifer," he said. "That first treatment went really well." They were already detecting a lot less cancer in his cells, and anticipating that after the second treatment the prognosis would be even better. "This is really shitty, what I'm going through," David said. "But it's going to be over soon, and I'm going to be fine."

He said he was sorry that we wouldn't be going to Australia, and I told him not to be silly. "Maybe we'll go next year instead," he said. "The doctors say I'll be able to do everything I could do before—

surfing, hang gliding, everything. The only thing they don't want me to do for about a year is bungee jumping, 'cause it's too much stress on the bones. But everything else, I'll be back to normal."

He apologized again for not calling me on Christmas, and we said good-bye.

I went out to run some errands and to the bookstore. I was wandering through Crown Books and my cell phone rang. It was David. "We had such a great talk, Jennifer, I just had to talk to you again," he said. He sounded very tired, dopey. I went out to my car to talk to him. We stayed on the phone for over an hour. Later when I got my cellular phone bill I saw that he had tried to call me eleven times before he finally reached me.

New Year's Eve

Jennifer, it's David, um, sorry your cell phone's not working right now, um, I'm surprised I got your machine. Um . . . I haven't been feeling really good the last few days so that's why I haven't called you. Not bad, not, um, not anything unexpected or whatever, just, you know, just as you expect I feel really weak. So I haven't forgotten about you, I'm actually thinking about you quite often, and, um, as always I love you a lot, and I'm hoping you're taking really good care of yourself and when I'm able to I will, um, call you again, and hopefully it'll be sooner than later, okay, Jennifer? Take really good care of yourself, I miss you a lot. 'Bye, sweetie.

His voice was very slurred, slow, drugged-out. He had gotten an infection in his bones and was taking morphine for the pain. Sometimes when he'd call, I could barely understand him, and I was constantly asking him to repeat himself. He still called almost every morning at six, L.A. time, which was nine in the morning in New York. Sometimes he'd call even earlier, five o'clock, four o'clock. He'd apologize, his voice thick, sounding completely out of it, childlike. "I'm sorry, Jennifer, I'm sorry. Are you mad at me? Please don't be mad. I shouldn't be calling you, I'll hang up now, okay? Don't be mad."

During several conversations we would all of a sudden be disconnected. The morphine was causing numbness in his hands, and sometimes he would just drop the phone. He'd call back, apologizing again. "Do you still love me, Jennifer? Even though I hung up on you? I didn't mean to."

By the end of our conversations, he'd become more alert, and I'd tease him about his earlier responses. He'd laugh, "Did I really say that? You must think I'm crazy."

I was still longing to see him, and his refusal to let me was inexplicable to me. Too guilty to tell him directly, I wrote him angry letters that I had no place to send. I'd spew my frustration onto the page: How could he deny me a simple visit? Me being family was bullshit. He made me this dependent, now he was abandoning me. When we spoke, I was always supportive, encouraging, but finally my frustration and need to see him got overwhelming. I was convinced that him seeing me would be good for him. He'd even admitted that to me—that he'd love to see me, and it would definitely help him; that Roxanna and Selena were encouraging it; but that he couldn't bear for me to see him this way.

I decided I was going to track him down. I hated that I was doing it, I wondered if I wasn't becoming just a little insane, but I started calling every hospital I could think of in New York, asking if they had a patient, David Cohen. Sloan-Kettering, Columbia Presbyterian, any hospital that had a cancer center. He was not registered at any of them. None of them had ever heard specifically of the treatment David was undergoing, but described similar treatments—marrow being removed, stem cells replaced . . . No one called it a bubble, but they did acknowledge that the patient would be in isolation.

After calling every hospital I could think of, I wondered if David hadn't purposely signed in under another name. Was he that determined to remain hidden? That seemed excessive to me; he was taking this privacy issue too far.

Finally I confronted him about it. He said he wasn't surprised. He'd had a feeling I might try to find him. "That's why I'm in the hospital under another name, Jennifer," he said. "Because I didn't want my friends to find me. Don't you think I knew that would happen?"

For the first time I got really pissed off. I told him he was cruel; that I wasn't like his other friends; that I was more needy, more dependent. I was a patient as well as family, my needs were different. But nothing, no ranting and raving, no pleading, could move him.

"But I have a better idea," he said. Once the infection had cleared up, the doctors had given him permission to travel. He wanted to see me, and suggested we meet. He first suggested San Francisco, then called back an hour later. Roxanna had pointed out that San Francisco was cold and damp at this time of year. What about Santa Fe? Like Camelback Mountain, he found it to be a spiritual place, and thought it would be a good place to heal, and to spend time with me.

"And maybe after I see you in Santa Fe, I'll think about you coming back to New York with me," he said. "Once you've seen how shitty I look, maybe I'll get over my stupid phobia and let you visit with us. Would you like that, Jennifer?"

I asked him when he thought he'd be well enough to make the trip, and he said in about two weeks. "I'll get rooms at a really nice hotel," he promised. "This makes me really happy, that we're going to do this. I'm sorry you think I've abandoned you, Jennifer. I really love you. I'm going to see you soon, I promise, and then you'll come back to New York, and meet everyone."

January 1996

Several days went by without a phone call. David was not due for another treatment, so the silence was very uncharacteristic. He had always warned me when he wouldn't be in contact. I started to panic, terrified that something had happened to him. The infection had spread to his whole body. He was dying. Dead. I was convinced of it.

I became like a child, totally lost. Who will take care of me? What will I do? I'll die. I called Jane, who I think was scared by my craziness. Her big, tough sister was losing it. She tried to reassure me, and comfort me, but it did little good. I was two years old, I couldn't listen to reason. "You don't understand, he's the only person who ever loved me," I said.

"I love you," Jane said.

"It's not the same," I told her. "He's the only person who really knew me."

Jane said I was acting like David was already dead. "He's going to die," I told her, "I know it."

Finally, after about six days, David called. He was doing fine, he said, he'd just had a difficult few days. I made him promise not to do that to me again. I understood if he wasn't feeling up to talking to me, but couldn't someone—the nanny, Roxanna, Selena, anyone, please call and let me know so I wouldn't worry?

David agreed that if it happened again, Roxanna would call me. I'd never spoken to her before, and David suggested he put her on the phone so we could meet each other. "That way it won't be so weird if she has to call you," he said.

"I'd call her in here now," he said, "but Holden's asleep on my stomach. He's so cute, Jennifer, I don't want to wake him." That was one of the few benefits of being sick, David said, getting to spend so much time with his family. Along with Roxanna and Selena, the twins and triplets had even been coming with them on his checkups at the hospital. "The nurses go crazy," David laughed.

We talked for a few more minutes and hung up. About a half-hour later, Roxanna called me. It was weird to hear her voice, after hearing so much about her for the last year. After David had said she'd be calling, I'd tried to imagine what she sounded like, but really couldn't picture it. Her voice was very calm, measured.

"Isn't this odd, Jennifer, to finally be talking?" she said, "I've heard so much about you."

"Me, too," I said. I admitted I was nervous talking to her, and she said she was, too.

We talked for several minutes. She told me that she loved my paintings, and that she couldn't wait to meet me, and to have her cat Puff meet Lewis and Baby. She joked that David was a terrible patient, very demanding, but that between the two of us, warriors both, we'd keep him in control. I asked why David wasn't letting me visit him or even contact him, why he was so secretive.

"Jennifer, I can't really explain it now," she said, "but once you've come to the guest house, and become part of our family, you'll understand everything." I didn't really see what there was to understand, but I had to be content with that. Roxanna was struggling with watching her husband fight cancer, I wasn't going to push her for explanations.

"I have to go now, Jennifer," she said. "I hear the other babies waking up." She apologized for cutting our conversation short, and handed the phone to David. He was very excited that we'd spoken to each other; he'd been nervous about it, and now it was done. "It'll make it that much easier when you come here after Santa Fe," he said.

About an hour later, Roxanna called back. She said she felt she'd been abrupt in getting off the phone before, and wanted to make sure I wasn't offended, which of course I wasn't. She said we'd talk again soon. Now that the ice had been broken, we could talk as often as I liked.

———

Mother." I had finally decided on Roxanna's Christmas gift, a painting symbolically depicting her and all her children, and including David and Selena. It was too big to take with me to Santa Fe, and I planned to give it to her when we met after David's treatment was finished.

———

I had been toying with the idea of buying a new car, if *Mr. Rhodes* got picked up for a second year. Except that it didn't. The news came from the network. We were canceled. No more *Mr. Rhodes*, no more Tom.

The staff rather cruelly made bets as to who would dump Tom first, his actress girlfriend, who we had heard hooked up with Tom at the Montreal Comedy Festival almost immediately after NBC's interest in him; or his manager. I, trying to cling to the most romantic option, said the manager. Mark said the girlfriend.

Mark was right. Several weeks after the show got canceled, we heard that Tom and his girlfriend had broken up. We of course didn't know the real reason why, but it was more fun to assume the worst.

So now I guessed it was going to be no more car, either. When I had told David about it earlier, I'd said I wanted a Volvo, but my real dream car was the Mercedes 500SL.

David said if that was the car I wanted, he and Roxanna would pay the difference between the two. I said that's crazy. He insisted that he *wanted* to do it, and of course eventually I said okay.

Now, even though my show was canceled, David still wanted me to get a new car, and he'd just pay for more of it. We talked about him and Roxanna coming car shopping with me. He asked if Selena could come, too. Of course I agreed. We talked about how much fun it would be picking out colors, going for a test drive. I still couldn't believe he was going to do this for me. He said it would make him really happy. We left it that when he was done with treatment, we would go buy me a car.

January 20

David was in a horrible mood. I'd heard him depressed before; angry; scared; but never this. He was pissy, complaining about everything. "I hate it here," he said, "I hate the hospital. I hate New York, it's so fucking gray here. I want to come home. I want to be done with this fucking shit."

He'd had another treatment, which had gone well, but he'd decided to check out of the hospital. "David, you can't do that," I said.

"Yes, I can, Jennifer," he said. "I've got money. I can pay the doctor to come to the condo. He can come twice a day if he wants, whatever he wants. I don't need to sit here waiting for him to see me."

They had hired a home nurse to help take care of him when he wasn't in the hospital, and David felt that between the nurse and the doctor visiting daily, he'd be fine. "If I stay in this place another second I'll go crazy, Jennifer," he said. "This isn't helping me get well."

I knew how important state of mind was in healing the body, and I agreed that if David's instincts were telling him he'd be better off at home, surrounded by his kids, then he should probably do it.

"You know, you're exactly right, Jennifer, thank you," he said. "You've helped me make up my mind."

January 24

I hadn't heard from David for four days. He'd promised me, sworn to me, this wouldn't happen again. If something had happened to him because he checked out of the hospital, it would be partly my fault. I had encouraged him. Something had to have happened—why else would no one have called me? I was terrified. I had to find him, there had to be a way.

I needed to find someone who knew David, who'd know where he was. I remembered the dedication he'd shown me in his book. Along with the dedication to Roxanna and his children was another page.

ACKNOWLEDGMENTS

To the intellectual and emotional cooks who fed the tummy of this tale.

The intellectual cooks: Barb Tyler, John Costa, Marnie Kale, and Rob Keen for providing the calcium that added strength and resilience to the bones of the tale.

The emotional cooks: Angelo DiCecco, Bernie and Katie Goldman, Phil and Annie Kessler, Lisa Ruben, Elliot Conner, Janet Demille and Lizzie Barber for providing the protein that sustained my energy through the writing of the tale.

The gourmet chef: Roxanna, last on this page, first in my heart—for making sure my mind eats from the four major food groups every day. You sweeten the successes and soften the stumbles. Thanks for being my partner through the fiery battles of existence.

I recognized two of the names—Janet and Angelo—but the only one I could put a location with was the latter. David had visited Angelo in Boston following his visit with me. Despite David telling me he hadn't told Angelo where he was, I didn't believe it. Angelo was David's best friend. He *had* to know.

There couldn't be that many Angelo DiCeccos in the Boston area, I figured, and in fact, I was right. There were none. At least none listed. So maybe he was unlisted. Or maybe I had misunderstood. Just because they *met* in Boston didn't mean that Angelo lived there. But he lived somewhere.

In a completely uncharacteristic move, driven by terror, panic, certainty that something had happened to David, I got the name of a private detective from my lawyer, Rod, and called him.

Within days the detective came up with a listing for every DiCecco on the East coast.

Dear Ms. Miller,

Per your request, we initiated an investigation for the purpose of locating the address of the above-named individual.

We have located several names with the last name of your subject. We also located only two individuals with the letter A as the first name. We checked the Boston area and found no one with the name Angelo.

The letter included the names and addresses of the two individuals with the letter A as a first name. One was Alfredo, the other, simply A. DiCecco, lived in New Jersey.

That was close enough to Boston, it had to be him.

s this Angelo?" I asked. There was a hesitation before the reply. "Yes. Who's this?"

"Are you the Angelo who knows David Cohen, the psychologist David Cohen? In Los Angeles?" He answered yes again, and again wanted to know who I was. I'd decided in advance that if I told him I was a patient of David's, he might think I was some crazed lunatic (which I supposed at that point I was very close to being) and refuse to talk to me, so I just said I was a friend.

"So?" said the voice at the other end. He did not sound the least bit happy to be talking to me.

"Well, I'm worried about him, you know, with everything going on," I said, "and I haven't been able to reach him and I don't know where he is. I thought you might know. I mean, is he okay?"

"How should I know where he is?" he said, "I haven't seen or spoken to David in over two years."

I couldn't be hearing him right. "What do you mean? That's impossible. He's been talking to you. He has cancer. Aren't you his best friend?"

"I guess I'm a friend, I guess. Look, who are you?"

"But he told me you were his best friend. There's a dedication in his book. He came to see you in Boston."

Angelo had no idea what I was talking about. "I'm telling you, I don't know anything about cancer, I haven't seen David in more than two years, and he's certainly not my best friend."

"But what about the gambling? I thought he was gambling for you. He didn't take money and make money for you?" I was stuttering, fumbling for words. This made no sense.

"I dunno. We've gambled a little, I guess. Look, I think I'm gonna hang up now."

I begged him to wait. "But I saw your name in his book. The dedications to you and Roxanna and his kids . . ."

"Look, I don't know who you are, but David doesn't have any kids."

"Yeah, he does. I've seen a picture. He has twins and triplets." My head was spinning.

He laughed, "Believe me, David Cohen has no kids. Good-bye."

It had to be related to Roxanna and her family's connection with the mob. It had to be. Angelo was suspicious, and he was protecting David. He didn't know who I was, maybe he suspected I was an angry patient, even dangerous. Maybe he thought I was someone related to David's abuse. Maybe I was from the IRS, tracking the gambling. Of course he wasn't going to say anything. It was the only possibility that made any sense to me.

Unless David was lying.

That was impossible. Absolutely impossible. Now, more than ever, I needed to talk to him. I had to get an explanation.

The only way I could think of to reach David was through their neighbor in Dana Point who was caring for their animals while they were away. I needed to find out where he lived. I felt I was invading David's privacy, but I had no choice. I called the private detective again.

———

El Encanto Drive, Dana Point, California. A thirteen-hundred-square-foot one-story house. It was not owned by David or Roxanna; it was rented. The phone connected to the house wasn't in David or Roxanna's name but was listed to someone else, a woman.

This was insane. What was happening? I tried to make sense of it. Maybe the El Encanto address was a cover to protect his family. Or an office, where he just kept papers. Or wrote. A place to get mail. David lived in a big house, a huge house, with a pool, two pools, a guest house. He had a boat, several cars. David, Roxanna, six children . . .

The private detective couldn't find anything like what I was describing. This was the right David Cohen; I had given him the license plate of David's car that I had recognized outside the office, I had David's psychology license number off his business card, his middle initial. I had the right guy. But nothing else. The detective was sorry, but that was all he could do.

called a friend of mine, David Regal, who I knew from my years in New York (we were in the comedy group Chicago City Limits together), and who had since moved to LA. I told David Regal what was happening. He said he'd make a call to another friend of his, who knew of a guy called a skip tracer. A skip tracer's basic job is to find people. People who have disappeared.

January 27

I called the skip tracer. Dan Hanks.

He asked me to give him every bit of information I could think of. License plate number, psychology license number, office address, age, description. In a daze I supplied whatever I could. Nothing connected in my head: I didn't understand what was happening.

"Don't worry, I'll find him for you," Mr. Hanks said. "If he exists, I'll find him."

29

Tuesday, January 28, 1997

I was driving north up Coldwater Canyon, toward the valley and home. I called my phone machine to check my messages. There was just one.

It was from the private detective. He wanted me to call him.

I quickly dialed his number. "Mr. Hanks, it's Jennifer Miller."

"I found David," he answered abruptly. "He's dead."

David was dead. My curse had come true. His knowing me had killed him.

Mr. Hanks met me at my house to fill me in on what he knew. He could tell I was completely flipping out, and admitted he probably could've broken the news to me a little more gently. "I guess I didn't realize what this guy meant to you," he said. He tried to comfort me, he told me to call him Dan, he put his arm around me. I was shaking.

"But I don't understand; he told me he was getting better. Why was he in San Francisco?"

I asked if it was the cancer, or the infection in his bones, or what.

"He was asphyxiated," Dan said. "He choked to death."

"What do you mean? Oh, my God, poor David."

I thought he meant the infection must have gotten into David's throat or something. Swollen it up, stopped his breathing. I couldn't believe this was happening. David couldn't be dead.

"It was like a bondage thing," Dan said. "He was tied up. Hand-cuffs, chains, all kinds of shit. They're investigating it as a homicide."

What?

They'd already autopsied the body, he reported. "And I don't know what he told you," Dan said, "but David Cohen never had cancer."

MEDICAL EXAMINER/INVESTIGATOR'S REPORT

The subject, Mr. David Cohen, age 33 years, resided with his wife at —— Bush Street #105 . . . Once inside the apartment, the subject [was found] unresponsive on the living room floor, covered by several blankets . . . Investigation at the scene revealed the deceased lying in a supine position, nude, on the floor of the studio apartment. No immediate trauma was noted. Purge was noted about the mouth and nares. The remains were cold to the touch. Rigor mortis was slight. Lividity was consistent with the found position. The subject had several silk scarfs[sic] about his head. Partially applied restraints were about the right wrist and right ankle. No obvious cause of death could be determined at the time of examination at the scene . . . A two-page note and medications were retrieved by crime scene . . .

Dan couldn't find any evidence David had ever been in New York, and he was certainly not renting property there. He had been living in San Francisco for some time, in a one-room apartment.

According to the police, instead of calling for help, Roxanna had disappeared. She apparently abandoned the body for several hours; then showed up with an odd story. The homicide detectives were suspicious, and were investigating.

"Oh, and that Angelo guy was right; he never had kids, either," Dan said.

I kept thinking, This can't be happening. This cannot be happening. It's like a dream, and I'm dreaming, I'm dreaming, this isn't real. It was so beyond reality it had to be a nightmare.

Almost everything I believed to be true for the last year and a half of my life was a total lie. I couldn't get my mind around it. How could that be? I was shattered. It's hard to even remember how unreal everything felt. From almost day one, when David had told me about his nanny, he had been lying. About everything, from the smallest detail to the greatest. And he had disappeared with almost a hundred thousand dollars of my money.

But the lies and the money and the betrayal were just overwhelmed by my grief. I knew the reality of the other, but the bigger reality was that David was dead. I never loved anyone else in my life and the only person I'd ever loved was dead. The one person in the world who had loved me. That wasn't a lie. It couldn't be a lie. Couldn't be. He loved me. He thought I was special. He was gone. What was going to happen to me? He was going to take care of me. I couldn't think beyond it.

I was so obviously distraught that Dan didn't want to leave me alone. He offered to take me to his house. "My wife's got all kinds of pills laying around she can give you," he said, kindly. Even in my anguish, I sensed that probably wasn't a great idea. I told him I'd be okay, and he left, and I sat there, just falling to pieces.

I knew Paul was working, doing audience warm-up, but I didn't know whom else to call. Somehow I got the phone number of the production office of the show, and they connected me to the stage.

Paul was in the middle of his routine, telling jokes to the audience, and the producer was reluctant to disturb him. I told her it was an emergency, and she went to get him. Paul asked the band to play while he answered the phone.

"What happened?" He knew it was about David.

"David's dead. He didn't have cancer. It was all a lie."

Paul's voice was shaky. "Okay, look, I'm going to come over, but I have to finish here. I can't just leave, I'm doing warm-up. Oh, my God. Are you sure? I'll come over, okay, soon as I'm done. As soon as we wrap, I'll come over."

While I was waiting for Paul I decided to call Angelo. I don't know why. For some reason I thought he should know, or I just wanted to hear his reaction. Maybe Angelo already knew, and I wanted confirmation that this really happened. Maybe I just wanted a connection with someone else who knew David.

I identified myself, and I told him his friend David was dead.

His answer was very odd, his voice cold, matter-of-fact. "Oh, really? Well, good luck to you." And he hung up.

Paul and I were walking around dazed, like we'd just come out of a war zone, a firestorm. Totally shell-shocked. Like me, David had told Paul he'd had cancer, and had called Paul a couple of times during the supposed treatment to report on his progress. Paul wanted to go to San Francisco. He couldn't—wouldn't—believe it was David who was dead, who had told all these lies. Couldn't be. He'd known him six years. He wanted to see the body, pictures, something.

We flew up to San Francisco, after arranging with Dan to meet some partners of his up there, other private detectives. On the plane Paul and I tried, unsuccessfully, to make some sense of what was going on.

A week or so earlier, as I'd started my search for David's hospital, Paul had come over, and I'd told him about David's visit to my house. Although he didn't say it at the time, Paul didn't believe me. He thought I must be so depressed it was coloring my judgment, that I was just *wishing* David could've been there.

When I told him about my first conversation with Angelo, when Angelo had said he hadn't seen David in two years, Paul, like me, thought that Angelo probably just thought I was a crazy person and was trying to get me off the phone. Paul still couldn't get it through his head that David might have made this whole thing up. It had to be that Jennifer was nuts.

I must've seen the doubt in his eyes because I showed him a Polaroid I'd taken of David petting my cat Lewis. It was clearly taken in my house. I may have been out of my mind, but I wasn't hallucinating.

"I had tingles up my spine when I saw it," Paul said. "It was just so wrong." Then I told him about the huge sum of money I had paid for therapy in advance, and the money I had given David for gambling. Paul shook his head in disbelief at the magnitude of it. Although he too had given David money in advance just prior to his "cancer," it was a few thousand dollars—nothing compared to what I had given him.

Stunned as he was, Paul admitted that even before this, he had suspected that something wasn't adding up. Along with being a comedian, an actor, and a writer, Paul was a magician, and had always a great interest in con artists and scams, and how people are able to fool people.

"I'd had inklings about this," he said, referring to David's absence. "Maybe because of the way he'd changed in the last six months. Nothing I could really act on. Vague thoughts that I dismissed as crazy talk. That's how I referred to it, crazy talk. I thought I was having some childish reaction because I'm feeling abandoned and deserted, my therapist is gone, and I'm just trying to negate and diminish any feelings that I might have for him."

He was amazed at the depths to which David had sunk, the total schizophrenia of the situation. It was like there were two Davids.

Now, on the plane, his thoughts were even crazier. He wondered if David and Roxanna hadn't even faked someone else's death so they could get away with this. The scenario in his mind was that if David had stolen this money from me, maybe he had stolen thousands of dollars from lots of different patients. What he had done was so fiendishly clever, Paul said, that now nothing seemed impossible.

I couldn't get my mind around such thoughts. My focus was still on the fact that David was dead, that I'd never see him, talk to him, again. The larceny, the emotional assault, still paled next to my grief.

We arrived in San Francisco, and the first place we went was to the police department, homicide division. It was like something out of *NYPD Blue*, except it wasn't a TV show. I couldn't believe I was standing there, in this place of shootings and stabbings and murder, with an investigation going on into David's death. It was totally surreal. Paul made a comment to the police captain about his clothes; he was very nattily dressed. The guy smiled, obviously pleased. "That's his trademark," his secretary whispered to us in an aside.

The homicide detective in charge of the case, Detective Atkins, took us into a little room with a desk and several chairs. Paul and I sat down across from him and another detective.

"I've been a homicide detective in San Francisco for a lot of years and I've seen a lot of bizarre cases, but this is the most bizarre," Detective Atkins said. He was talking partly about some journals they had found, David's and Roxanna's. He had them in front of him, and we were attempting, surreptitiously, to read them upside down. There was stuff about "Controlling the evil beast," and "I am an evil beast," and something in Roxanna's along the lines of, "I can almost trust him now. He almost fooled me, but I think I can control him now, I think he's docile."

This couldn't be happening. This was a joke. This was David. An evil beast?

From both the police and the private detectives we were hearing such impossibly weird things it was hard to keep track or make sense of them. At one point, either the skip tracer or one of his partners mentioned the police finding a cage in the apartment, large enough to accommodate a human. According to the private detective, Roxanna had told the police it was David's plan to go into the cage and starve himself to death. She also told them he was possessed by the devil, and had been seeing an exorcist. She refused to give the police the exorcist's name because it was a secret. That nobody could know where he lived, that he had bodyguards and people were always trying to kill him. The police weren't exactly sure who would try to kill an exorcist, or why, and wouldn't it hamper business to not advertise, but nothing was making much sense to them at this point. In any case, in the police report, which included a partial description of the apartment, there was no mention of such a cage.

There were also references in David's journal to gambling, and gambling debts, and the police later told the private detectives that they'd found records of large losses on David's computer. Paul told the detective that David had stolen money from me, and they asked how much. I told them, almost a hundred thousand dollars. I was crying. "But I don't care, I don't care about the money."

Paul wanted to look at the photos of the body taken at the apartment. He looked at the first photo, and he kind of cringed. There was a long pause. "I dunno, I . . . I guess, I guess that's him. That's his bald head. That's his earring. Yeah, I guess it's David." The detective asked if I wanted to see them too, and I shook my head. I couldn't bear the thought of it.

Later, when I was able to face hearing what the photos revealed, Paul described them to me. There was a black leather studded collar around David's neck, "very thick, almost three inches wide, really ran the whole length from his chin to his collarbone . . . with a ring and a chain on it.

"His face was all swollen and red on top of the collar. It was hard to recognize because it was so swollen . . . And it was clear that he couldn't breathe, he was like pulled or something."

Paul said he couldn't remember if David was completely naked, but he remembered him being on a bed, and seeing a lot of flesh, and his wrists were tied.

Roxanna had told the police that David's death was an accident, and although the detective didn't seem to want to tell us very much more, it was clear they thought it strange that Roxanna had abandoned the body, instead of calling the police. In fact, David had only been discovered because the apartment manager had come into the apartment at the request of David's father, who had called him from Arizona. The police naturally felt that in the case of an accidental death, the more normal reaction would have been to call 911. The exorcist story also appeared to seem a little too kooky for their tastes.

We stayed there for about an hour, answering questions, getting as much information as we could. The detectives said they would look into the money, to see if Roxanna had it, and if we thought of anything else to please let them know.

———

We left the homicide division more confused than ever. Gambling, evil beasts, an exorcist . . . ? This was David? David Cohen? So normal, so happy. Loved life. Preached integrity. Paul and I couldn't acknowledge it. Paul said to me at one point, "If anyone had said to me, Who's the most honest person you know? I would've said David."

———

Before we left San Francisco, I wanted to see Roxanna. To meet her, to see her, to hear some kind of explanation.

Paul and I had arranged to meet the two private detectives who were Dan's partners. I think we met them at a restaurant, a McDonald's or something.

Dave and Fred. Paul remembers thinking at the time that they were like something out of *Get Shorty*. One was a short, fat guy; the other tall, with long black hair and a long overcoat.

They filled us in on a few more details they had learned from their buddies at SFPD. More about Roxanna's leaving the body; a two-page note the police had found near the body. They had Roxanna's address, and agreed to take us there.

We stood on this seedy street in some low-rent area of San Francisco. The private detectives assured us they were carrying guns, and I just looked at them. What were they talking about?

I couldn't stop comparing where we were, outside this dingy little apartment building where David had died, to the life David told me he led—a Ferrari, a boat, a mansion with two swimming pools, a waterfall and a Jacuzzi and a Zen garden.

Roxanna wasn't home, and the manager told us she often went for walks in the park at about this time, and he was sure she'd be back soon. He seemed completely unaffected considering just days ago he'd found a bound, naked, dead person in his building.

Paul was pretty sure he would recognize Roxanna; at least he hoped so. He had met her one night when she and David had come to a sitcom taping to watch Paul do warm-up.

It was starting to get cold and we'd been there at least a couple of hours, just standing on the street, trying to look unobtrusive. These two detectives, Paul, and this short, thin, deathly pale figure with thick, black uncombed hair. I think the detectives expected us to get busted for loitering at any minute. Still, I insisted we wait. I was not going back to L.A. without talking to Roxanna. I was desperate to talk to her. Every woman who walked by, I'd whisper to Paul, "Is that her? Is that her?"

"No. No. No. I don't know." He was starting to doubt his memory of her. Suddenly he hissed, "That's her, that's her!" A woman was walking down the street toward us, with longish, brown hair, but otherwise fairly nondescript. David had described her as simply beautiful.

"Roxanna, it's Jennifer." She turned. At first she looked perfectly normal, not yet registering what I was saying. Then a look came into her face that I can only compare to that of a terrified rabbit, a deer caught in headlights. Sheer panic. Just as fast, a veil descended, and her face totally changed.

Later, when I was inside talking to her, Paul and the detectives discussed what they had seen. "Did you see that?" said one of them, either Fred or Dave. "Did you see her face change?"

"Like an actor getting into character," Paul said.

Even I could see that only six days after David's death she didn't appear to be a grieving widow, but I chalked it up to some inner strength, the spirituality David had told me about.

I insisted on going in to talk to her alone. Paul said he'd give me ten minutes, then he was coming in after me. I told Roxanna, "I have so many questions."

She paused for a moment. "I bet you do," she said, and led me inside.

What happened? What happened?" I kept repeating it, crying. I wasn't even talking about the lies yet, but about how he died. Why did she leave the body, why didn't she try to save him? I didn't understand.

She spoke to me very slowly, like she was talking to a small child, or a dangerous person with a gun. She'd stare at me, then glance away, then come back to look at me again. Leaving the body was just something she had to do, she said, and if she told me, I wouldn't understand. (According to Dave and Fred, she hadn't given the homicide detectives much more of an explanation.) I was completely confused and kept telling her, "I *don't* understand. Why did David lie to me? Why? Why did he say he had cancer? All your children? Why did he lie? Did he care about me at all? Did he love me? Why? Why?"

Roxanna was sitting on the bed and I was sitting on a chair facing her, in the room where David had died. It was beyond weird. The place was very small, just a bedroom with a kitchenette, and I kept thinking, if there ever *was* a cage in here, it would've taken up the whole room. It creeped me out to think what might've gone on in there. I wanted to wash myself.

"David loved you very much," Roxanna said.

"Then why did he steal from me, Roxanna? Why did he lie to me? *You* lied to me." I was crying, as I had been pretty much since I came in.

Again, she was very slow in her speech, very methodical. "I don't know why he lied to you, Jennifer. I don't know." She was ignoring my question about her own lies.

"Where's Shadow?" I wanted to know. I saw her cat, Puff, but where was David's dog?

"Shadow? Um, Shadow's . . . Shadow's at a friend of David's. That's where he is."

I asked if there even was a Shadow, or if that was just another lie. I wanted to know how far the lies extended. Was every single thing except Roxanna's existence completely fabricated? I wanted to know that something could be true, please let little bits and pieces be true, because if *something* was true, then maybe he had loved me.

"Yes, there is a Shadow," Roxanna said, very slowly. "It so happens he's at a friend of David's."

Suddenly the door opened and Paul walked in. He'd given me twenty minutes and was starting to get nervous. He did not trust this woman.

He came in and right off the bat was very confrontational. He wanted an explanation of what happened and why all the lies, and where my money was and he wanted it now. Roxanna refused to look at him, only addressing me.

"I can't speak for David," she said to me, "but he had his reasons." Either Paul or I asked where all the money was that I'd given David, including the twenty-five thousand. "It so happens I don't know where that money is," Roxanna said, "I'm sure he spent it." She said when he showed up with the twenty-five thousand, she assumed he'd won it in Vegas.

I said, "But you knew he was visiting me; you spoke to him from my house. He wasn't in Vegas; you had to know the money came from me. Casinos don't hand you cash."

"It turns out I didn't know," she said.

She frequently prefaced her answers with something like "It so happens" or "It turned out." Paul later told me he thought it was a mechanism to distance herself from the answer. "And she used that voice," he said, "that calm voice and big eyes in that wholesome Midwestern face, trying to make everything seem so reasonable."

Paul was getting more and more hostile with her, and I was getting more and more hysterical, and Roxanna was continuing to virtually ignore him.

"Jennifer, you know what?" she said. "He's going to be back."

"What do you mean?" I said.

"He's still going to be there for you. He's still looking out for you. You still are part of the family."

"What do you mean, going to be back?" I said. "Like reincarnated?" Paul was rolling his eyes at this point.

Roxanna looked at me, leaned toward me. "What would you say about David's spirit?" she asked me.

I said I didn't know, that it was good?

"He had a wonderful spirit," Roxanna said, "like in your painting. One of the greatest spirits ever, don't you agree?"

I said yes.

"What does that mean to you, Jennifer, the greatest spirit ever?" Roxanna asked. I didn't know.

"God," she said.

"You think David's God?" I said. This was getting a little weird.

"I think David is God and I think he's coming back in three days," Roxanna said. "And he may not look like David but I'll know it's him."

Paul jumped in at this point. "You told the detectives he was possessed by the devil; now he's God. Which is it?"

Roxanna wouldn't look at him. She took a deep breath, like she was going to say something very important. "David went to kill the devil," she said. "He went to kill Satan. He wanted to die and I helped him. We had planned to do it later, but this time is okay, and he's coming back in three days."

This going-to-kill-the-devil stuff was way too much for me, but I've always had a healthy respect for the idea of reincarnation, and am very open to ghosts and aliens and all of that. And I was so freaked out at this point that I was thinking, Okay, maybe it's true. Maybe he *can* come back. I know it's not true, but I'm hoping it is true.

Still, the whole story didn't fit right. What she had told the detectives (that it was an accident) versus what she was telling me. And it still didn't begin to explain all the lies and all my money.

"I don't know, Roxanna, I'm having a little trouble with this," I said. "I mean, God? I'm sorry, but I'm having a little trouble believing that."

Paul at this point was thinking, Yay, Jennifer, there's the Jennifer I know! She's still there! Because before that he thought I was totally gone.

Paul said later that he felt I knew deep down this was completely insane, but I was rationalizing it in my mind, trying to buy into Roxanna's viewpoint because she was all I had left of David.

I told her, "I want to believe you, Roxanna, I really do. I wish he was coming back. He meant so much to me." I was crying again.

Roxanna started saying again that he was definitely coming back, and I was going to stay in their family, and Paul had just about had it. He saw her reeling me in, and he's thinking, she's going to try to maintain a relationship with Jennifer and get more money from her.

"Listen to her, Jennifer, listen to her. Look at this look in her eyes!" Roxanna looked straight at him, not saying a word. "Have you ever seen eyes like that before? Did you see the interviews with the Manson family with Squeaky Fromme? That's the exact same look they have, look at it, look at that face!" She kept staring at him, and he kept going, getting angrier and angrier.

"Look at her, she's abusing you, she's taking advantage of you, trying to make you believe this crap! David is dead! I saw the pictures! God wouldn't die that way! God would not die in fucking S&M sex!"

He just lost it, he was screaming at her. He had a suspicion about what had happened, and he didn't care if she knew it. "She's probably on drugs! She probably killed him! Look at her!"

I wanted him to calm down, to stop yelling at her. It did seem like things had gotten really weird here, and that Roxanna wasn't making much sense, but I was so freaked out at this point I didn't really know what to think. I wondered if maybe she was a little crazy but even more, I wanted to believe. "Paul, there's things we don't know about the world, maybe there *is* reincarnation . . ."

Roxanna started to say something to Paul, agreeing with me, and he said, "Roxanna, don't you fucking start this shit with me. It doesn't work with me."

He turned to me. "Jennifer, I'm sorry, I care about you and she's doing to you what David's been doing for months and I can't sit by and watch it happen.

"Look, I want to get you out of here," he said. "She doesn't give a shit about you. She killed David. She probably wants to steal more money from you, and those two hired guns outside that we brought with us care more about you than she does." Bringing up the hired guns was no accident. During his tirade he noticed her face had gotten really scary looking, very cold and hard, and he was a little nervous about her, not sure exactly what she was going to do. All he knew was that somehow David had died, and who knew how it happened?

I agreed we should leave, asking Roxanna if we could keep in touch. She was still my only connection to David. She said of course I could, and gave me a phone number. I wondered if it was real and she said it was. Paul wanted a private word with her, and asked me to leave.

Reluctantly I stepped out into the hall. Paul closed the door behind me.

He got right into Roxanna's face. "You're talking to me now. I don't buy any of your shit." She started to speak, but he cut her off. "Shut the fuck up. If you ever come near my friend or ask her for money and try to get anything out of her, I'm going to fucking find you and you're going to be sorry. Do you understand?"

She answered in a really loud voice, loud enough for me to hear. "There's no need to threaten me."

"I'm not threatening you," Paul said. "I'm just telling you what's going to happen. Leave my friend the fuck alone." And he left.

The private detectives gave us a ride back to the airport, and we headed back to L.A. We barely spoke on the plane, exhausted. Drained, physically and emotionally.

I kept my curtains drawn, night and day. It was not a choice, I simply didn't have the energy to open them. I didn't care that it was dark, didn't notice I don't think. I couldn't process what had happened, didn't understand it. Everything David had said was a lie, lie, lie. Nothing he had promised me was going to come true. I was completely empty. I cried constantly. I lay in bed, barely eating, never sleeping. I was still taking Prozac for depression. A stimulant, it was battling the sleeping pills, and I was caught in a vicious cycle. I got shrunken and small and pale. Why, why, why did he do it? For the money of course, but I still couldn't make sense of it. Why me? Why so cruel? This wasn't possible. Couldn't be. I'd lost everything I believed in, the very ground under my feet.

I had no show to go to, no work, nothing to distract me. I had no parents to lean on, I was barely speaking to them. I talked to Jane and I told a few friends the story, parts of it at least, what parts I was not ashamed to admit; but I saw only Larry. He was overwhelmed, I think; helpless to do anything, and he just watched me.

The days dragged by inches. Sometimes I took two or three baths a day, just for something to do. Were they comforting? I don't remember. It just passed the time, watching the tub fill up. Getting in. Waiting. How was I going to get through the next minute?

I got thinner and thinner. I ached inside. So this was grief. This was mourning. Now I knew pain. All that stretched ahead of me was barren. I had dreamed, believed, thrilled at the thought of a happier future, and it was gone. In fact it never was there to begin with. I had nothing, no one.

"... And I'm stabbed in the gut, bleeding to death, and they've forgotten I even existed."

At the same time I was starting to go through the paperwork on David and Roxanna that the private detectives had given me. Reading it in between crying. Although it was beginning to register that David had *stolen* from me, it didn't help me. It didn't make me angry so I could go, "Well, fuck him"; it just compounded my distress, made me even more confused. I realized that right from the beginning he had lied, but I still couldn't reconcile that with the man I had known. Sweet, patient, loving. Thief, con man, manipulator. He loved me. Did he love me? He thought I was special. He *said* I was special. Was it only for the money? He cared for me. Why did he betray me? I'd never see him again. I should hate him. I didn't, couldn't, although I was starting to hate myself for my stupidity.

As I looked further into who David was, the paperwork the detectives had given me, and additional investigation, showed at the least a very secretive and strange life.

David and Roxanna (whose maiden name was Alton, unlike the Italian name David had told me), lived in a small, rented house in Dana Point owned by a couple named Kessler, who lived in Canada. These were the same Kesslers mentioned in David's acknowledgment page. When the private detective had called the phone number at the house, they found it was now rented to someone else, who said they did not know David and Roxanna.

There was of course no boat, no mansion, no fancy cars. David had declared bankruptcy in April of 1995. He was listed with two social security numbers, both of which also came up with a woman's name. In November of 1996, for a period of a few months, he kept a P.O. box in Maine, on the other side of the United States, which appeared to be maintained under this same woman's name.

In 1995, the only phone number the detectives could find listed at the house on El Encanto was 714-555-5555, the traditional non-phone number.

David's father was listed among the papers, and I called him in Arizona. I was seeking information of any kind, but, primarily, where was my money. I had barely gotten out that I knew David, and was calling to say I was sorry and could I . . . when his father hung up on me. The next day, when I called back, the number had been changed to one that was unlisted.

The private detective also informed me that David and Roxanna, along with giving up their rental, had closed all their bank accounts in Dana Point sometime in August before leaving for San Francisco. It appeared they were not planning on coming back.

I called Roxanna, fishing for answers, not telling her I was looking into their lives, or what I had discovered. Remarkably, she had given me the right phone number. I tried not to tell her the versions of any stories I had heard from David, but asked for her version first. Whether what she told me was true or not, I had no way of knowing. I already knew she was a liar from her telling me about the babies waking up, and David's cancer and being in New York and joining them at the guest house, so I could only assume the worst.

I asked her about the surgery David had undergone for so-called scarring from sexual abuse. She said it was to remove kidney stones. His bruises (supposedly from falling down the stairs—in their one-story house) were, she said, from a fight David had gotten into on Venice Beach.

I asked Roxanna about the book, to which I owned the film rights.

"It's at the agent right now."

I asked about the publisher that wanted it. The big million-dollar deal.

"Um, it is at the agent, and it keeps getting held up, and I don't know why it's getting held up. I know that David called the agent like two weeks ago, and I know that, I know that the agent had cancer."

I couldn't believe what she was saying. I wanted to scream at her, "You've used that one! You can't think of something else?!"

Clearly there *was* no book deal, and I was pretty sure not even an agent.

As I looked even further, I found that almost *every single thing* had been a lie. From the private detectives, Roxanna, and the police reports, I learned David was, indeed, a licensed psychologist; that much was true. But almost nothing else.

I sat down one day and tried to list all the lies I could come up with. They were innumerable: The cancer. The chemo. The radiation. The bubble. The hoarseness in his throat. The nanny. New York. The twins. The triplets. Selena and her mother, Julie. Selena's boyfriend Dominick. The mob lawyer father-in-law. The swimming pools, Jacuzzi, guest house, waterfall, cars, motorcycle, home gym. Opening his clinics. The trip to D.C. to get credentials. The sexual abuse. Winning a triathlon. The boat. The pool parties. His best friend Angelo (who it turned out was married). The appointments for January. The successful gambling on my behalf. The car accident. His laryngitis. His fake exhaustion hiking. On and on and on.

And the details within the lies. On the twins alone: They love Barney. Vanessa's picture. Their Halloween costumes. Trading candy for toys. The dedication to them in his book. Taking them swimming. Who likes the water, who doesn't. Vanessa is the braver one. Darian loves the car. How they like to be held . . .

Hundreds and hundreds and hundreds of lies. How did he keep them straight? Did *he* believe them? I wanted to believe he was just crazy, mentally ill, not a con man. But then where did Roxanna fit into that? And if he was just crazy, his craziness conveniently netted him a great deal of money. And where *was* the money? My money. Who had it?

I was feeling totally stunned by his deceit, and also still horribly depressed and wishing he wasn't dead. I asked Roxanna if I could go to David's funeral. I had no idea if this man was loving, evil, cruel, crazy, healer, or con man. It didn't matter.

The coroner was holding the body until further investigation could take place, but Roxanna promised she'd tell me when the funeral was. Not trusting her promises, I kept in touch with her just to make sure.

Finally the coroner released the body to Roxanna. According to the private detectives, in spite of all of the bizarre and mystifying circumstances, the police couldn't find enough evidence to charge her with anything. I wondered if I should tell anyone that at her apartment she had told Paul and me that David wanted to die, that they had planned it together, and that she had helped him. And I wondered, wasn't assisted suicide a felony in California?

Roxanna actually told me twice that she had, in effect, assisted in planning David's death. The second time was in a phone conversation two weeks before David's funeral. I was asking her—pleading with her—to explain why David had lied to me, and why she had lied to me. She offered no explanation for her own lies, but insisted that David had lied to her too, referring to the twenty-five thousand dollars in cash he suddenly appeared with after visiting me. He claimed it was gambling winnings, Roxanna said, and repeated that she had no idea the money came from me. What else could he have lied about, she wondered. He made her believe he was God, she said, but if he could lie to her about the money, and if everything else (including his three-day resurrection) was a lie, then that meant she helped kill her husband. I gasped at her statement, and I sensed that she suddenly understood its implications. She quickly went on, "I mean, I had no intention of him dying, it was purely, purely an accident." She repeated it again, "It was purely, *purely*, one hundred percent an accident."

———

Roxanna finally called and gave me the details about David's funeral. He was going to be buried in Arizona near his mother, who had supposedly died of brain cancer. By this point I doubted even the simplest of facts, and she could just as easily have been still alive for all I knew.

I made plane reservations, booked a rental car, and left for Phoenix. My first funeral.

34

I really didn't know what to expect when I got there, but it was not like funerals I'd seen on TV. First of all, there was hardly anyone there, ten people at the most. They all seemed to be connected more to Roxanna—I believe her mother was there, her sister, her friends. The only person who seemed to be more a friend of David's was Janet, who was also Roxanna's friend. So she did exist. None of the other people so lovingly mentioned in David's acknowledgments page seemed to be in attendance.

The casket was sitting there, white, draped in flowers, waiting to be lowered into the ground. I couldn't believe David's body was in there. It was devastating to me. How could this be? I'd sat across from this man for over a year, and now he was this . . . what? What does a body look like? Was he shriveled up? Normal-looking? Thin? Bloated? Wasted away? I couldn't bear to think of it, and couldn't stop thinking of it.

Roxanna had asked if she could put the "The Healer" spirit stick in the casket with David, that I had given him for his birthday. I said of course she should bury it with him, that I had bought it for him and I wanted him to have it.

The only other person who seemed to be there specifically for David was his father. No brother, no sister (if they ever existed), no friend other than Janet. Your last party, and nobody comes. It struck me as very sad, and very strange.

His father was wearing what I can only describe as the worst hairpiece I've ever seen. Jet black, thick, shiny, perched on the top of his head like an ill-fitting motorcycle helmet. Burt Reynolds would've been horrified. When I mentioned to Roxanna how dreadful it looked, she said it was his real hair. Her response chilled me—did she and David lie about *everything*?

It was very weird being there. I felt like two different people emotionally. David was dead; I was distraught, confused. Even though he'd done this horrible thing to me, I needed to say good-bye. Grief was still winning over anger. And yet at the same time, another part of me was trying to figure out this life, this person who I thought I knew but didn't. I was observing everything, the lack of attendance, people's behavior.

Again, I'd had no experience with funerals and how people act at them, but Roxanna, as when I'd first seen her outside the apartment, did not seem to be grieving. She appeared calm, cool, very matter-of-fact, dressed casually, smiling at times. Only when David's father was saying Kaddish over the casket, did I see the lightest evidence of tears. Even as I was dazed and crying, my cynicism crept in: since David had supposedly gambled away all the money he stole, maybe she wondered how she was going to pay for the service.

The man conducting the main part of the service read some Buddhist thing; I believe it was Janet who read a short poem, and we were all invited to light incense. I wondered how anyone could have Buddhist beliefs and do what David did.

Roxanna had introduced me to Janet before the service, and she and I had spoken briefly. "David's been tormented his whole life," she told me. "He's finally at peace. You should just be happy for him." I asked her, But why would he lie to me; I don't understand all the lies. "Jennifer," she said, "it's really best if you don't ask questions."

I had brought with me one of the sweatshirts I had ordered on *Mr. Rhodes* to give to Roxanna. My friends couldn't believe I'd even come to the funeral, but giving Roxanna a gift? I didn't fully understand it either. I knew that this was the same person who had acted so bizarrely and coldly in San Francisco. And I knew she'd been part of the scam. And that she was a liar, and possibly crazy, with her resurrection theories and stories of demonic possession. But at the same time, she was my only connection to David, and I was not ready to give him up yet. I was so all over the place emotionally that no matter what I thought of her, no matter that I felt a slight chill in her presence, I could not sever that connection so easily.

Roxanna, Janet, and I walked over to my rented car. I reached in and grabbed the sweatshirt, and handed it to Roxanna. Janet said to Roxanna, "Well, he's definitely gonna cut the sleeves off that."

"What?" I said.

"I mean, I meant, David *would've* cut the sleeves off," Janet said, and she and Roxanna looked at each other.

———

I dropped my rental car off at the airport, passed through the metal detector, and prepared to board my flight back to Los Angeles. I was getting my boarding pass when the woman at the gate stopped me. She called a security guard, and they insisted on searching my purse. I kept asking why this was necessary, what was the problem, but they wouldn't answer. They said only that FAA rules allowed them to search people at random. Finally, after digging around fruitlessly in my purse, they let me board.

I went to the bathroom and immediately understood why they'd been so suspicious. I looked like hell. Blotchy skin, hollow-eyed, pale. My clothes were dark, my hair a tangled mess from wind blowing at the funeral. I'm sure they thought I was a drug addict with a bomb. I went back to my seat and cried all the way back to Los Angeles.

———

I was back in L.A., David was buried, it was time to go on with my life. I just had no idea how I was going to do that.

I didn't want more therapy, ever, but I thought, at least temporarily, I needed someone to help me through this—to sort out the truth from what I had lived for the last eighteen months. I probably tried about seven or eight different therapists, looking for someone I could feel comfortable with. They all seemed either too distant, not smart enough, too formal. Weirdly I suppose I was looking for someone more like David. Except not insane or a criminal.

I'd see each one only once, and I'm sure my insurance company, upon receiving the bills, wondered what the hell I was doing. Mostly I sat in their offices crying as I told the story; and these supposedly dispassionate listeners would sit there, gasping, "Oh, my God!" shaking their heads in disbelief, their mouths open in shock.

They all agreed this was the worst thing they'd ever heard of involving a fellow therapist. Therapists merely sleeping with their patients seemed almost therapeutic in comparison. Some of them, I think, doubted that David and I had never had sex; to them that would have seemed normal.

None of them could begin to explain what had happened, they seemed at least as confused as I was. They were shocked that David hadn't referred his patients to other therapists; it was completely unethical and irresponsible. Of course, when I pointed out that David lied, stole money, stayed at my house—that fact became fairly insignificant.

Although I wasn't together enough to wonder about it at the time, I'm sure many of the people I saw couldn't understand how I felt so little anger toward David, why I would want to go to his funeral, how I could grieve for someone who had done something so wrong to me. It's perhaps hard to understand, but it is not so unusual.

There are stories in the news of children horribly abused, who from their hospital beds still cry for the parents who beat them. Their parents are the only ones they rely on, the only ones they feel love them.

I heard a tale once of a little boy, set on fire by his father, who still wanted his father to visit him in the burn ward. The father has done a terrible thing to the boy, but in the boy's mind, who else will take care of him?

Patty Hearst fell in love with her kidnapper, because of a phenomenon called the Stockholm Syndrome, in which the victim of a kidnapper falls for their captor. Kept blindfolded and locked in a closet, Patty nonetheless fell in love with her captor, Cinque, and emerged from her experience sharing (at least temporarily) his political beliefs, even going so far as to participate with him in armed bank robbery. Because her captor was the one she depended on for everything, by necessity she turned to him. She had no choice but to trust him, and even forgive him everything. He held her life in his hands.

Even when Patty Hearst was released, her feelings for Cinque didn't vanish in an instant. Psychologically battered, she was confused, unsure what was true. It didn't matter what people were saying about him, or even what she had seen with her own eyes and endured under his control.

There is a psychological denial mechanism called "cognitive dissonance," also known as "self-justification." We use it to convince ourselves we have not made a mistake, that we were not fools. It can be as simple as convincing ourselves that we like the food we ordered in the restaurant, even though in reality it's not very good; or that we made the right choice in buying a new car, even though it keeps breaking down. We don't want to be wrong. Being wrong says something about who we are.

And because we don't want things to conflict with our beliefs, we refuse to accept them. We work around them. I had to believe I was right about David, or I had made a terrible, terrible choice. I couldn't get my mind around how wrong I'd been, the fact of it was impossible. There had to be some truth to the things I believed. And if I was right about him, then deep down he was good, and I still love him, and he was wonderful, and he loved me, and I miss him.

And like the little boy, even if I did see what David had really done, and how wrong everything was, it didn't matter. He was still a father to me. And even though he was dead, in my distraught mind there was still no one else in the world who could take care of me. And that, of course, was the final irony. Because David had become a mother and father to me, the one person who had put me in this position was the one person I believed I needed most to help me out of it.

————

My insurance was running out, and I felt tapped out financially in the therapy department. And, frankly, I didn't want to put any more money into it than I had to, feeling quite honestly that I'd given more than my fair share to the profession.

Paul had told me that toward the end of his therapy, when he had believed they were winding down, David had abruptly decided that he didn't think Paul was done. "What he used with me," Paul said, "was that I'd gotten so much out of it, and my life was so much better, that it would be even better if I would just . . . He said it as a challenge, knowing that I respond to challenges, but in a very, very subtle way.

"It's hard to convey how subtle it was," Paul said. "The things that he did . . . it's not like he was a pimp slapping us around to get us to work for him. It was literally brilliant."

David had told Paul that it was up to him. "But if you stop, there could be some regression, you could go backward and lose the work that you've done. If money is an issue I'll do it for free."

"It was always that," Paul said. "He'd always make it that money was not an issue, so you'd feel bad if you thought it *was* an issue."

Right before David took off, Paul gave him some extra money to cover continuing, an amount which at the time he thought was reasonable, because, as he told me, "I'd paid a lot less for the year before."

"That's because I paid for you," I said.

So I was not really looking to plunge a lot more money back into the therapeutic process, and besides I was genuinely concerned about my finances. I thought I should check out a place my friend Larry had been going—to a place where they did therapy on a sliding scale, depending on your income.

I figured if I explained what had happened, how much money a fellow therapist had stolen, and that I wasn't working, I could get some short-term therapy for a minimal amount of money. I called up and made an appointment with a therapist named Jim.

The way the clinic worked is that many of the people there are still in training, not yet fully licensed; some quite inexperienced. I think Jim was totally overwhelmed by my story and unsure what he could do to help. Like everyone else, he was just horrified by the story. I was, as always, explaining what happened and crying constantly, and at one point Jim asked me if this whole thing had ever made me feel like killing myself.

I admitted that the thought had crossed my mind when David got sick, the idea that I wouldn't want to live without him, or even couldn't live without him, but that I didn't feel that way anymore.

"Well, how would you do it?" he asked. "If you were going to kill yourself, how would you do it?"

It seemed like an odd question, but I later learned that one of the first things new therapists learn is that if a patient talks about actual methods of killing themselves, they are more likely to be serious. I'm not sure, however, that the therapist is supposed to actually *encourage* creative thinking.

"I dunno. I mean, I guess there's a million ways," I told him. "Put my head in the oven, take pills, jump off a building, drive into a tree, exhaust fumes, shoot myself, razor blades . . ."

"You have a gun?" Jim interrupted.

I told him I did. Before I'd moved into my house, I'd bought myself a 9mm semiautomatic Beretta, and I had learned how to use it. I'm a surprisingly good shot.

Jim and I talked some more, I was still weepy, and then my forty-five minutes were up. No more running over. We arranged to meet later that week.

A couple of days later Jim called me at home. He felt I needed some-one more experienced, that the clinic mostly put these newer therapists together with your more basic run-of-the-mill neurotics (my words), and that my situation was a little . . . unusual (his words). He said he'd try to get me a referral to someone farther along in their training at the clinic, and he'd get back to me. I said fine, and we hung up.

That night, Larry and I had arranged to go out to dinner. We ate Thai food, then rented a video at Blockbuster. "Let's get ice cream," I told Larry as we were heading home. We stopped at the liquor store, grabbed a carton of Vanilla Chocolate Chip Häagen-Dazs, and went to my house.

I set the ice cream on the counter to soften up, and Larry put the video in the VCR. I went to check my messages. The light was blinking.

"Jennifer, it's Jim. Are you there? It's Jim. Are you there, Jennifer? Answer me. Jennifer?" Click.

"Jennifer, it's Jim again. Are you there? Are you okay? Okay, if you don't answer, I'm calling the police. Jennifer? I'm calling the police. I'm calling them now." Click.

I walked into the living room. "I think that therapist I saw the other day called the cops. Do you believe it?" I told Larry. I was looking for Jim's business card in my purse. I'm not sure if I paged him or it was a direct number, but either way, I was speaking to him within minutes.

"Jim, it's Jennifer Miller. I was at dinner. I went out to eat. What do you mean, you called the cops?"

He said he thought I was killing myself with my gun, and I told him, slowly, that, No, I was out eating dinner. But it worried me. "Look, please call the cops back and tell them I'm not killing myself, okay? I'm watching TV. Just 'cause I own a gun, Jim, doesn't mean I'm using it or have any intention of using it." He admitted that he'd overreacted, apologized, and said he would call them right away.

Within minutes my phone rang. "It's too late," Jim said. What the hell did that mean? "They're there already," he said, sounding panicky. "They're 'on-site.' "

On-site? Please let that not mean what I think it means. Still holding the phone, I turned my head to look out of my living room window. My backyard was filled with beams of light moving through the shrubbery. Dark shadows behind the lights. I spun around. Out of my front window, in my front driveway, more lights. More shadows. Front and back, multiple bright lights. Shadows. Flashlights. Behind the flashlights were cops. A lot of cops. Swarming over my front yard and back. With shotguns.

Larry and I looked at each other in shock, just flipping out. There were cops in my yard! My heart races when I'm getting a speeding ticket. I quickly opened the door so I could explain to them that this was all just a big mista . . .

"PUT YOUR HANDS UP! PUT 'EM UP, NOW, NOW, NOW!"

Eight of them. In my house. Seven men, one woman. "Put your hands behind your back!" I was told.

"This is a mistake, this is a mistake . . . this guy, call him, he'll expl . . ."

They told me to shut up, not to move. They handcuffed me, my hands behind my back. Pushed me on to the couch. Larry tried to intervene, they promptly handcuffed him too.

"Do you own a gun?"

I said I did. "But it's registered, it's, it's legal." I was stuttering, really scared. I hadn't done anything wrong, but for some reason, it was terrifying.

"Where is it? Where's the gun?"

I told them where they could find it, and three of the eight cops went upstairs to retrieve what they must have thought was a very heavy weapon. Their big police boots clomping up my spiral staircase. Lewis and Baby freaking.

"You don't understand, this . . ."

"Be quiet," the woman cop said, apparently pleasing her supervisor to no end.

"Doing a great job, Miles," he told her. "Aces. Handling this right by the book." He actually gave her a thumbs-up.

What did he mean, "by the book?" This is how they treated people who they thought were suicidal? People who thought the world was a harsh and cruel place?

Larry tried again to explain, and they warned him if he didn't shut up, he'd be arrested. He shut up.

"Please, we were eating Häagen-Dazs," I tried again. "Watching a video. My gun isn't even loaded . . ."

"Get outside," I was told. The woman grabbed my arm, and they took me out into my driveway. Me, in my driveway. Eight cops, with shotguns. Cop cars.

I felt totally humiliated. "Oh, God, please let my neighbors not be watching. Please let them all be away," I was praying. I'd lived there a little more than six months. My neighbors were quiet, nice, conservative people. In my nice, quiet, suburban neighborhood. And I was backed up against a cop car, handcuffed.

"Please, what are you doing?" I pleaded. "Let me call the therapist, he'll tell you."

"It's too late," I was informed. Once they're told a person might be suicidal, there's nothing they can do. They have to complete the assignment. What the hell did that mean?

It meant they were taking me to the hospital. The mental hospital. The loony bin. The snake pit. Oh, God.

"We were just watching a movie," I begged. "You saw me through the window. You were watching. You saw me." I was shaking, just terrified.

Nothing I could say would change their minds, and in fact I didn't say much after they told me again to be quiet. I did ask if we could go to Sherman Oaks Hospital, only a few blocks from my house, and I was told no, we were going to the county hospital. In Sylmar. Miles away up the freeway, where God knows what kind of psychiatric facility is available.

They put me into the back of the police car, my hands cuffed behind me. I told them the cuffs were hurting me, they didn't answer. A now uncuffed Larry locked up my house, and swore he'd follow me to the hospital in his car. And we left. I was praying that no one had seen this. And for it to please be over. The only plus was that for a moment I was completely over my grief about David, because I was thinking, lucky for him he was already dead.

I sat in a small waiting room at the county hospital, waiting for a psychiatrist to come talk to me. The cops handed me a piece of paper, explaining my rights concerning the gun, which they were confiscating. "Sign this," I was told.

According to the paper, it seemed that if you actually pulled out a loaded gun and threatened someone with it, you wouldn't be able to get your gun back for seventy-two hours. But if you threaten your *own* life, even if it's just someone else *saying* you threatened it and then taking it back, you lose your gun for five years (except if you pay your lawyer a huge sum of money to go to court and get it back for you). This applies even if your gun turns out to be upstairs, in a locked box, and unloaded.

In other words, if I'd pulled out a gun and threatened to kill Jim, I'd have had it back on Monday.

The cops left, their responsibility for my emotional well-being having been met. Larry sat with me and we waited for the psychiatrist to arrive.

"My name is Julio-Doctor-Montano." Oh. My. God. He didn't even speak proper English. This was the guy who was going to decide if I needed to stay in a psychiatric ward for seventy-two hours' observation or if I could go home and eat ice cream.

Larry put a restraining hand on my arm. Now, more than ever before, it was important I maintain my cool and put on a happy, happy face. Don't offend the nice doctor, I could see the pleading in Larry's eyes.

Dr. Montano asked me if I wanted to kill myself, and I very calmly said, No, I had just gone out to dinner; we were about to watch a video, et cetera, et cetera. I was trying to stay really light and casual, but I was actually really, really scared. This guy didn't know me at all. If he read me wrong, got the wrong idea; if he thought for a second that I was suicidal, I'd be stuck in that place. A county hospital psychiatric ward. I was shaking, and not wanting him to see me shake. I explained that Jim was a new therapist, and therefore overly cautious. I was fine. I'd had some problems with this other therapist, but I was fine. I didn't say, If you try to keep me in this place for seventy-two hours I will *definitely* kill myself.

After talking to me for about three minutes, Dr. Montano said he didn't understand why I'd been brought in, and pronounced me fit to go home.

Larry drove me home, and sat in my house and watched while I called Jim and screamed at him. How could he do this?! Here was another therapist fucking me over! Was I supposed to give him my daily schedule from now on? *He* was the one who brought up methods of suicide. I went out to fucking dinner, for Christ's sake!

He couldn't apologize enough, "I'm sorry, I'm sorry, I'm new . . . ," but I didn't care. I'm sure I could've been more forgiving, I know he was only trying to do what he thought was best, but I'd just been handcuffed, yelled at, pushed around, had guns pointed at me, and taken to a mental hospital in a police car. I was in no mood for forgiveness.

Larry and I decided to forgo the video, but ate the ice cream and then Larry left. I locked the door behind him, set my alarm, and sat down at the dining-room table.

I felt completely weird and confused and unreal. What had happened to me? How could this be? I'd blindly given away a hundred-thousand dollars. I'd fallen hook, line, and sinker for a con man. And now, as if everything else wasn't enough, I'd been taken in handcuffs to a mental hospital. I couldn't understand how my life had come to this.

What About Bob? is a Bill Murray movie about a crazy patient who follows his therapist around and drives him insane. Basically a very unhealthy therapist/patient relationship. Several months after all this happened I was talking to a guy I know, Simon, and it occurred to me that if Dr. Montano had asked what movie Larry and I rented that night, *What About Bob?* would've been the perfect movie to cite. It was not a brilliant joke or anything, but it seemed funny to me. And Simon, I think, was taken aback that I could laugh at this. I think I had come off as so weak during everything that happened, that people (including myself) had forgotten what a strong person I was.

That person still existed; it had just taken me a little while to track her down.

After deciding that perhaps Jim wasn't the right therapist for me, I had ended up with a woman therapist; her name was Buf. Between visits to her, I still spent most of my time at home. Still not eating, not sleeping. Eventually I started going to movies to distract myself, but frequently I would start crying in the middle and have to leave.

My sister Jane came to visit. We went out to eat together, went window-shopping. I was still somewhat angry with her for letting it slip to my parents that I was in therapy. She knew I had been very depressed about David having cancer, and was worried about me, so a month or so earlier she had told my father. He called, claiming he'd be visiting Los Angeles, and would like to see me. I told him not to bother. I said David had been a better father to me in a year and a half than he had been my whole life, and if he came to L.A., I wouldn't see him.

He wrote me a letter that stated simply, "I'm sorry you find us so wanting as parents. Hopefully one day you'll change your mind."

Of course now I felt guilty and mean for saying those things to him; and horribly stupid, especially in light of how wrong I had been about David.

Jane could stay only two days, but it was good seeing her. It shook me out of my inertia. We even had fun together. And of all the people in the world, she knew our family. She was probably the only person who could even begin to understand how this could happen to me.

I saw Buf for several more weeks. She was nice enough, sympathetic, but I felt no connection to her. I was spending even more money on therapy—money which I didn't have—and for what? After a few weeks of moping in her office, I decided I'd had enough. I was going to take my chances.

When I had gone to see David I was certainly not as happy as I could be. I had definite issues with intimacy and vulnerability and connection and all those things. And I was lonely and drifting. But with him I had become this train wreck, unrecognizable. A tangled mess, stumbling and flailing. I needed to breathe. I said good-bye to Buf, although she cautioned against it, and as I stepped out into the street outside her office, I remember breathing a sigh of relief. I was free. I could do this. David had controlled everything, every thought, every move. Now it was my turn to drive. My car, my gas, my route. And the Pluto Dude nowhere in sight.

I started seeing my friends (I had a lot more of them than I thought, and much closer ones than I thought), forcing myself to see them, horribly humiliated at what they had seen of me. I pushed myself to do things: playing poker, reading, working in my garden, painting, returning to horseback riding, impulsively adopting a big, crazy puppy. All the while examining, examining.

And I started telling people who didn't know the story, people I'd lost touch with over the time with David, about what had happened. I found I was not as much of a freak as I thought, not so alone in falling into an abyss. Everyone had their own stories, although maybe none quite so peculiar.

When Simon and I were sitting there, and laughing at the notion of *What About Bob?*, and the man who brought new meaning to the word "*Psycho*-therapist," and the tale of my "*Not* so nice Jewish doctor," Simon said, Boy, it seems like you're really over this, but you can't possibly be. Not yet, how could you?

And I told him, You know what, I am over it, and his eyebrows raised. But I knew. True, I had gone on this most bizarre journey, and gotten really lost along the way, but Simon didn't know me, and I did.

I had been asking myself many questions during the past months. How did David do it? How was I so gullible? How best to get over it? And I was figuring all of those out. But there was still one big question in my mind, one which I knew I might never find an answer to. An answer to what could be the biggest lie of all.

Was David even dead?

Even though I was doing well, and getting past what had happened, I knew that my judgment might be colored by a desire to have David still be alive—so I could confront him, so he could give me my money back, so I could get justice.

Knowing this, I asked my lawyer, Rod, what he thought. Putting all the facts together, even Rod, who is not prone to flights of fancy, could not exclude the possibility that David had perpetrated an even more enormous scam, and that at the very least there seemed to be more to the story than a simple accidental death.

There were so many strange incidents, so many things that didn't add up, so much secrecy, that it couldn't help but make us wonder.

First of all, I guess, was why would David *want* to die? And of course we only had Roxanna's word that that was his desire. Paul and I had learned that David had taken money, or attempted to take money, from other patients before disappearing. One of course was Paul himself, who gave David around two thousand dollars for future therapy. Another was a woman, Bridget, a psychology graduate student from whom David unsuccessfully requested an additional ten thousand dollars (she had just completed her training as a therapist, and David offered to refer clients to her in exchange for the money). Each request was carefully tailored. Another was a woman named Sheryl, who had given David fifteen thousand dollars for therapy right before he disappeared.

(Sheryl also told me that she had connections in the travel business. Instead of the allegedly luxurious, no-expenses-spared trip he took to

Australia, she had arranged his accommodations and gotten him the cheapest possible rates.)

So of the four patients of David's that Paul and I *knew* about—myself, Paul, Bridget, and Sheryl—David had gotten or asked for money from all of them. How many other patients were out there that we knew nothing about? Five, ten, twenty? Paul said David had a thriving practice. Was the money he took from me the most he got from anyone? Or was I just the tip of the iceberg?

Who calculatedly cons people out of money, closes all their bank accounts, gives up their home, skips town, and then arranges to have themselves killed, as Roxanna had told me?

But what better way to escape with potentially hundreds of thousands of stolen dollars than to appear to be dead?

My first inkling of doubt had come in San Francisco, at the police station, when Paul had first looked at the pictures. There was a definite hesitation as to whether the photograph was of David. "I guess . . . That's his bald head. That's his earring. I guess that's him," Paul had said. Even at the time, distracted as I was, it struck me as odd.

Much later, when I asked Paul to describe the pictures to me, he said he was pretty sure it was David, at least he thought so. Except that now time had passed, there were definite discrepancies between what he remembered, and was in the medical examiner/investigator's report.

> . . . Investigation at the scene revealed the deceased lying in a supine position, nude, on the floor of the studio apartment. The subject had several silk scarfs[sic] about his head . . .

Paul had said David was on the bed, tied to the bed. He had also mentioned a three-inch-thick black collar around his neck, which is not mentioned in either the investigator's report, or the autopsy. They certainly described everything else.

> . . . There is a blue and multicolored scarf tied around the upper head, obscuring the eyes and forehead area . . . beneath this scarf is a 3 to 3 1/2-inch-wide, tan-colored, Ace bandage–type of wrap that

is wrapped approximately five times around the [head] in an over-lapping fashion. This Ace bandage also covers the eyes and forehead area, and portions of the ears. There is a small amount of vomitus and purge-like red-brown material present around the mouth, extending along the right side of the face.

This seemed to be nothing like Paul's description of what he had seen, although his description of the restraints seemed to match more accurately.

... On the right wrist are two locked handcuffs. These two gray-metal, locked handcuffs are connected to each other by two gray-metal chained links ... Present on the right hand is a black leather glove. ...

There is a handcuff link present around the right ankle ... Below the handcuff attached to the right ankle is a black leather restraint. The black leather restraint has a black shag-type clothing lining on its surface. The restraint is secured by a belt-loop type of cinch placed on the fourth loop and snugly, but not tightly, applied to the right ankle. Adjacent and not attached to this leather restraint is another identical design-type leather restraint with the belt-type clasping mechanism open and attached. ...

There was more to Paul's description: "His face was all swollen and red on top of the collar. It was hard to recognize because it was so swollen. ... And it was clear that he couldn't breathe, he was like pulled or something."

The medical examiner's report stated that, "*No obvious cause of death could be determined at the time of examination at the scene.*"

How accurate was Paul's memory? Did he recognize David or not? A bald head, an earring; those aren't so unusual.

In addition, when Paul had first heard about David's death and the stolen money, his first instinct was to wonder if this wasn't more of the scam, and that maybe David wasn't dead.

As far as I know, except for Paul looking at those evidence photos, only Roxanna identified the body.

When I had given the sweatshirt to Roxanna, and Janet had mentioned that "David's gonna cut the sleeves off that," it struck me as a little weird. People often make mistakes right after someone dies, still referring to them in the present tense, but this sweatshirt was not even meant for David, it was meant for Roxanna.

I had asked Roxanna several times where David's beloved dog Shadow was. Each time she seemed clearly uncomfortable, evasive, "Uh, he's with a friend of David's," she'd say.

If Shadow *was* with a friend, it was a friend who cared enough about David to be saddled with his dog but not enough to show up at his funeral.

Why didn't Roxanna just admit there was no Shadow? It would be so much smaller than all her other lies. Or could it be Shadow was with David?

Who beat David up? David clearly had gambling losses, or at least his computer indicated he did. (That would certainly help Roxanna explain why there was no money remaining for her to return to me.) The private detectives had wondered if David didn't have someone looking for him, someone to whom he owed a lot of money. Not someone innocent, like a patient, but someone who was in the business of loaning money, and someone who very much expected it back. David had been beaten up badly enough to have bruises all over his arms (according to David, from falling down stairs; according to Roxanna, from getting into a fight on the beach). Did David fear that the next step would be a lot more severe than a beating?

Paul and I also wondered if David's beeper constantly going off during sessions could have been his bookie calling. I, of course, had thought at the time that it was all of his patients calling their wonderful, attentive therapist. In retrospect, it seemed that no one could have that many patients. Who was paging him?

At one point I had pointed out to Roxanna a discrepancy between David's actual birthdate, and a birthdate the private detectives had found. He told me his birthday was September 6; it was in fact September 9. "That's good," Roxanna said, when I told her. "That means they haven't found him yet." This was weeks after David's death. I asked her what she meant, and she said it meant nothing, and refused to elaborate.

Were there people looking for David? People he owed money to? What better way to prevent being killed than to say you're already dead?

David's body was discovered after his father called the apartment manager, concerned about his son. Concerned about what?

David's father changed his number to an unlisted one right after David's death. Changing your number is a fairly big deal. You have to tell everyone, every friend, every relative, every business associate. It's a drag; it's inconvenient. At a time when you'd think you'd be expecting people to call expressing condolences about your dead son, why would you make that impossible? Under anything but very odd circumstances, it seems a rather unusual thing to do.

Was it even his father at the funeral, in the rather obvious wig that Roxanna denied? Why were so few of David's friends there? Was his death such a secret that Roxanna didn't tell anyone? Why did Janet tell me it would be better if I stopped asking questions?

Why did Angelo, not a best friend but admittedly a friend, react so coldly and with so little interest when I told him David was dead? "Oh really? Well, good luck to you."

As I was mulling over everything, including David's visit to me, I remembered David asking me for my signature on a blank piece of paper. He had told me he liked to collect signatures, and of course I believed him. But now I wondered, why did he do that? I pay most of my bills with Quicken, using computer checks, which are kept in my office downstairs, next to my guest room. Many months after all this happened, as I got down lower in the stack, I found a fair number of checks missing.

When I had talked to Sheryl, even more interesting than David getting money from her, was a story she had to tell that she'd learned from a friend of hers, a woman who used to live in the same apartment building as David when he first lived in L.A.

Prior to meeting Roxanna, according to this friend of Sheryl's, David had been seriously dating another woman. He was popular in the building, polite, quiet, paid his rent on time. According to Sheryl, after David met Roxanna he broke up with the other woman, started living with Roxanna, and his personality and behavior totally changed. The landlord had told this friend of Sheryl's that David stopped paying rent on time; people in the building noticed he became difficult, angry, belligerent.

Could Roxanna have had some hold over David? If she had masterminded this, who would even know? At the very least, she knew David was lying extensively to me, did nothing to warn me about it, and in fact actively participated in the lies. Her lies corroborated David's cancer, his treatment in New York, his children, his fancy home; covered up the fact that David was secretly closing his practice while continuing to take money from his patients; and that they had given up their rental house in Dana Point, closed all their bank accounts, and fled to another city. Why would she do all that? Though she claimed David lost all the money gambling, I found it very hard to believe she had not benefited in some fashion from the payments I gave David for my "lifetime of therapy."

It occurred to me that David had been seeing Paul for five years, and it was unlikely that he had been planning this con for such an extended length of time. At one time, he was just a therapist—although Paul did tell me that David always took money in advance, even from the beginning. I wondered if David meeting and marrying Roxanna had anything to do with what ultimately happened. Clearly the evil was present in him, but was Roxanna his dark muse or merely a loyal wife drawn in by the brilliance of his manipulations?

Roxanna had told me that when David sounded dopey in his phone calls to me, it was from all the medications he was taking. Prescription drugs—Klonopin, Depakote, Ansaid, and Prozac—were found in the San Francisco apartment, but the toxicology report listed no drugs of any kind found in the blood or urine of the body.

The police found evidence in the journals of previous S&M sex between David and Roxanna, making this accidental death appear much less suspicious. There were tales of gambling losses. Of demonic possession.

But when were those journals written? By whom? How true were they? Creating a journal is easy, you just start writing stuff down, whatever you need to make your story work. David's lies to me started within the *first week* I met him, when he told me about his nanny, and continued for a year and a half. Layer upon layer, carefully crafted to create an entirely different reality.

Neither I, nor anyone else, saw evidence of David's belief in the devil; he didn't even know if he believed in angels. He told Paul he didn't believe in God. Roxanna told me demons talked to him; that he was crazy, phobic, terrified of newspapers and Kleenex. There was plenty of Kleenex in that office, boxes of it, mere feet from David's chair; he couldn't have cared less.

If you're that crazy, that psychotic, how do you turn it off just during office hours, or when a patient calls you on the phone? If you're seeing demons, how do you control their visiting hours?

From everything I had been told, there were definite discrepancies between what Roxanna told Paul and me; and what she told the police. Almost a year after the body was found in the apartment, I spoke to Inspector Repetto, one of the homicide detectives on the case. Like Detective Atkins, he found the whole situation strange, to say the least. "I've been a cop for twenty-seven years; this was the most bizarre and unusual interview I've ever done," he told me. "On first appearance she appeared normal," he said, "then I thought, whoa, what's up with this?"

When the landlord and the police initially came upon the body, Roxanna was nowhere to be found. The police left several messages on the phone machine in the apartment asking her to contact them, which she eventually did. At her interview, she never even discussed David until the police brought it up. Never mentioned her dead husband. She'd been in Las Vegas, she told them, showing them receipts to prove it. The detectives brought up David's death, and asked Roxanna why she went to Las Vegas. Roxanna told them the plan was to go there after David's death, and wait for him. "Who decided that?" Inspector Repetto asked her.

"The council of spirits decided that after David died I should go to Las Vegas," Roxanna told the detective. It was supposedly some sort of resurrection that she and David had planned. That David would come back three days after his death, and she'd meet him in Vegas.

"She put him in a straitjacket and chains," Inspector Repetto said. "Trussed up over the pole in the closet, the pole where the clothes hang." According to Roxanna, the devil would battle with David and try to take over his body, so they would bind the body to prevent the devil getting in.

"Roxanna left David hanging over the pole for five hours," the detective said, causing death by positional asphyxiation. Positional asphyxiation is a condition in which the lung muscles, kept in one position for a long period of time, become so fatigued that they stop working. "When Roxanna returned to the apartment, David was dead," Inspector Repetto said. "She took him down, laid him on the floor, and went to Vegas."

Although Roxanna's resurrection story to the police fit in with her comments to me about David's return, something (other than the whole insanity of it) still struck me as odd. If Roxanna was instructed by the "council of spirits" that after David's death she would meet him in Las Vegas, wouldn't that mean the death was preplanned? Didn't the police find it a contradiction to have a plan in place, to be implemented after an accident?

Roxanna had also told Paul and me that "David wanted to die, and I helped him."

Of course all the discrepancies paled next to the bigger question. Was it even David's body at all? And if David wasn't dead, then who was? I started to wonder, How hard would it be to plan a murder?

Picture a dark bar in San Francisco, in a seedy part of the city. An S&M bar. People dressed in black leather, studded collars around their necks, whips, chains . . .

A couple enters. Donna. Dirty blond, mid-thirties. She's with a guy, Rick, maybe five-foot-seven, balding, stocky, an earring in his left ear. They approach the bar.

As they cross the room we can see they are known here. They've been coming here for weeks, almost as if they're looking for someone. Waiting for someone. Shopping. The bouncer nods. Rick and Donna nod back. Their attention is drawn to a man seated at the bar, empty barstools on either side of him.

Rick and Donna look at each other. Finally. They approach the man, who has a statistical resemblance to Rick. He is around five-seven, mid-thirties, balding, stocky, an earring in his left ear.

As Rick approaches the man, he signals the bartender, who draws a couple of beers. Rick and Donna sit next to the man. One on either side of him. They smile. And as people do in any bar, they strike up a conversation. Introduce themselves. Rick and Donna, meet Frank. Rick buys him a drink.

The night goes on. Frank buys a couple of rounds, Rick and Donna buy a couple of rounds. Rick and Donna drink a little slower than Frank, but Frank doesn't notice. They're learning a lot about their new friend. He's new to town. He has no friends here. As a matter of fact few, if any, know he's even in San Francisco at all.

Not surprisingly, Rick and Donna learn that Frank likes rough sex. Sex games. This is an S&M bar after all. Coincidentally, Rick and Donna like the same things that Frank does. Leather, chains, tying people up, controlling them. Isn't it great that they all met?

It's late, and Rick and Donna invite Frank back to their place. Donna has a great idea for a game. "Sure, why not," Frank says. What does he have to lose?

———

Finally it's over. For a while there, when Frank was pleading, it got really ugly. But Rick and Donna can't think about that now. They cover the body with a blanket. Rick gathers up some belongings. He takes a wad of cash that he's hidden, twenty-five thousand dollars, maybe more. They each know the plan by heart, they don't need to talk about it. Rick thought it up. He's brilliant. He knows Donna's story is just insane enough to put people off track. He tells Donna he'll see her soon, and kisses her good-bye. And he's gone.

Donna watches him from the window. She knows she'll see him in a few months. She places a note next to the body. It's in her handwriting, but Rick composed it months ago when he was planning this whole thing. Donna shuts the door behind her, and goes to Las Vegas.

———

Just a scene from an imaginary thriller. All speculation. But I'm a writer; that's what writers do. David was a writer, and apparently much more devious than me. And it's not so hard to move from imagination to reality. Just takes enough incentive, motivation. Cunning. Maybe brilliance. Everyone who knew David said he was brilliant, from his former patients, to the therapists who shared his office.

How does this person, this embodiment of craftiness, die so stupidly? Or does someone so crafty fool everyone? David was never just one step ahead of me, but hundreds. Using incredible detail, he created a totally false world. He manipulated everyone around him in individually tailored ways. Who knows where that manipulation ends?

It's hard to believe it was simply ironic; that he concocted this richly detailed mock life, conceived of all this deception, got away with all that money, only to die accidentally.

And of course, if the scenario I imagined had taken place, asking Roxanna to identify the body would have been like the art expert being asked to authenticate his own forgery as real.

———

I think David kept in touch with me to stop me looking for him. The longer he had to get away, the longer he had to cover his tracks. But finally I came looking anyway. For once, he had misjudged me.

———

Who knows, maybe David *is* dead. But was it an accident? My writer's instinct kicked in again. A wife sees all her money wasting away on gambling debts. All the money she and her husband had worked so hard to get. I suppose lying can get exhausting. Having to pack up your life, move away, only to see everything you've stolen trickling away.

Or perhaps David *did* think he was possessed, and was God, and was going to kill the devil. All at once. Maybe Roxanna was as crazy as he was and really believed it when he said, "Honey, I'll be back from the dead in three days, don't wait up."

It just seems to me that death shouldn't be so complicated. There's an accident, someone dies, people mourn. Simple. No weirdness, no unanswered questions.

Most people don't live their lives in secret.

Again, everything is speculation. Nothing you could hang your hat on, nothing conclusive, just a lot of stuff that doesn't make sense.

I'll never know exactly what happened. But when I look at all the money involved, the treachery, the cunning, the lies, the evasion, the strangeness of these two people's lives, nothing would surprise me.

———

I tried to be as objective as I could during the writing of this book, and one day it occurred to me that maybe everything was much simpler than I was making it, that maybe I was just letting my writer's brain and my imagination spin out of control. Looking for clues, seeing mystery where there was none. I called Paul and asked him what he thought.

"All I can say is this," he told me, "even today, when I see someone on the street who looks like David, I look very closely."

So, how *did* this happen to me? It was a question I had been asking myself over and over. How could someone so smart not figure this guy out? How could I have been so stupid?

Intellectually I could understand it. I could see all the things that came together perfectly to make David's job easy: A trusted friend's recommendation; David being a doctor, an authority figure; success as the therapy progressed; a terrible need for a father's attention.

But when I think that this actually happened to *me*, I am sometimes dumbfounded.

When I was a child, and having trouble in school—bad grades, talking too much, rebellious—typical kid stuff—my parents took me to have my IQ tested. It was 155. No dummy in anyone's book.

Of course I'm well aware that having a high IQ doesn't make you necessarily smart in the ways that can save you. Except I *was* smart. Savvy, cynical, even suspicious. Street smart. I lived in Manhattan for five years, not the kindest place in the world. I knew not to get on a subway car that was empty. I knew when someone might be following me, or stared a little too long at my purse. I was always very aware of what was around me. I was intuitive about people, almost always right about my perceptions of them. Any friend of mine would tell you I was bright, clever, had good instincts. I'm funny, creative, imaginative. I read. Books, newspapers. I see a lot of movies. Watch a lot of TV. News, documentaries, thrillers, mysteries.

Paul and I got together a lot after this all first happened, comparing notes, sharing stories, and one of the things he said one day was that he couldn't believe I'd let David get all that money. Because if nothing else, money was something I was careful about. "I don't want to use the word stingy," Paul said. "Use the dictionary to find something else. But you're pretty tight with money."

Paul was being polite, I *am* somewhat stingy. Yet I had let this man con me out of almost a hundred thousand dollars, and actually a lot more if you included money I paid him in the first months of my therapy. I just wrote check after check and handed them over. I handed him cash. I never questioned it, never doubted it.

In the past I'd read or heard about people who gave some scam artist their hard-earned life savings, and I would always roll my eyes. How could they be so naive, so gullible? Or a woman who married a guy who was already married, and gave him everything. Couldn't she see it coming a mile away?

But you don't see it. If you're vulnerable enough, and someone knows how to tap into those vulnerabilities, you're lost.

From the first day I walked into that office, David could see that I was desperate for attention, support, validation, affection. And he knew that I had just sold a screenplay. The perfect target. He must've jumped for joy after I left that day, and his lies started almost immediately thereafter.

I'd never felt loved by anyone, and he offered me love. I'd never felt protected; he offered a lifetime of protection. He bent over backwards to show me how important I was, how special. Told me, and showed me, over and over and over.

I'd always heard that little girls are supposed to fall in love with their daddies, but the concept had always seemed bizarre to me.

When my father died at the end of 1997, my brother delivered the eulogy at his funeral. He spoke beautifully of my father's love of knowledge, of learning, of art, travel, history, medicine. He spoke of his love of flowers and gardening, his work ethic, his dedication to his patients (many of whom were in attendance, crying). He said that my father worked for free when people had no money, and that he was a loving healer. At the end of the eulogy, my brother broke down, clearly moved, and went back to his seat. Jane and I looked at each other, our thoughts unspoken but the same. Not once had my brother mentioned what kind of father he was.

When my mother passed away a year and half later, it was the same. Jonathan spoke emotionally of her exquisite taste and beautifully decorated home. Of her fashion sense, and the fact she always looked beautiful, even when just going to the store. He talked of her creativity, and of the gold jewelry she designed and made herself. His voice cracked as he described how she loved to bake, but not to cook, and how she and my father had cruised around the world. And all those things were true, and I felt terrible sadness as he spoke about her. But, again, there was not one mention of her as a mother.

———

So I fell in love, I suppose, with David. He was the daddy I always wanted, a mother in a way, and in some ways my first boyfriend. He told me I was pretty, smart, sweet. He listened intently, where my real father might easily have dozed off. Of course one thing he was listening to were tales of my professional success, and when monies were coming in. How could I miss the coincidence of him adding hours, and needing an additional twelve thousand dollars at a time when I'd be netting almost exactly that? Or as soon as my show looked like it was going to series, his idea of a lifetime in advance?

Of course because I didn't want to hear it. Little girls don't want to hear anything bad about their parents.

"Your need for him was like an infant needs its mother," Paul told me later. "You never had parents, and he gave you one, he gave you a family, and that's exactly what you were, a toddler, emotionally speaking."

It had always been my problem in life that I functioned strictly from my intellect, and David found a way to completely circumnavigate that intellect. Straight to the emotional core.

After this first happened, people would ask me, "Didn't it strike you as weird, all this wonderful stuff David was offering you?"

And I'd say, No, no, no, I totally trusted him. Only when I looked back, and really thought about it, could I see that the doubts had flashed into my mind, even if only briefly, all along. The problem was that I was so desperate for the things that David offered me.

"But what he was doing was so obvious," somebody said to me once, "how could you not see it?" They seemed almost angry that I could be so gullible. I told them I guessed it was like being on a lifeboat. Maybe there's things about the boat that don't seem quite right—there's a part that's all rusty, or a leak forming on the side, or it just seems off somehow—but it's saving your life. There are no other boats, *this* boat is your only hope. So you ignore or discard the things that aren't quite right, or maybe you don't even see them at all. You can't afford to see them. Because if you see them, and you abandon the lifeboat, you're lost.

I wasn't the only person David conned and betrayed, but I was probably one of the easiest. So hungry, I grabbed at everything, pushing aside anything that got in the way.

Ironically in keeping with the ocean theme, a friend of mine made the analogy that David was like a shark, spotting a wounded victim. "You're a wounded person floundering in the ocean, and this shark sensed the floundering and the agitation and honed in on you."

"But he didn't even have to go looking for me," I told him. "If we're doing the analogy of shark and the victim, I swam right into his mouth."

As I look back, there were so many clues I missed; or more accurately, saw and discarded.

That day he called me on the phone, when I thought, what's wrong with him, why is he calling me? My flash that he was a David Koresh–type brainwasher. His being too generous; that there must be a motive. A thought I had one day that he was full of shit and this was all bullshit. My image that this is what David does, he turns people against their families. Twice having him give me the wrong phone number. His story about believing he'd be alone his whole life, contradicting his story about having a daughter, Selena. Forgetting his arrangement to not ask me to cash the checks, when his memory was impeccable. Baby, the lover of everyone, being terrified of him.

The car accident, of course, was another one. Paul and I learned that David had used the same car accident excuse, but on a different day, months apart. If Paul and I had only spoken before . . . (Although who knows if David somehow wouldn't have been able to explain it.) But David knew Paul and I never discussed our therapy together, I'd even told him as much. He was in no danger of being discovered.

One day I remember asking David, "Do you even live in Dana Point?" I have no idea now why I asked, the question just sparked in my head.

"Jennifer," David said, total surprise and hurt in his voice, "what kind of a question is that?"

I had a dream about David one night. In the dream, amongst the rest of what was going on, David had told me he had to leave for some reason. I had woken up and written the dream down.

> . . . David lied to go be with this guy, and I thought, if he can lie, he can lie to me. And now I know him to be a liar. He gave me an old phone message to listen to, it was a confusing message but I couldn't understand it. I couldn't hear the message and what I could hear made no sense. But it was meant to con me.

All the clues were right there in front of me. Gifts. My beautiful instinct trying desperately to protect me, and I ignored it.

———

Paul also had had some hints along the way that he had pushed aside.

Primarily he had noticed a change in David's behavior over the last six months of therapy. His sessions weren't as good, Paul said; they weren't as productive.

"I thought I was blocked," Paul said. "But he was not as attentive; his beeper would go off during the sessions. And this is a small thing, but he would swing his feet like this; he'd have his legs swinging on the chair and they would bump against the couch. It was very annoying, and I'd ask him not to do it, and he'd do it like every session. Twice or three times in one session he'd forget. It was a very small thing."

Except it wasn't a small thing. Previously David had been exquisite in terms of memory, and paying attention to people's discomfort. Something was going on, and I'm sure Paul wasn't the only one who noticed it.

But who could question it? The brilliance of being in David's position was that any doubts or suspicions a patient brought up could be justified as *their* problem. You're in denial, you're afraid of intimacy, you're projecting . . . That's what made it all the more heinous, that he would tap into the weaknesses in people that *he* had brought out, and use those weaknesses against them.

David, of course, had had a perfect explanation for my dream of him conning me, as he did for everything. It was Pluto trying to distance me from him, or the man in my dream was actually my father, or I had a fear of intimacy or whatever. Perfect, beautifully wrapped explanations for everything.

For a long time I tried to believe that David was just very disturbed, meant no harm, didn't really know what he was doing. Because at that time I needed to believe that he did care about me. But the more closely I looked, his behavior was of someone who knew *exactly* what he was doing. So much so that it was almost a cliché.

David would frequently say to me, "I promise you, Jennifer," or, "Do you believe me?" Almost every day. In Gavin De Becker's book *The Gift of Fear* (a great book by the way, and I wish I'd read it years ago) he talks about the clues that can point out a criminal, or *a classic con artist*. There is one he calls the "Unsolicited Promise."

> [Promises] are the very hollowest instruments of speech, showing nothing more than the speaker's desire to convince you of something. . . . The reason a person promises something, the reason he needs to convince you, is that he can see that you are not convinced. You have doubt (which is a messenger of intuition), likely because there is reason to doubt.

De Becker also talks about something called "Forced Teaming."

> Forced teaming is an effective way to establish premature trust because a we're-in-the-same-boat attitude is hard to rebuff without feeling rude . . . [F]orced teaming . . . is intentional and directed and it is one of the most sophisticated manipulations.

Paying a therapist in advance is completely unethical. But the way David presented it, he made you *want* to participate in this mischief with him. "He'd preface things sometimes when he'd do things," Paul recalled, "by saying, this isn't standard, I could get in trouble for this, but . . . He brought you into his confidence. Brought you together into his risk-taking venture."

It was like when he told me he'd still see me even if I had no money, and of course *I'd still see him even if he lost his license.* In the car on the way to my house, laughing at the unconventionality of his visit. "We better not tell anyone."

Another clue De Becker offers is "Too Many Details."

> When people are telling the truth, they don't feel doubted, so they don't feel the need for additional support in the form of details. When people lie, however, even if what they say sounds credible to you, it doesn't sound credible to them, so they keep talking.

No one had more details to offer than David. Thousands and thousands of details.

And finally, De Becker talks about "Loan-Sharking."

> The more traditional loan shark gladly lends one amount, but cruelly collects much more. Likewise, the predatory criminal generously offers assistance, but is always calculating the debt.

"For you, Jennifer, I'll lower my fee, phone calls are free, our sessions can run over, I'll always be there . . ." When David took money for the so-called gambling, he first showed me, "Look what I've given you, Jennifer. Five thousand dollars!" It's yours, he told me, look how I care about you. He was always so generous. Giving, giving, giving. But only with one hand.

In this particular part of his book, when De Becker had talked about forced teaming, the unsolicited promise, too many details, and loan-sharking, he had been illuminating a point about a rapist.

Ironically, that was my original title for this book: "Therapist."

After this all happened, and I started to tell more of my friends about this story, one of the most frequent things they would ask me was, "Do you think David helped you?" And that to me was the most interesting question of all, and perhaps the hardest to answer.

There is a song by Alanis Morrisette, from her album *Jagged Little Pill*:

YOU LEARN

I recommend getting your heart trampled on to anyone
I recommend walking around naked in your living room
Swallow it down (what a jagged little pill)
It feels so good (swimming in your stomach)
Wait until the dust settles.
You live you learn
You love you learn
You cry you learn
You lose you learn
You bleed you learn
You scream you learn

I recommend biting off more than you can chew to anyone
I certainly do
I recommend sticking your foot in your mouth at any time
Feel free
Throw it down (the caution blocks you from the wind)
Hold it up (to the rays)
You wait and see when the smoke clears
You grieve you learn
You choke you learn
You laugh you learn
You choose you learn
You pray you learn
You ask you learn
You live you learn

Before I met David I was virtually a girl in an emotional bubble. I had told him I felt like a ghost, that I'd gone through life without the experiences of other people, and it was true. I never got to make my mistakes as a child or as a teenager. I never had a boyfriend break up with me, or had him cheat on me. I never got to have a first love and all the happiness and heartache that goes with it, or learn what it's like to be dumped or betrayed. I never made stupid choices, loved the wrong boy. I never lost someone that I loved. I never cried, felt no joy, no pain.

Because of David, in some ways I did get to experience all of those things. They ended up happening to me late, and maybe that made them more severe, like an adult getting the measles. And I could have done with not having to experience them all at once, but things aren't always perfect.

Before my experience with David, I would never have dared admit to anyone the things that I have admitted in these pages. And I still pause, and shudder a little, to think that other people are going to read these things about me. I'm reluctant to share credit, but I suppose the biggest testament to David, whether it was intentional or not, is that one way or another, it is because of him they are here to be read.

So I suppose some might say, "Okay, so he did help you; it's just that your therapy was very expensive." But that completely discounts what he did, not just to me, but to all his other patients. The price can't be measured only in dollars.

It would be awful to have money stolen by someone hacking into your computer and getting your bank code, or by stealing your checks and forging your name, or even by a swindler over a phony investment that you believed in. And those things are terrible—there is the financial loss, and a feeling of violation. It leaves you angry, and wanting justice, and you might call the police and report a crime and maybe you're even angry with yourself, "How could I have left my wallet on that counter?"

But this wasn't a wallet. I could forgive myself so much more easily for a wallet. David told me that all my defenses had been wrong, that there *was* someone in the world who could love me and care for me.

He made me believe I had wasted my life by not loving and not trusting and not relying on someone else, and so I did. I abandoned all those defenses and believed. And the person I believed was David.

It was about so much more than money. What David did was immoral and unethical and cruel, and it was criminal.

———

What I went through, during and after therapy, changed me of course. What a waste if it didn't.

Because I was in such turmoil, my friends saw a completely different side of me. I couldn't hide how shaken I was, or how much I needed. But rather than disgusting them, as it did me, they say they like me as much or even more. And because I believe them, I try to not be so disgusted with myself, although I don't often succeed.

I'm more understanding now of other people's weaknesses and mistakes in judgment, or at least I make an attempt to be. Sometimes my critical eye looks in, and I have to stop and remember. But at least I know to stop. I understand that if this happened to me, it could happen to anyone. I was starved for attention, but there are many weaknesses. Love, good health, financial security, a great deal on a car—everyone needs something. I used to not forgive people for being human.

I'm stronger, because this didn't destroy me when I thought it might. I learned that I have the capability to weather terrible things, and that makes things seem not so terrible. I know that nothing is permanent.

I try to pay closer attention to what people tell me and show me about their own struggles and dreams, to listen below the surface. And I absolutely listen much, much more closely to my own instincts.

Those are good things, and I am glad for them. But at the same time, there was a price exacted. I have to fight a lot harder now to be a good person—it can be very tempting to want to say, "I got shit on, I can shit on someone else." Sometimes I can't help but wonder, why am I bothering doing this good thing? What would this person do for me? I didn't used to think that way.

I am not rich, although I have done well by many standards. I worked hard, and made good money, but the money I gave David I could not afford to lose. I am of course worse off financially than I would have been; and, as David knew, lack of money was always one of my greatest fears.

While intellectually I know that not all people are untrustworthy; emotionally, I'm not so sure. I am much more cynical now, very suspicious of people's motives. I doubt I'll ever trust someone a hundred percent. I know that I got fooled once, and I'm not stupid enough to think it's impossible it couldn't happen again. Never say never. I trusted someone a thousand percent, and was completely, utterly wrong. How can you possibly know who's good and who's bad? Really, really know?

Even if one day I do meet someone and fall in love and get married, I suspect I'll always emotionally hold a little back; and keep my finances separate; and maybe even keep secret where I hide my gun. (I can see the guys lining up now.) That these are even my thoughts is unfortunate.

What David did to me made me feel like a fool, and totally shook my faith in myself and everyone else. For some time after this happened, I had no idea who I was.

———

But I suppose the most important question is, how do I feel about myself *now*, now that all the dust has cleared?

Sometimes I wondered if David used to go home at night and think, "Boy, I got her good today." If he was that calculated and cold. Did he laugh at my naïveté, gloat over the checks?

Or was there a part of David that really did care for me? I obsessed over this question for weeks, asking every therapist I saw. "Was I really special? Did David really love me? They all comfortingly said, "Of course you are," "Of course he did." What could they say? And, in fact, they didn't know the answer any more than I did.

It's very easy for people to say, about any failed relationship, it went bad at the end, so the whole thing was bad. The love affair failed; the person was always a bastard. But things aren't black and white. David may have genuinely cared, and been crazy, and been trying to help me, and known he was ripping me off. Genuinely cherished me, and emotionally and financially raped me.

I realized I would never know how David really felt. If his motivation was purely selfish, or if behind his greed there was any truth in the things he told me. Even if I could ask him, even if he swore blind on his children's lives. And of course the next step was to realize that it had to not matter if he cared about me or not, loved me or not.

How David did what he did, I understand. *Why* he did it had to become unimportant to me.

A few months before my father died, he told me he knew he hadn't been a very good father to me, and he asked me to forgive him, and I told him I did.

I think that if you had asked my father or my mother, they would say they loved me. And I think that they believed they did. But I wonder, then, how they define love. I think I know now what love should be, and theirs is not my definition. Love is a lot more than just saying it, or feeling it, especially when it's for a child, who doesn't know how to ask for what she needs, and hasn't yet learned what she deserves.

While I hated my parents at times during my therapy with David, I do not feel hatred now, although I am certainly angry. But how can you hate someone you feel sorry for? And I understand, I think, how it happened. My parents were barely loved, and it all flows down from there. Sadly, for them and for me, they didn't have the strength or the courage to defeat their own childhoods. And I suppose I do hate that they didn't try harder, or weren't less lazy, or didn't get help, or weren't so blind, or didn't recognize that they weren't equipped to have children.

Any sympathy or understanding for them doesn't help me with my rage at having the life I had. It does not make it easier. And I would be lying if I didn't admit that it disgusts me that the only person to ever show me what I think love should be had a vicious ulterior motive. It's unfair; it was so wrong, I didn't deserve that. But now, so what? It's done, and I have a choice. I can go back to believing I'm worthless and unlovable, and I will become bitter and miserable and turn cold and vanish back into the emptiness; or I can believe what David led me to believe, no matter what his reasons were.

During that time with him, in spite of who he turned out to be, I came to believe I was special. Lovable and deserving of love. The person that believed that was there all along, lurking inside, waiting, and finally she made herself known. Love, and amazingly even the mere illusion of love, has that power.

Author's Note

This is a true story. However, the names of David's patients, Roxanna's maiden name, and the names of those who David claimed to have been his friends have been changed.

If I hadn't hired a private detective to find David, it's very likely that none of us, none of his patients, would ever have known what happened. I'm sure there are still patients out there who have no idea what happened to their beloved therapist, and probably assume he died of cancer. If anyone has anything they care to add to this story, they should please contact the publisher.

Epilogue

In August of 1999, two and a half years after the police found a corpse in David's apartment, I received a fax. It was sent to my home phone number from Southwest Airlines, confirming a flight reservation.

I called the airline to tell them that the fax had been sent to the wrong number. The reservation agent told me that the ticket had been purchased on-line, and assured me that my phone number had been given by the person making the reservation. I thanked the reservation agent, and hung up.

I was about to toss the fax away, when I looked at it again. Something caught my eye, the departure and arrival dates of September 6 and September 9. An uneasy feeling came over me. David had told me his birthday was September 6 but he had lied. On the autopsy report, his date of birth was listed as September 9. The flight on the reservation originated and ended in Phoenix. David was from Phoenix, and that's where I had attended the funeral. Why would confirmation for a flight originating and ending in Phoenix be sent to Los Angeles? The first name on the reservation was David, the last name was Teume . . . David had that habit of using the letter *U* for "you." *Teume* couldn't mean "to you and me," could it?

I wondered if I was just being ridiculously paranoid. Was I looking for clues to Paul McCartney's death, or was it genuinely disturbing?

If even one thing had been different; the dates by just one day, if the city had been Tucson, if the name hadn't been David, I would've thought nothing of it. Just a misplaced fax. But of all the wrong phone numbers for this to be sent to . . .

I took a breath, and I asked myself, if this was David, why would he send this? To scare me? To reassure me in some bizarre way? Was it part of a sick game? Was he going to try to come back for more?

As unsettling as the fax was, the most terrifying thing was to think that one day I might just get a knock on my door.

Maybe it *is* just coincidence. But if it isn't, and the fax is from David, the implications are chilling. If he is alive, and the body in the apartment was not his, then he is a murderer. He is still out there. And he wants me to know it.